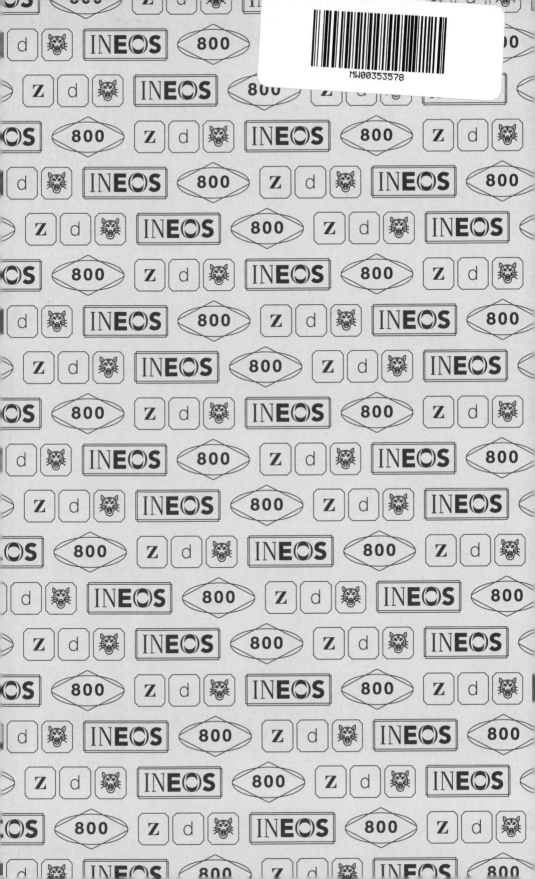

GRIT, RIGOUR & HUMOUR

Also by Sir Jim Ratcliffe

The Alchemists: The INEOS Story – An Industrial Giant Comes of Age

Grit, Rigour & Humour

The **INEOS** Story

Sir Jim Ratcliffe
Dominic O'Connell
Quentin Willson
Patrick Barclay
Sean Keach
Steph McGovern
Lord Sebastian Coe
Sir Andrew Likierman

bantam

TRANSWORLD PUBLISHERS

Penguin Random House, One Embassy Gardens, 8 Viaduct Gardens, London sw11 7bw

www.penguin.co.uk

Transworld is part of the Penguin Random House group of companies
whose addresses can be found at global.penguinrandomhouse.com

First published in Great Britain in 2023 by Bantam
an imprint of Transworld Publishers

A CIP catalogue record for this book
is available from the British Library.

ISBN 9780857505224

Typeset in 11.5/15.5pt Minion Pro by Jouve (UK), Milton Keynes
Text design by Couper Street Type Co.
Printed and bound in Great Britain by Clays Ltd, Elcograf S.p.A.

The authorized representative in the EEA is Penguin Random House Ireland,
Morrison Chambers, 32 Nassau Street, Dublin D02 YH68.

Penguin Random House is committed to a sustainable future
for our business, our readers and our planet. This book is made
from Forest Stewardship Council® certified paper.

When it comes to it, success in business is all down to people. Thanks to all the INEOS team over the past twenty-five years.

Contents

A Word from Head Office

Sir Jim Ratcliffe

FOR THOSE READERS WHO KEEP a 'bucket list' of places to explore, the Kimberleys in northern Australia are worthy of consideration. They should appeal if you like remote, if you like places where the hand of man hasn't yet tampered, where we see unspoiled, unpolluted, undeveloped, unpopulated land in the same state it was in a million years ago.

I chanced upon them four years ago in April 2019. My children had decided to have a crack at the Marathon des Sables. I was injured and unable to join, and irritated. In these circumstances a distraction helps assuage disappointment, and so I teed up an island-hopping, around-the-world circumnavigation of the Southern Hemisphere. It did the trick. I never gave a second thought to the allure of desert marathons and the suffering of my two sons, as a couple of mates and I cycled and fished our way across the Pacific. Between cycling from one set of colossal unearthly stones to another on Easter Island, to catching my all-time-record GT (giant trevally) in the Cook Islands (safely returned, I might add), to feeling the ground tremble every time a Cook Islander smashed into another in a local rugby match, one being carted off in the back of a pick-up with a broken leg (a far cry from Bruno Fernandes clutching his untouched face in the Liverpool debacle recently), we had a 'Boyzone' time.

There followed Vanuatu and the Great Barrier Reef, which were both a bit overrated, I thought. But then we found the Kimberleys. An oasis of remoteness.

We pitched up in Kununurra, top-right Western Australia, staging post for the Kimberleys. We checked out the 'Aussie Sports Bar' in the evening and enjoyed a wry 'gay Poms' look from the hefty barman when we ordered three gin and tonics, extra ice. A schoolboy error, which I am pleased to say we narrowly survived. My abiding memory, though, of this very authentic, as-they-should-be Aussie bar was the car park. There were probably thirty vehicles sitting there. Every single one was a pick-up. Every one was customized. Seriously cool shit. Maybe this was where we got the true inspiration for the Grenadier pick-up, who knows? If one ever finds its way to this car park, then we know we have made it.

Grant Simmer had raved about the Kimberleys. He was the young navigator on *Australia II* when they finally prised away the America's Cup in 1983, ending the longest winning streak in sporting history. He was also CEO of our first attempt to regain the Cup and break the longest losing streak in sporting history. Despite our valiant efforts we failed, but more to come on this subject later in the book.

So it was, with Grant's ringing endorsement in our ears, that there was a frisson of excitement the following morning as we boarded our private charter heli to the Kimberleys, home of the fabled barramundi, one of the world's finest sporting fish and target of our aspirations.

The Kimberleys are a long way from anywhere. That's what remote means. It was too far for a single hop in the heli, and so we get to the nub of our story. We had to put down at an especially remote (!) refuelling station, midway, situated in endless Australian bush country.

We landed in a cloud of sand and dust and sand in blisteringly hot temperatures and were met by a forthright and thoroughly capable lady who manned the station solo. The pilot was given his fuel marching orders with clarity and politeness but with a tone that brooked no discussion or deviation.

She then turned to us and invited us into her small cabin. We sat down as I recall in a surprisingly pleasant lounge with clear evidence of the female touch. To one side was a small functional table laid with kettle, teabags, mugs and milk. And beside these was a lemon drizzle cake pre-sliced. This most charming lady had baked us a cake. It doesn't get better than this. We enjoyed her company for half an hour, supped tea, ate cake and listened to some of her stories about pilots lost in the bush. Some never to be found. Well, in one piece at least.

It's a tough land. Little water, inhospitable, easy to get lost. Easy for something to go wrong. Not easy sometimes to extricate oneself if things do go wrong.

So it was quite impactful when I looked across to the far wall of the lounge, where all these intrepid heli pilots would enjoy tea, to see a large whiteboard with various messages written and papers stuck. In the centre in capital letters was written 'DON'T DO DUMB SHIT'. The Australian bush is unforgiving to careless heli pilots.

And so this brings me to my point (finally, I hear you say).

Why has INEOS been so successful in such a short period of time in an industry that has been around for over a century? We have grown from nothing in 1998 to revenues of $65 billion and EBITDA peaking at $10 billion in a mere twenty-five years. Not only that, but I would guess we will grow by another 50–100 per cent in the next five years, given what I can see in the pipeline.

Well, sorry to say there is no easy nor short answer to that question, otherwise everyone would be 'at it'. However, there are indicators.

All board meetings in INEOS commence with safety.

Note: In INEOS safety comes before finance and profit. Every single recordable injury is described by the relevant management team to Andy and me in our monthly board meetings. Cause, consequence, learnings and actions are presented and collectively agreed.

INEOS starts and ends with safety. Every employee knows this. We unashamedly have bonus metrics based on safety. It requires constant attention, or it slips quickly. This means developing a corporate attitude and commitment to safety from all employees.

So, back to our Aussie cake. Producing chemicals can be as dangerous as heli flying. We have explosion risk, toxic chemical risk, fire risk and physical risks from manual work and working from height.

We have become relatively sophisticated about risk. We try to be predictive. We apply consequence unashamedly to poor or careless behaviour. We have seven life-saving rules. A breach results in dismissal, or, if you are a contractor, a significant fine.

But at the basic, fundamental end of the risk spectrum it starts with 'Don't do dumb shit'. I recognize that it is a rather earthy expression and not to everyone's taste, including our head of HR, Jill Dolan. However, it says what it means on the tin. INEOS, with 25,000 employees, has had seven fatalities over twenty-five years. The first was in Germany, where there was a strict safety system on a palletizer which disconnected the power before entry. The employees/management had disconnected the safety system in order to bypass the protocol and quickly get at the machine if it jammed. It resulted in a fatality. It was unthinkably stupid. There are many such examples.

The rather hardboiled expression 'Don't do dumb shit' features in the INEOS Compass, which evolved some years back as an attempt to encapsulate the INEOS DNA or culture. It is an amalgam of expressive words and phrases, good and bad, that we like and that we don't like.

Sitting at the centre of the Compass are the three words that I believe most closely express our tenor, our way. Grit, Rigour, Humour. It applies equally to our sports ventures. Business doesn't always go swimmingly. It can be challenging, unpleasant, even dirty. We can't have people shy away from facing up to the tough times. Grit is an essential quality. Rigour is the opposite of winging it. Lack of rigour doesn't cut it in INEOS. Do your job fully, and well, and with pride. Prepare thoroughly and if you don't know the answer to a question say so, but never twice. In my humble opinion the Americans do rigour better than anyone because they exist in such a competitive marketplace. The UK is slipping. And humour simply makes the world go around. Life is short and to be enjoyed. Personally, I struggle if life is too dry. You need to enjoy some banter, and don't get too hung up on the woke agenda.

Wrapped around these three key words in the centre of the Compass is the phrase 'Manners maketh man'. Now I must confess that again this phrase rankled with the head of HR because of its masculinity. However, please read it as gender-fluid. Which frankly it is.

I worry that some of the younger generation haven't learned some of the basics of good manners, as we have steadily emasculated school teachers, police and increasingly parents from demonstrating some consequence for poor behaviour. Call me old fashioned if you wish, but I expect INEOS employees to exhibit good friendly manners and respect. Non-negotiable for me.

You will find the INEOS Compass at the beginning of this chapter!

If I move on now to where INEOS is headed in the future, it is clear that we are currently going through a period of considerable transition. The Law of Sod many of you will recognize as being most reliable and so this major transitional upheaval for INEOS is taking place regrettably in an economic trough. We are in the midst of a series of fascinating deals at a time when inflation and interest rates are peaking at their highest levels for a decade or more.

We wrote the book *The Alchemists* five years ago. At that time Sports, Oil & Gas, Fashion and Auto were all nascent. I would add China and the Middle East to this list of new journeys. In none of these had we travelled far along the learning curve and therefore we were unsure of our strategy, or management teams or commitment. We have subsequently learned a lot about (and from) these new challenges, first and foremost being that you don't know what you don't know. As a consequence, there are bumps in the roads that you don't necessarily anticipate. It's also difficult to identify whether you have the right management teams if you don't understand enough about the business. Like any challenge, it demands Grit, Rigour and large doses of Humour when you hit the bumps. It doesn't matter if it's Football or Oil & Gas or China, you have to recognize that there is an immense amount to learn before you feel at ease with strategy, direction and management.

Today I feel we have made good progress in all the areas above. Sport has settled, and we can see good progress in the America's Cup and Football. Cycling and Formula One are both run by the world's best pros, and we don't presume to be able to offer a great deal of advice – well, maybe just occasionally when Toto or Dave get their tyre choices muddled (☺). Oil & Gas has seen the arrival of two very senior pros from BP and has been transformed. Belstaff will show its first profit for a decade or more, and it recorded its highest ever sales level in 2022. And Auto have finally sold a car! I have fallen in love with the Grenadier, which always brings a smile to my face when I open the garage door and the unused G-Wagen keys gather dust on the garage hook.

Even from where I sit today I cannot guarantee the success of Oil & Gas and Auto. Only time will tell. But I guarantee that we will apply our abiding principles of Grit, Rigour, Humour to these two potentially enormous businesses for INEOS.

Oil & Gas is facing huge challenges as it is battered by the 'wannabe greenies', who haven't yet figured out that we cannot exist for many decades to come without fossil fuels. Yes, the world will eventually master and then build sufficient green energy generation and storage to meet the demands of 10 billion humans, but certainly not in the near future. So, just as bulk commodity chemicals were as popular as a 'fart in a lift' in the early 1990s to the stockbrokers in short trousers, so it is with Oil & Gas today.

To illustrate the absurdity of the current green agenda, the Natural History Museum has a wonderful anthropologist called Professor Chris Stringer, who eloquently and passionately describes the ascent of men. He is a natural storyteller and a joy to listen to. However, he has been banned from speaking at INEOS because we have an oil and gas business. One might ask how this stately institution heats its cavernous home, but that would be inching towards bitchiness.

All that said, every cloud has a silver lining. Banks are reluctant to lend into this fossil fuel energy field, the majors have cut back on exploration and the general appetite to step into this essential energy source is considerably diminished. So rather like our lift analogy in chemicals twenty-five years ago, we will continue to scrutinize opportunities that come our way.

Automotive is another huge industry in flux. And again, related to the energy transition, but also for reasons not entirely clear to me, increasingly regulated down to minutiae. A regulator's paradise. Pages of interminable detail on the dimension of the A-pillar and on the location of the spare wheel on the back. Surely the customer can choose. But regardless, we have broken through with our first product. And it does have a lovely compliant A-pillar and spare wheel, but seriously I believe it serves a unique function in the automotive world which today is unusual. There are countless SUVs to choose from, but there isn't really a car that performs peerlessly off road whilst being a joy to drive on road. It's rugged, unbreakable, comfortable and to me looks cool, although granted that is in the eye of the beholder. It is manufactured in a state-of-the-art car plant built by Mercedes in 2018, with robots as far as the eye can see. There is no excuse for anything but the highest build quality.

Only time will tell whether the Grenadier will become a staple diet for those who need to be able to negotiate off road terrain on occasions. For certain, it is the most capable of all production vehicles on the famous and intimidating Schöckl mountain, where Magna engineers perform durability tests for twelve hours a day. We plan to increase the product range with the introduction of an electric version of the Grenadier in 2026. Slightly smaller, range of 400km and still capable of ascending the Schöckl. In addition, we have in mind a couple more models, but more of that later.

China and the Middle East are regions where our ambitions have grown. Whereas Europe, and particularly the UK, are squeezing the life blood out of manufacturing, with overburdened legislation and excessive energy costs, stemming from poor energy policies, China has blossomed. In its pursuit of self-sufficiency, it has built an immense industrial infrastructure of the highest quality. To illustrate, if you take ABS plastic, which is useful for car dashboards and refrigerators, amongst myriad other uses, China was barely a player in 1990, with a trivial market share. Europe and America owned this space. Today they dominate world production with over 6 million tonnes in a world market of 10 million tonnes.

As a consequence of this drive for full independence of essential products, the Chinese market is very large and growing for our range of chemicals and plastics. The Chinese and ourselves have much to learn from each other. We enjoy each other's company. They are hardworking, highly educated, serious about their business and honest to deal with. All things I hope we can say about ourselves. Whereas we have a long-standing European relationship with PetroChina in refining, we have just entered a far-reaching joint-venture business with Sinopec in China. This again will be a journey that I fully expect to be fruitful for both partners. Our relationship will interweave technology, manufacturing expansion, safety disciplines, Western and Chinese management styles, and hopefully humour too. For ventures of this scale, importance and complexity to be successful, there needs to be mutual trust, a win-win attitude where the JV contracts are never ever taken out of the bottom drawer, and equal contributions to the prosperity of the venture made by each partner.

The Middle East journey for us is different. This is driven by competitive raw materials, because the home market is inconsequential. We enjoy again good relations with the head of Aramco and TotalEnergies, where trust exists on both sides and we enjoy each other's company. INEOS has some unique technologies which will bring something new to the Kingdom, adding value and creating new sophisticated job opportunities. Whilst we have considered several investments in the Middle East over the last twenty-five years, on this particular occasion the stars lined up, the projects look attractive, and we are well underway.

We are a global business. We manufacture and sell throughout the world. We invest our capital (several billion dollars a year) optimally, i.e. for the best returns. We have seen many changes over a quarter-century of existence and many challenges to which we have had to adapt.

Early on we were predominantly European, with two thirds of our profits coming from this large, sophisticated market. Germany, Belgium, Norway and France led the way. We struggled with competitiveness in Italy and withdrew. The UK has been a disappointment. Skills are not what they were, energy is expensive, unions have been aggressive (unlike Germany, where the unions focus on encouraging employers to invest for future growth), although to be fair they have been much more constructive and willing to engage in proper discussions about the genuine health of our businesses over the last ten years, and the government has been uninterested or lacklustre at best. America has been resurgent on the back of world-beating energy costs and frankly fine management. Whereas Europe has slowly squeezed the life from much of its manufacturing base with carbon taxes, complex legislation, high labour and social costs, America has gone into overdrive.

Furthermore, Europe has a lousy energy strategy, resulting in prohibitively expensive energy costs, at the last count five times higher than in America. Whereas the USA has taken shale exploration and extraction to technical levels never seen in the oil and gas industry before, together with a consistent and intelligent approach to nuclear energy, Europe has ignored the science and run scared of shale gas, letting minority activists dictate nuclear strategy. Remember, nuclear energy is not only green, it emits no carbon emissions, it also has virtually no variable costs and hence once built is extremely competitive. The major growth spurts in the world economy in the last two centuries can be clearly correlated with step changes in energy cost. Europe today finds itself unable to be competitive in steel, cement, plastics and ammonia (fertilizer) – the bedrock of a strong economy. The USA is the reverse.

And hence in our petrochemical and plastic industry in the USA, there have been immense levels of investment on the back of low-cost energy and raw materials. Maybe as much as half a trillion dollars has been invested in the last fifteen years, with the beneficial knock-on of closing old polluting facilities that can no longer compete. Renewal is a critical component of improving the world's global carbon footprint. Whereas we have seen the carbon tax 'stick' in Europe, which has emphatically failed to work, we now have a 'carrot' in the USA called the Inflation Reduction Act. Almost half a trillion dollars of government grants and assistance are now in place to attract the world's best green energies and technology to the USA. If you wish to invest in hydrogen, carbon capture, solar or wind, head west, young man.

And so today we see that the INEOS profile has flipped, and the USA is now by far our largest profit earner. Europe attracts much less of our investment. The USA, China and the Middle East are currently ahead of Europe in these stakes.

We are a far different company from five years ago and I suspect in five years from now we will have grown and changed even more.

We have a thirst for challenges that will not go away. Our many CEOs and management teams will make sure of that. But we will never forget that our core business, which drives and funds INEOS, is petrochemicals, unloved in some quarters, maybe, but essential to life as we now know it. And that our core values of Grit, Rigour and Humour will ensure, I hope, that we will always do things well and professionally.

Twenty-five years have gone by in the blink of an eye.

2

Firm Foundations, The Core Business

Dominic O'Connell

AT ONE EDGE OF THE Grangemouth oil refinery and chemicals plant near Edinburgh sits a squat grey cylinder. The site's sprawl – 1,700 acres of refining columns, steam generators and process plants, all connected by a dizzying spider's web of pipes – conceals the cylinder's true size. Up close it is a beast, forty-four metres tall and fifty-nine metres wide, large enough to swallow 560 double-decker buses.

Peek underneath and you discover this is not a simple concrete drum. It perches off the ground on a forest of steel piles, most of which go forty metres out of sight down to solid rock below. In all, seventeen kilometres of piles were sunk into the marshland on which Grange-mouth sits to make a solid base.

Why go to such trouble? The answer hides inside the tank. A one metre thick concrete wall surrounds a layer of insulation, and beyond that a thin steel liner which would break if the structure were to move even a fraction. Into this will be poured about thirty thousand tonnes of shale gas, brought by ship from the United States and kept liquid by freezing it to minus 160 degrees Celsius. The anonymous grey structure is in reality one of the world's largest Thermos flasks.

Its construction, and the scheme to build a fleet of ships to bring the frozen gas from America, was not part of an industrial strategy drawn up in Holyrood or Westminster. Nor was it a plan hatched in the board-room of one of the giants of the oil and gas industry, such as BP or Shell. Instead the tank was built by Grangemouth's current owner, INEOS. Over twenty-five years the company's founder, Sir Jim Ratcliffe, and his two fellow shareholders, Andy Currie and John Reece, have created one of the world's largest chemicals enterprises, with annual sales of $65 billion and twenty-six thousand staff, by stitching together a string of assets, many of which, like Grangemouth, were deemed surplus to requirements by their previous owners. In the process, all three have made themselves billionaires. They have courted controversy by ruth-lessly cutting costs, confronting unions and shifting the company to and from low tax jurisdictions, while Ratcliffe has shifted his own per-sonal tax affairs offshore. They also, as the plan to import shale gas from America shows, have been unafraid to risk big money to give their plants a future, and the best possible chance of making a profit.

All this has been done with little heed to the conventions of how big companies operate. You cannot buy shares in INEOS. Unusually for a company in a sector with a powerful thirst for capital, it has never listed shares on a public market, instead preferring to raise finance by taking out loans and selling bonds – IOUs that promise investors a guaranteed rate of interest for a set period of time, but no ownership. It does not have independent directors, it does not publish a single set of accounts that take in the full sweep of its activities and it has little in the way of the central functions – human resources, legal affairs, marketing – through which most modern companies control their operations. Its businesses are less like the arms and legs of a human than the limbs of an octopus, able to function with a degree of autonomy from the centre.

Despite its status as one of the UK's largest homegrown companies, Ratcliffe's creation has for most of its life been little known outside the world of chemicals. That has changed rapidly in the past five years as it has diversified into a new set of ventures: sport, with investments in cycling, Formula One and football; fashion, through the luxury brand

Belstaff; and automotive, with the Grenadier four-wheel-drive vehicle going on sale in late 2022. If Ratcliffe is successful in his bid to buy Manchester United, one of the most famous football clubs in the world, its profile will increase substantially.

INEOS began life in Europe but now its largest businesses, and its biggest opportunities for growth, are in the United States, the Middle East and Asia. This geographical shift is one of three big challenges it faces. High energy costs exacerbated by the Russian invasion of Ukraine, the rising price of permits to emit carbon dioxide and stricter regulation make it difficult to justify investment in its traditional European stamping ground. The urgent need to tackle climate change and pressure to curb the use of plastic is the second test: INEOS has cut its carbon dioxide emissions and plans to do more, but achieving net zero, where all its emissions are either eliminated or offset by other activities, will be a technical, regulatory and financial marathon. Paradoxically, some companies' reluctance to own oil, gas or petrochemicals assets because of public and investor pressure to divest may present INEOS with some big takeover targets and the opportunity to rapidly increase in size. Finally, the age of the three shareholders – Ratcliffe is seventy, Currie sixty-seven and Reece sixty-six – means they must deal with the difficult question of succession, and what INEOS will do without them.

Owners and managers

Jim Ratcliffe sits in morning sunshine at a long table in INEOS's Knightsbridge headquarters, eating a mandarin. He is tall, thin, and, perhaps because of his long hair, looks dishevelled, more like an irascible woodwork teacher about to lose patience with the class than one of Britain's richest men. When asked a question he frowns, looks straight ahead out of the window and gives a thoughtful response, often punctuated with a joke or a surprising expletive. It is a cutdown version of how he thinks INEOS management should operate: the company mantra of grit, rigour and humour.

The greatest of these may be rigour. Ratcliffe gets exercised about people who pretend things are not what they are.

'The first thing in all our meetings is safety. It is by far the most important thing we deal with. But you have to start with the truth, the unadulterated truth. We need to know if there have been any near misses, any issues at all. Otherwise you can't make sure it's the safest place in the world to work. If somebody drops something off a piece of scaffolding, then we don't want management to hide it. If we know things have been dropping off scaffolding, then we can do something about it.'

This exasperation extends to politicians, the state of public services in the UK and the fate of manufacturing in Europe, all of which more later. It also helps explain the two big oddities of INEOS as a corporation: its loose structure and the way it finances its operations. If it were listed on the London exchange, the likely market value of almost £40 billion would put it just outside the top ten of the FTSE 100, on a par with Lloyds Banking Group. That would bring considerable prestige. Ratcliffe would be much more in the public eye and, probably, a pillar of the business establishment.

But being a publicly traded company would mean much more scrutiny of executive pay, independent directors on the board and the constant need to satisfy a disparate group of shareholders. Particularly galling for Ratcliffe would be the army of analysts employed by financial institutions to research companies and issue recommendations to buy or sell their stock. Ratcliffe doesn't want to talk to analysts 'in short trousers', as he puts it, a putdown that rather dates him, being an echo of Nigel Lawson's dismissal of the 'teenage scribblers' who dared question his judgement as Margaret Thatcher's chancellor.

Analysts do not like surprises from the companies they cover. Unexpected developments make their judgements look silly. It is a stock market truism: companies that have left-field events in their earning statements see their shares marked down. In Ratcliffe's case, his wariness comes from direct experience with his own foray into public markets. After a career in chemicals and private equity, he bought a speciality chemicals business from BP in 1992, renamed it Inspec and floated it on the London stock market two years later. It was the precursor of INEOS.

The shares did well, until in 1997 an economic downturn torpedoed sales at its Antwerp unit (it had bought a big bulk chemicals plant there from BP). Analysts did not like the surprise, the shares fell, and the advice was to ditch the Antwerp business.

'As soon as you have a bad quarter, it's "management doesn't know what they are doing"', Ratcliffe says. 'The result is that the managements of public companies have a strong temptation to be less than completely honest, massaging their numbers to appease analysts and investors. They do it. We did it. Every quarter you are thinking, can we smooth this out? perhaps release a few provisions [amounts reserved against potential losses] or, if you have a great quarter, can I hold some of this back for later when things might get a bit worse?

'I became a cynic. You just waste an immense amount of time with these people, and they have all got their own agendas. It wasn't an environment I particularly enjoyed. I remember once having a talk with the chairman [of Inspec], and pointing out that whenever we had a chat with one of the stockbrokers a week before the results were out, the share price would always move a little bit in the right direction. It is not a coincidence.'

INEOS was in part born out of this frustration, and Ratcliffe's conviction that analysts and the wider market were wrong about the value of the Antwerp plant. He could use this blind spot to make money. He bought it himself, and formed a different company, INEOS, to house it. To fund the purchase, he put in his own money (as did other executives) and secured backing from the Scottish private equity company

Murray Johnstone. The bulk of the money, however, £72.5 million out of £84 million, came from the sale of bonds to a broad spread of investors, including many from the United States, where corporate bonds were a more common form of financing. The INEOS modus operandi was set. No involvement with public equity markets, finance raised from bond sales and, crucially, ownership of the company contained in a small, like-minded group of people, with Ratcliffe holding a majority stake. He owns 60 per cent of INEOS; Currie and Reece hold the remaining shares between them.

Michael Tory, founder of the boutique investment bank Ondra, which has worked with INEOS, says the decision to use bond finance rather than the stock markets has been crucial to its success.

'Debt is superior to equity for this industry for two main reasons – first, a normal bond is typically of longer duration than the industry cycle, which means debt providers are less concerned about short-term fluctuations. All they care about is getting their interest and principal repaid and they can ignore interim volatility. Equity investors should think like this but can't – they have their own performance metrics and incentives,' says Tory.

'Second, relying on debt is better aligned to value creation. It promotes long-term investment for fixed asset renewal, operating efficiencies for cash generation and discipline and respect for capital since, unlike equity, there is no printing press to issue more money if capital is misallocated.'

INEOS's decision to eschew the stock market came at roughly the same time as wider questions began to be asked about the efficiency of the public company system. One common complaint is the disconnect between shareholders and management, who often have different views and frequently lack a proper means of communication. Investors in public companies are a broad and diverse spread of institutions and individuals, ranging from traditional fund managers who take an active interest in their portfolio, to giant funds who own shares only because they are part of a stock market index, to high frequency traders who are in and out of shares in fractions of a second, and all the way down to individuals who have bought shares as part of their savings, or just for fun. The companies in which all invest are run by professional managers incentivized by pay packages focused on short- and medium-term financial targets.

The fractionalization of ownership means it is difficult for individual shareholders to have much say in how companies are run. Warren Buffett, the guru of American markets whose company Berkshire Hathaway has one of the most enduring records of investment success, frequently urges shareholders to think more like 'owners' of companies, with a proper interest in long-term returns. That is rarely the case. Howard Marks, the veteran Wall Street investor who founded Oaktree Capital Management, summed it up in a memo to clients last year. 'Most people buy stocks with the goal of selling them at a higher price, thinking they're for trading, not for owning. This means they abandon the owner mentality and instead act like gamblers or speculators who bet on stock price moves. The results are often unpleasant.'

Company directors are also frustrated. Recent research by Tulchan, a corporate affairs consultancy, which included interviews with twenty-six FTSE 100 chairs, found a state of deep disquiet about the relations between companies and their shareholders. The chairs accused investors of a box-ticking approach to stewardship, the outsourcing of voting decisions to advisory firms, and a general lack of interest in the whole public company sector.

At INEOS, a small group of shareholders runs the company. This is a big strength, but also a potential Achilles heel. The agency Fitch, one of the powerful international ratings organizations that judges the credit worthiness of corporate bonds, notes the potential problem. '[The] corporate governance limitations are a lack of independent directors, a three person private shareholding structure and key person risk ... as well as limited transparency on strategy around related party transactions and dividends.' In other words, investors should be aware of the risks of having a giant organization so reliant on a small group of people.

Chain reaction – how INEOS grew and grew

Pick up a Bic ballpoint and tap its hard hexagonal barrel. Then pull out and bend the clear tube inside that holds the ink. The first is polystyrene, the second polypropylene – two plastics found in countless items used in everyday life: cars, toys, furniture, computers. Like nearly all plastics, they are made from oil and gas. The stream that comes out of the oil well is separated into groups of molecules roughly the same size. One set is pushed through chemical reactions that turn them into the right kind of building block, a chemical Lego brick. Another chemical process makes all the bricks snap together. The result is plastic, a long, stable chain of molecules that makes an ideal industrial material.

Making those building blocks – bulk chemicals, as they are normally called – is INEOS's main business. It turns oil and gas into the raw ingredients used in plastics and other industrial processes and makes some plastics itself. A couple of examples are found in the ballpoint pen. INEOS makes benzene (a ring of six carbon atoms) and ethylene (two carbon atoms bonded together with four hydrogen atoms sticking out of the ends) and combines them to make polystyrene pellets. It makes propylene, a slightly longer molecule than ethylene, and, by linking all the molecules into a chain, turns it into polypropylene.

The scale of modern plastics making is mind boggling. According to Global Data, in 2021 ninety million tonnes of polypropylene were made worldwide, and about sixteen million tonnes of polystyrene.

Most of these materials were invented in the rapid flowering of industrial chemistry that followed the Industrial Revolution. The pace of discovery quickened between the world wars and raced ahead again in the two decades after 1945. The technology to refine oil and gas had been understood for hundreds of years before that, but rapid advances in pure science and practical chemistry allowed scientists to develop commercial processes to turn hydrocarbons into useful materials for manufacturing.

The prolific Birmingham-born inventor Alexander Parkes is credited with developing the first plastic, a type of cellulose, in 1850. The first synthetic plastic, Bakelite, came in 1907, with Belgian chemist Leo Baekeland beating Britain's James Swinburne to the patent office by just one day. In the 1930s nylon, polystyrene and polyethylene were first made and quickly commercialized, while polypropylene followed in the 1950s.

Many of the discoveries were made by chemists working for oil and gas companies, which were keen to find new uses for their products beyond heating, electricity generation and fuel for automobiles. They began to build chemical plants alongside their refineries. Several major centres for chemical manufacture formed in the last century – in the north of England with plants built by ICI (Imperial Chemical Industries, the now defunct company that was for decades Britain's largest manufacturer), in the Ruhr valley, where the Rhine allowed transport of feedstocks and finished products to and from Germany's industrial heartland, in Antwerp, where Bayer, BASF and BP capitalized on easy access to a giant port, and on the Texas and Louisiana coasts of the Gulf of Mexico, where the US oil majors already had a big presence and were joined by Dow Chemical.

Thirty years ago, however, cracks began to appear in the established order. Bulk chemicals is, like the production of most commodities, harshly competitive. An economic downturn quickly eats into margins and can lead to big losses. Cutting output in the face of falling demand is difficult. Plants can be throttled back, but stopping production completely is expensive, and bringing a refinery or chemicals process plant back online is time-consuming and complicated. The comfortable competition between the big players – BP, Shell, ICI, Hoechst, Bayer, BASF, DuPont, Dow and a gaggle of others – was being disrupted by new players from Asia and the Middle East. They built giant modern plants and, in some cases, had access to very cheap feedstocks of gas and oil, meaning the old guard had to run fast just to stand still.

Shareholders began to put the established companies under pressure to find ways out of this boom and bust business. A case in point was ICI, a giant corporation that prospered on the back of the new chemical industries for most of the twentieth century. By the 1990s, however, it was struggling under a mountain of debt and the share price was flagging. Successive management teams gradually broke the company up, selling the pharmaceuticals business (which lives on as the drugs company AstraZeneca) and concentrating instead on specialty chemicals. It was thought that they would provide a steadier stream of earnings, and be less susceptible to competition. Eventually the break-up ran its course and the last remaining ICI business, Dulux paints, was sold to AkzoNobel in 2008.

Some oil and gas companies were also wondering whether they should retain their chemicals units. The margins were small compared with the riches that could be made in finding and developing new oil wells, and some investors judged them both a distraction to management and a drain on capital.

'It is never top of the agenda,' says Brian Gilvary, the former finance director at BP who subsequently joined INEOS to chair its energy division. 'The margins are seen as being relatively low, and it is viciously cyclical. If you wanted to be the rising star in an oil and gas company, you probably weren't on the chemicals side.'

In hindsight, Ratcliffe's timing was immaculate. He started his business career in 1974 at Esso (for a fuller account of Ratcliffe's career and the development of INEOS, you can read *The Alchemists, The INEOS Story*, Biteback Publishing 2018). He was born in October 1952 in Failsworth, a former mill town halfway between Manchester and Oldham. Aged nine, he moved with his family to Hull on the Yorkshire coast. He was educated at Beverley Grammar school, an academically selective state school whose alumni include William Howe de Lancey, chief of staff to the Duke of Wellington at the Battle of Waterloo.

After completing a degree in chemical engineering at Birmingham University, Ratcliffe joined BP as a graduate trainee, only to be let go shortly after joining because a medical assessment showed problems with eczema, not thought ideal for someone who would be working with chemicals. He went to Beecham Pharmaceuticals, trained as an accountant, and later moved to Esso, the British subsidiary of the American oil giant Exxon, and from there to Courtaulds, the UK's top producer of man-made fibres. In 1987 he made his move out of industry, being headhunted to join the UK offices of the American venture capital firm Advent International. Venture capital companies make their money by buying unloved or undervalued firms, reviving their fortunes, and selling them.

Four years later he struck out on his own after identifying a BP fine chemicals business – 'fine' chemicals are more complicated molecules, often made in batches, for specific applications – as a potential target. He teamed up with Dr John Hollowood, a chemicals entrepreneur who had recently sold his own venture, to mastermind the deal. BP sold the outfit, which had plants in Carshalton in south London and Hythe in Hampshire, for £37 million. Four private equity firms put in money: Advent stumped up £10 million, HSBC Private Equity £3 million and Candover and Charterhouse £2 million each. The new managers also put their money at risk, Hollowood investing £250,000, Currie (then manager of the BP unit, who joined Ratcliffe's new venture) £30,000, and Ratcliffe £141,000. He mortgaged the family house to raise the cash.

The deal was ready to go in September 1992 but was nearly sunk by 'Black Wednesday', when the British government frantically tried to salvage its doomed position in the European Exchange Rate Mechanism. An early step towards monetary union, the mechanism pegged different European currencies at fixed rates. The pound joined at too high a level, and crashed out on 16 September. In an attempt to defend sterling, Chancellor Norman (now Lord) Lamont, increased interest rates sharply before accepting defeat and withdrawing the UK from the mechanism – a humiliating episode that played a part in the defeat of John Major's government five years later by Tony Blair's Labour. But at the highest point of Lamont's rate hike, the Bank of Scotland, which was lending to the Ratcliffe consortium, pulled out, saying that it would be unsustainable for the fledgling outfit.

It was a short-lived storm. With Britain out of the exchange rate system, rates went back to where they had been and the deal was back on. A week later Ratcliffe's first company, with him as chief executive, was born. Hollowood was chairman and Currie sales and marketing director. It was called Inspec, a shortened form of International Speciality Chemicals. Currie remembers being confident about its likely success.

> 'We had plans to shut one of the facilities, the one at Carshalton, and when we had done that we knew margins would go right up and it would be much more profitable. It was quite liberating too to be out of the bigger company.'

Inspec quickly bought two speciality chemicals companies in the US and floated on the London market in 1994 at a value of £164 million. It was a big payday for the initial institutional investors, and even more so for the individuals who had put money in. The management shares went up by just under two hundredfold, leaving Ratcliffe with a (paper) profit of £28 million.

Inspec's biggest deal, and the one that inadvertently contained the seed of INEOS, was the purchase of another BP facility, a plant in Antwerp that was one of Europe's biggest producers of ethylene oxide. In 1995 Inspec paid £84 million for a site roughly the size of the City of London which employed four hundred people. Currie judged that BP had overlooked its proper potential, and under new management output tripled. But it was a step into the cyclical world of bulk chemicals and two years later when recession loomed, the plant's sales stuttered, and Inspec shares tumbled.

The company's advisors said the Antwerp facility should be sold. Ratcliffe in effect did a management buyout, purchasing it from Inspec in 1998. It was INEOS's first asset, and the one that set the operational and management style, and financing methods, for all that was to follow.

INEOS grew rapidly in the first half decade of the new century. It swallowed up four businesses from ICI, the first of which was its Perspex operations in October 1999. It then bought the chlorine and fluorine businesses, followed by European Vinyls Corporation, a struggling joint venture between ICI and the Italian oil company, Eni.

Even after the spree of deals, the company was a relative unknown. When Dow Chemical merged with Union Carbide in 2001, it had to sell some of its operations to get clearance from the US competition authorities and Bob Learman, who worked at Dow, had the job of putting together a presentation for prospective bidders. Their identity was kept secret until the last minute. 'I was going up in the lift to do the presentation. I turned to the mergers and acquisitions guy and said: "You should tell me now who I am presenting to." He said, "It is a British company, INEOS." I said, "Who?" I had never heard of them.' INEOS bought the Dow businesses, and Learman is now one of Ratcliffe's senior lieutenants.

Picking up unwanted assets piecemeal had made INEOS a sizeable organization for a private company. It had also established the company's reputation as a good home for businesses; Ratcliffe was known as a sharp operator and hard negotiator, but he had not shut down companies and he had operated plants safely. When chemicals operations were put up for sale, the INEOS name was normally on the list of possible buyers.

By the early years of this century, Ratcliffe was on the hunt for something big. He tried, and failed, to buy Basell, a joint venture between BASF and Shell, missing out to Access Industries, a private group owned by the Ukraine-born businessman, Leonard Blavatnik.

Another mammoth was waiting, however. In 2002, BP had begun a review of its petrochemicals arm. 'We were asking whether we were still the right owners of the businesses,' said one former BP director who was directly involved with the process. 'The conclusion was that our bulk chemicals operation, particularly the ones aimed at plastics markets, were still good businesses, but the market had become commoditized, and there was more competition on the way from China in particular.' BP's public position was that the business would be spun off and floated on a stock exchange as an independent organization. The board, however, was also considering bids from other chemicals companies.

INEOS was, on the face of it, an unlikely contender. Its annual turnover was about $7 billion. Innovene's was $22 billion. Innovene had sites right around the world, including the Grangemouth refinery and chemicals plant in Scotland, a refinery in Lavéra, near Marseilles, a giant chemicals facility on the Rhine between Cologne and Düsseldorf, and the Chocolate Bayou gas-cracker outside Houston, one of the biggest in the US. INEOS had no experience in refining, and it was uncertain whether David had deep enough pockets to afford Goliath. Ratcliffe eventually won the day in 2005, beating off Reliance Industries, owned by India's richest man, Mukesh Ambani. INEOS paid $9 billion. At a stroke, it had entered the big leagues.

The sale was traumatic for many Innovene staff, particularly senior management, who had expected to be running their own company. Many left, but others quickly adapted to the new way of working.

Patrick Giefers, who was BP's head of HR at the Cologne site and is now site manager, said the focus became costs – actual costs, rather than costs viewed through a remote head office prism – and investment. 'As an example, for BP employment costs were all about headcount. If you reduced headcount it was a good thing, even if you outsourced the work to an external company and didn't really save any money. You were able to say, "I have reduced the headcount." Whereas at INEOS it is – how much are we spending to do the job? And after an initial period, it was – what do we need to invest in to make the plant better? I think if we had stayed in BP ownership this site would either be much smaller or it might already have closed.'

Three years after the Innovene deal was concluded, the banking crisis struck, and Ratcliffe had to battle with bondholders to retain control of the company. After that storm passed the deals continued. In 2011 INEOS transferred the refinery assets it took on with Innovene (at Grangemouth and Lavéra, in France) into a joint venture with the Chinese oil company PetroChina. Grangemouth also gave INEOS its biggest public exposure in the UK, when a dispute with unions over terms and conditions – in particular pensions – dominated the headlines for months. Matters came to a head in 2013, when Ratcliffe decided that the site, of vital importance to the Scottish economy, and one of the few large manufacturing employers left in the country, would close. The unions caved in, and Ratcliffe rescinded the decision.

An attempt to secure feedstocks for the European operations at the right price led to a whole new set of deals. INEOS built a fleet of tankers to import shale gas from the US to feed Grangemouth and the Rafnes site in Norway, and then bought from BP in 2017 the Forties pipelines system, which brings North Sea oil and gas ashore. In the same year the company made a move into oil and gas production, buying the North Sea assets of Denmark's Dong Energy, which had decided to focus on renewable energy. Another deal with BP came in 2020, when INEOS bought its remaining petrochemicals business for $5 billion. In December last year it signed two petrochemical joint ventures with Sinopec, including taking a half-stake in the giant Shanghai SECCO complex, originally built by a joint venture between the Chinese company and, naturally enough, BP.

How it all works

Andy Currie walks behind his desk, picks up an A4 sheet of paper and runs his finger down a long table. 'This is part of the list for this year – we have just been working it out,' he says. The paper contains a string of dates and times, with company names beside them. It is the masterplan for how INEOS runs itself, a cascade of meetings of the executive committees of the twenty largest companies in the group. Each committee meets six or seven times a year, two to three hours at a time. Ratcliffe and Currie, whose role at INEOS corresponds to that of a chief operating officer, attend nearly every meeting. Reece, who is the finance director, attends fewer, but will spend more time with particular companies when a finance issue needs addressing.

It is an unusual way to run a large multinational. Chief executives at big companies usually try to reduce the number of people reporting directly to them: have too many, the theory goes, and you risk getting lost in the weeds rather than focusing on important issues. At INEOS the top executives, who are also the owners, have direct contact with a large number of operational staff. It sounds more suitable for a small organization than one with large, complicated and far-flung operations.

While there is no control experiment – it is impossible to know how INEOS would perform if it had a traditional structure – it seems to work. The intimate involvement of the top three is balanced by the degree of freedom they give to their managers. The INEOS head office does not have to spend much time managing group-wide functions; these are delegated to the subsidiaries.

INEOS executives who have worked at other organizations, frequently at other large oil and gas or chemicals companies, bring up speed of decision-making as a key difference. They also cite the trio's long experience as a competitive advantage. 'Between them they have a great breadth of knowledge, but they have also done the job and know the industry inside out. They usually have angles you have not thought about,' one INEOS manager said.

Mike Nagle, chief executive of INEOS's US olefins and polymers business, says that in most big companies, managers are constrained by competing central fiefdoms. 'It can be a mess. The IT department tells you your costs are going up. You ask them why and it's because their property cost is going up. And that's because human resources needed a new building or whatever. It can be a doom loop. At INEOS if I need a new piece of software it's up to me and my organization to sort it out. There is no one else to look to.'

Andrew Gardner, chairman of Grangemouth and chief executive of the Forties pipeline, says that the conflicting demands of the BP hierarchy could lead to farcical situations. 'I was once asked to do a paper for presentation to the board at the end of the week. But my boss wanted to have it for two days to work on it before it went to the next level, and so did the next level, and the level after that. So to have it ready in time I would have had to start work two days before I was asked to do it.'

The freedom can be disconcerting. When the Dow businesses were bought by INEOS, they were kicked out of their existing offices. 'They [INEOS] said – OK, go find an office. And some IT. You are thrown into the ocean and it is sink or swim,' Bob Learman says.

The system would not work without a reservoir of trust. Gardner says that a manager's initial proposals are given a thorough going-over by Ratcliffe and co, but the level of scrutiny can recede over time. 'After a while, they work out whether you can do it or not. And they let you get on with it, within reason.'

Ratcliffe says not all managers can be happy with the system.

'You could call the system FIFO – fit in or f*** off. Some people like it, some people don't. It emerges when things are not going as they should, the tension builds up and you start to get quite focused on the competencies of the people. Eventually you get to a point where, yes, we can make it work, or you have to make some changes.

'That model – the independence where people are their own bosses, they won't have interference from head office, they have to sort out their own tax, all that – comes from private equity. You incentivize the management really well and let them get on with it.'

Managers, however, are expected to help out their colleagues in other parts of INEOS.

'We always say you are not expected to do missionary work, but you are there to look at best practice. You need to be an open book with your colleagues across the business. If we see it not happening, we get on to it straight away.'

Ratcliffe concedes, however, the federated system is not the only approach.

'At Exxon, for example, they make it [greater control by head office] work, and they make it work quite well. But I don't like amorphous lines of responsibility. If I want to know who is behind that success or that failure, it is hard to find out. And it makes it hard to incentivize people properly. I've had experience with both – at Courtaulds managers were quite independent, not at Exxon, and then at Venture Capital it was complete freedom.'

The federated structure can lead to complexity. INEOS's main site in Germany, a sprawling complex the size of Monaco that sits on the Rhine between Cologne and Düsseldorf, was part of the Innovene business sold by BP in 2005. Before INEOS arrived, all the staff worked for one company, BP. Now they work for four, each a different INEOS business. 'There are obviously lots of potential frictions – what one business wants may not be what another wants, and they all work on the same site. But – it does work,' says site manager Patrick Giefers.

Blue-collar workers have a shared bonus pool. Each business pays into a central pot, and it is distributed between staff. Bonuses for white-collar workers depend on the performance of the business for which they work. And staff who work for more than one unit get a share of the bonus from each individual business. It could – perhaps should – be an industrial relations nightmare. That it does work says something about the degree of personal trust between Ratcliffe and the unions. He recounts the story of his first meeting with the leader of the site's unions. 'He said, "We are interested in the future of this plant, and the jobs that our children are going to have here." It was a completely different outlook to what you might get from unions in other parts of the world. He wanted to know that we were going to be responsible owners.'

Below Ratcliffe, Currie and Reece sits another layer of management, five key consiglieres who run one or more of the key divisions. Most arrived at INEOS through the acquisitions done over the past twenty-five years and have risen through the ranks. They are Gerd Franken, chairman of Olefins & Polymers Europe, Bob Learman, chairman of Oligomers and O&P, US, Kevin McQuade, chairman of Styrolution and Aromatics, Rob Nevin, chairman of INEOS Sport, Acetyls and Inovyn and Ashley Reed, chief executive of INEOS Enterprises and chairman of INEOS Automotive.

Each executive committee meeting starts with the same subject: safety. Currie, an avuncular, white-haired man whose voice still carries more than a trace of his south Yorkshire roots, says nothing is more important.

'It is a potentially dangerous industry. It starts and ends with safety. You can't hurt your people, and you can't operate a plant if it is unsafe. Every meeting starts with the same standard slides on safety, and we are very focused on it.'

Of special interest are 'hi-pos' – incidents that hurt no one but had the potential to do so. 'If a brick or a scaffolding pole falls, we want to know why. Because next time it might hurt someone, so we have to have a system where it will not happen again.'

Cliff Bowen, a convenor at Grangemouth who sits on the executive committee of the union Unite, says the focus on safety penetrates down to individual workers.

'All my members, all the staff here, know that they can stop the site if there is something unsafe. And it works both ways. Safety at petro-chemical plants is often about following the correct protocols. If you are outside in the middle of the night and it is freezing and blowing a gale, you still have to follow that procedure and not take a short cut.'

That focus on safety and procedures came into its own during the COVID-19 pandemic. Grangemouth couldn't shut down, but it did have to bring in strict staff separation rules. 'It was another protocol to follow,' says Bowen. Gardner states with evident pride that only two people were infected at work. The additional shift cobbled together to take over in case of mass illness was never called into action.

There is a close attention to cost, and in particular the ripping out of cost when a new operation is acquired. It aims to cut about one quarter of expenditure on taking over, and all planned spending must go to the relevant executive committee while the new business is bedded in.

'We normally find lots of credit cards – hundreds of them. We have a template of how to do this, but it is a shock to the people working there,' says Currie. 'Usually – but not always – new managers from other parts of INEOS are installed to foster the new ways of working.'

The centre does come into play when large investment decisions are required. Executives talk of putting proposals to 'Incap' – short for INEOS Capital. There is still an INEOS Capital registered at Compan-ies House, but Reece says that it is not a formal decision-making body. 'When they say INEOS Capital, it is shorthand for the three of us [him, Currie and Ratcliffe],' Reece says. Investment plans normally have to clear the hurdle of generating a 20 per cent return on capital before they will be considered.

When it comes to deciding what next to buy, INEOS executives will normally always ask whether the asset in question is one of the best of its kind, and whether it will be able to make money in boom times or bust. 'It is a very simple philosophy – we want things that are first or second quartile, so that we are the big pig at the trough, basically,' says Ratcliffe.

The pandemic required many companies to ask staff to work from home, and home-working has remained a feature of post-pandemic life. Its adoption varies widely – some small companies have ditched their head office altogether, others insist on a certain number of days a week in the office, while others give their staff a great degree of flexibility to switch between the two. At INEOS, working from home is frowned upon. It is well known that Ratcliffe hates the idea.

'I'm 100 per cent against it,' he says. 'People don't work, they get lazy and they get into bad habits. They walk the dog, they prune the roses. The thing about coming to work on a Monday morning is that a switch clicks – you are at work. Go home on a Friday, the switch clicks again, you are at home, you can relax and do all those things. I don't think people do work at home. There is too much temptation and not enough supervision. I do not believe in it.'

In practice, INEOS may not have been completely immune to the wider shift in working culture. Managers say they do not permit it, but in the same breath talk about practicalities and getting the best out of people, a code, perhaps, for realizing that there could be some sensible exceptions to the blanket ban.

Another thing that marks INEOS out from other large companies is the relative scarcity of women at the top. Thanks in part to government-backed targets, the number of females on FTSE 100 boards has grown rapidly in the past decade. At the start of last year just over 40 per cent of all FTSE 100 board members were women, up from 12.5 per cent in 2012. The most senior women at INEOS's head office are Jill Dolan, head of Human Resources, and Debra Smeeton, head of Group Tax. Two of the divisional chief executives are female: Lynn Calder at INEOS Automotive, maker of the Grenadier four-wheel-drive vehicle, and Fran Millar at Belstaff, who also runs INEOS Hygienics.

Ratcliffe insists INEOS is a strict meritocracy. Is it not odd that a meritocratic system keeps selecting men? 'There is no bias, absolutely not. When people offer themselves up for a job, we select the best person.' And Ratcliffe sees no argument for INEOS exercising positive bias and promoting women to try to balance gender representation at the top.

'That would mean that if I have a really good guy going for a job, and an average woman, I have to say to the guy – sorry, you don't get the job. I'm not going to do that. We are competing against some quite tough people around the world. It's just like a football team – if you don't send the best people out, you don't win the game. If you finish up with a bunch of mediocre people, it just turns into a shitshow.'

Some INEOS executives are happy to defend the company's record on promoting females.

'I think it is unfair to blame the company for what is an industry and societal issue. There simply weren't that many women in chemicals fifteen years ago, and it does take time for them to rise to the top. There are excellent female managers in INEOS, and they will get there,' one said.

Show me the money

Bruce Springsteen played Hyde Park on 28 June 2009. It is regarded as one of the better live performances from his long and illustrious career; a recording was released as a film the next year. John Reece was watching but slightly preoccupied. The next day he and Jim were due at a crunch meeting with the company's lenders at Glaziers Hall on the south side of London Bridge.

How it worked out would determine INEOS's fate – whether the trio would retain sole control, and if so, how much the banks would want as their pound of flesh. If it went badly, they could be pushed out and the company either broken up or sold. 'I remember thinking that if Bruce can stand up in front of thirty-five thousand people, then we should be OK in front of three hundred. Of course the difference was that everyone in the crowd wanted to see Springsteen, and the lenders didn't really want to see us,' Reece says.

The Glaziers Hall showdown was the culmination of a protracted and at times turbulent set of negotiations between the company and the hundreds of different financial institutions that had provided it with finance by buying its bonds and loans. It was an existential moment, the toughest test it has yet faced, and showed the limitations and potential weaknesses of INEOS's chosen method of financing. Shunning public equity markets meant the three owners had retained control of the company, but reliance on debt funding left it at the mercy of lenders when markets turned down.

The problems began late in 2008 as a knock-on from the banking crisis. A splurge of high risk lending, notably in the US housing market, led to a crisis of confidence in the world's biggest banks. In the US Lehman Brothers went bust, and there was a taxpayer-backed protection system put in place for the rest of Wall Street. Nearly all of Detroit's big car companies received soft loans and other government assistance as demand for their products dropped like a stone. In the UK, Lloyds and Royal Bank of Scotland were bailed out by the government in one of the biggest commitments of public funds since the Second World War.

A recession was on the way, and INEOS was one of the first to sense its arrival. Given their widespread use, demand for bulk chemicals is a reliable lead indicator of industrial downturns. INEOS managers noticed orders beginning to dry up towards the end of 2007, and its first quarter earnings at the end of January 2008 were below expectations. By September 2008 orders had, in Reece's words, 'fallen off a cliff', and there had been a costly strike at Grangemouth earlier in the year, which further drained profits. INEOS was still carrying much of the debt taken on three years earlier to fund the Innovene deal – in total, $8.5 billion spread over bonds and loans held by about 230 different institutions. If trading got worse, INEOS might not be able to afford the interest payments on the debt. That would put the company in default and possibly let the lenders seize control.

INEOS was not alone in feeling the pinch. In the first week of 2009, LyondellBasell, then the third largest chemicals company in the world, applied for Chapter 11 bankruptcy in the United States. It was struggling under the $23 billion of debt taken on when it was created in 2007 from the merger of Basell with Lyondell, an American chemicals company.

In the end, INEOS was tripped up not by missing an interest payment, but by the small print of its loans. Most corporate bonds have some kind of covenants attached – terms written into the lending documents that specify that the borrower must stay within certain financial conditions. These can include a minimum level of profitability, a ratio of profits to interest payments or a ceiling on dividends to shareholders. Covenants are designed to give lenders an extra level of protection by making sure a company maintains sufficient financial strength to pay the interest on its borrowings. Infringement of covenants normally puts a borrower into default.

The covenants on INEOS's debt were triggered by a rapid fall in the oil price, which dropped from $100 a barrel to $40 in the space of a few months. The Grangemouth and Lavéra refineries need about ten million barrels of oil to run – to keep them 'wet' in the chemical engineer's jargon. The barrels are constantly replaced as the plant is run, but they are part of the company's assets. As the price of oil fell, so did the value of the *in situ* oil, so much so that covenants in the INEOS bonds were triggered.

The threat of default and its aftermath clearly still rankles with Ratcliffe.

'If the value of your stock [the oil] falls, accounting rules mean you do have to take it on your profit and loss statement. But it was not cash out the door – it was, really, meaningless. But it opened the doors to the banks, and they came in and took between seven and eight hundred million dollars out of us over the next three years.'

Battles between companies and bondholders, and between the various groups of bondholders, are relatively common in the United States, where bond finance is a more established method of corporate funding. Some institutions specialize in 'distressed' debt, hoping to swoop in on a potential insolvency and find an angle that will make them rich, and possibly leave the problems with others.

INEOS wanted the lenders to give them breathing space on the covenants, time to restore profits and make sure there was no further breach. In return, it offered to pay upfront fees and increase the interest paid on the bonds. The first offer was rejected, and the second accepted. Along the way, the management rejected proposals that would have seen one set of lenders do much better than others. As can often happen in debt renegotiations, the senior lenders – those with the first call on the company's assets in the event it went bust – wanted to restructure the loans to ensure those holding the junior loans got nothing. 'We weren't going to do that,' says Reece. 'We felt it was wrong.'

The Glaziers Hall meeting proved decisive, with two-thirds of lenders voting in favour of the company's proposals. In July 2009, INEOS announced it had reached an agreement with the bondholders: a waiver of the covenants in return for fees and extra interest payments totalling about $800 million.

Michael Tory of Ondra Partners said the lenders in the end became convinced that Ratcliffe, Currie and Reece were the right people to run the company.

'The banks and bondholders supported INEOS's management since it was clear that Ratcliffe, Currie, Reece and the senior team were the best possible – and most effective – managers of the company's assets, especially in the difficult situation in 2009.'

Ratcliffe says practical considerations also played a part.

'We are one of the biggest chemicals companies in the world. We deal with dangerous stuff like hydrogen cyanide, and our processes are high temperature and high pressure. What does a bank know about running something like that? Would they really want the responsibility?'

Could INEOS face a similar debt crunch again? It could, but it appears much less likely. The company has less debt relative to its overall size and profitability than it had in 2009. Gross debt is now about €16 billion and it reliably makes EBITDA profits (a selective measure of profitability that excludes interest, tax and depreciation payments) of €6–8 billion a year. Gross debt that is twice profits is a relatively light load by private equity standards.

It has not struggled to attract lenders; in the past five years it has gone to the market fifteen times, raising about €15 billion in a mix of refinancings and repricing of debt. 'As the market improved between 2010 and 2015 we were able to bring the cost of the debt down dramatically,' says Reece. The debt is not raised by INEOS as a whole but by seven different financing vehicles, each with its own borrowings. The top company in the INEOS structure is INEOS Limited in the Isle of Man. It pays UK corporation tax.

Despite a tough year for corporate bonds in 2022 (and the turmoil in the wider bond market caused by rising inflation and rising interest rates, with the chaos of the UK's disastrous September mini-budget on top) it was successful late last year with a plan to refinance an outstanding term loan early. It offered €1.1 billion worth of loans for sale, but given the level of demand expanded the offering to €2 billion. 'That loan was not due until 2024, so we didn't have to do it, but we thought given what was happening in the credit market it was best to make a move early,' Reece says.

Since then INEOS has raised a further tranche of loans and bonds, launched at €2.2 billion but upsized to €2.6 billion in February 2023. It has also changed the fine print of the bond terms. They are now 'covenant-lite', a term commonly used to describe loans with few conditions attached. Another unintended stumble over oil stocks in refineries is unlikely.

That does not mean there are not risks. The biggest obvious threat to a chemicals company with big operations in Europe is the rising cost of raw materials, chiefly oil and gas. Russia's invasion of Ukraine in February 2022 sent the price of both soaring, although prices have fallen back to close to pre-invasion levels since. The Cologne plant has paused production at its ammonia plant (which makes chemicals used in fertilizers) because of the high price of gas, and has throttled back other operations too. Its total gas use has fallen from five terawatt hours a year to just one, and there is the threat, so far unrealized, of gas rationing by the German government should supplies become even more constrained.

INEOS has, however, moved to reduce the risk by importing cheap shale gas from the US. It feeds the Grangemouth and Rafnes facility in Norway with its own fleet of liquefied natural gas tankers that shuttle back and forth across the Atlantic.

The other risk, although it may be receding, is a global economic downturn. Economists forecast the UK and US will go into recession this year, although they are split about how long and how deep it will be. Last year, with China pushing hard on its zero COVID policy, Ratcliffe confesses he was 'anxious' about the state of order books, and recent board meetings have revealed the extent to which the surge in energy prices has shut down many European manufacturers. 'The dive back in August was similar to what happened in 2008, if not to quite the same level. China is coming back, the US will be OK, so there might be a recession, but I think it will look a bit better this summer.'

INEOS is also taking on more debt to build – not buy – its biggest chemical plant yet. Project One in Antwerp will be a 'cracker' – a plant that turns natural gas into ethylene – and will replace the current facility which was the original INEOS asset, bought out of Inspec in 1998.

With a capacity of 1.5 million tonnes a year, it is significant for the whole European chemicals industry, one of the few new large plants to have been built in the past five decades. Naturally enough, it will run on shale gas imported from the US. Ratcliffe thinks it will be the last plant the company builds in Europe.

Jason Meers, a former Barclays and Ondra Partners banker who is chief financial officer for the new project, says the rationale for building a new plant – a rare thing for INEOS – is two-fold. First, INEOS needs more ethylene for its own operations, and demand from third parties is growing. Second, the plant is INEOS's future in Europe; it will have half the carbon footprint of the existing assets, and will be built with 'future proofing' in mind, and that it will be able – provided the right technologies emerge – to be a net-zero carbon emissions plant by 2050.

'Many operators don't really have a plan for net zero – they just have their existing plant and will eventually shut it down. Much of it is thirty or forty years old and making a substantial cut in carbon emissions, even if you could afford it, is just too difficult,' Meers says.

The financing for the new plant is different from a run-of-the-mill INEOS fundraising. It will cost €5 billion, including interest payments on the loans taken out to fund construction. INEOS will put in €1.5 billion and borrow another €3.5 billion. The export credit agencies of the UK, Spain, Italy and France will together underwrite €1.2 billion of loans, with another €800 million partially underwritten by Gigarant, an investment vehicle backed by the Flanders government. Commercial banks will provide the remaining €1.5 billion with a fifteen-year loan.

The involvement of the export credit agencies says something about the size of the project, and the work it will generate for contractors in each of the four nations. About three thousand people will work on its construction, and once operating it will employ 450. It will, Meers says, be built with a flexible approach to achieving net zero carbon emissions – by using hydrogen as a fuel, by taking more power from renewable sources, or from carbon capture and storage, where carbon dioxide generated in the plant is taken off to be stored underground. 'The idea is to keep the options open – it might be a combination of all three,' Meers says.

INEOS hopes Project One will produce its first ethylene in 2026. Construction work has begun, but one big potential obstacle still awaits.

An unwanted industry

The protesters crept in quietly, but there was little need for stealth. Just after dawn on 3 October 2020, a group of Extinction Rebellion supporters walked into an area of woodland earmarked for Project One. They put up banners and tents and chained themselves to trees and fencing. 'Investing in the production of more single-use plastics is absurd nowadays, isn't it?' a spokesman told a local news website. 'If this factory is built, the Port of Antwerp's carbon dioxide emissions will increase by more than 5 per cent, while they urgently need to be reduced.'

The protest didn't last long. Police arrived in the afternoon and carted most of the protesters off, making several arrests. The opposition to Project One has not melted away so quickly, however. While it has been approved by the Belgian government and construction continues, an outstanding challenge remains from ClientEarth, an organization with a long track record in mounting legal objections to developments it believes will harm the environment. An earlier attempt to overturn the decision to approve Project One failed, and the new challenge is likely to be heard before the Flanders government's Raad Voor Vergunnings-betwistingen, or Council of Permit Disputes, later this year.

It is not the first time INEOS has found itself on the receiving end of environmental protests. Extinction Rebellion supporters tried to blockade Grangemouth a couple of months after the Antwerp protest. One of the protesters was David Carruth, a 29-year-old rural postman. 'In all good moral conscience, when you know what's happening, you have to act,' he told the *Daily Record* on the day. 'We need drastic structural change in our society and maybe direct action will do the trick. We have to get out there and fix this. We have to try.'

The protests – and more recent similar ones outside INEOS's London office – show the company is, reluctantly, front and centre in the battles over climate change and the environment. It is a classic ideological clash: INEOS says it is working hard to cut carbon emissions and bring on stream new kinds of plastics made from alternative materials, including plant-based feedstocks to replace oil and gas. Many of the protesters reject the mitigation and improvement argument entirely. They say any new plants that will use hydrocarbons in the future, any new oil and gas or plastic production, is wrong, and foolishly shortsighted given the rapid and serious nature of climate change and environmental degradation.

There appears no immediate prospect of a meeting of minds. Asked if he can imagine a world without plastic, Ratcliffe shakes his head.

'Do people want to live in a cave? No clothes, because your clothes are man-made fibres. No heating, no lighting, no possessions. The only thing you can do is make a fire. How do you think electricity gets into a building? What insulates the cables? How do you make anything – how do you make a factory to make paper without plastics? What do you think your iPhone is made of, or your car? There is nothing – you can hardly make anything without plastics.'

Reece points out the protestors outside the London offices were wearing hi-vis vests. 'They are all made of plastic. The end result of what they are saying is that we should all go back and live in a field. The government has said no to fracking for gas in the UK. I would say come back and see us when there is no hot water in your shower.'

Cliff Bowen, the Unite convenor at Grangemouth, shares a similar disdain for some views on greening the economy. 'A green job is not a pizza delivery guy on an electric bike. A green job is a technician working on a new technology that will cut carbon emissions.'

Ratcliffe does want to change what INEOS does to meet climate change goals.

'You can do it in a better way, which the chemical industry is getting better and better at. But you can't flick a switch and do it overnight. We have quite challenging targets – net zero by 2050 – but the one I am focused on at the moment is a cut of 30–35 per cent in carbon emissions by 2030.

'It is an investment of tens of billions of dollars. We are converting furnaces, changing technologies, using more biomaterials. Each business has a path as to how they will hit the target by 2030, and it all requires investment and it all takes time. You can't just start burning hydrogen in your existing furnaces – you will damage them. You need to adapt . . . And you have to extract carbon dioxide from other exhaust gases – how do you do that? It is more chemicals, more new technology.'

Regulations in Europe and the UK will eventually force a big change in chemicals manufacturing. Both plan to be net zero (or 'climate-neutral' in the EU's case) by 2050. The European Union banned, in theory, many kinds of single-use plastic two years ago, and in the UK single-use plastic utensils, including cups, plates, trays, bowls and food containers, will be banned from October 2023.

Individual INEOS business units are puzzling over how to meet the CO_2 goals. At Grangemouth, Scotland's biggest industrial site and the country's biggest single user of gas, emissions have already been cut from five million tonnes a year in 1999 to three million. Going further and capturing the carbon emitted is a tricky job; there are multiple sources across the site, and in some of them CO_2 is only a small fraction of what comes out of the chimney.

The next step will be a partial switch to hydrogen power. INEOS plans to build at Grangemouth a large new plant to make hydrogen from methane, a component of natural gas, using high-temperature, high-pressure steam. It will not be 'green' hydrogen, the term given to production that uses electricity from a renewable power source to break up water atoms. This is 'blue' hydrogen, made from hydrocarbons. The carbon dioxide produced, about one million tonnes a year, will be sent north by pipeline to the Acorn carbon capture project, which envisages the greenhouse gas being stored offshore in disused North Sea oil and gas fields. Acorn is a joint venture between Storegga, an independent British carbon storage specialist, Shell, North Sea Midstream Partners and Harbour Energy. It missed out on selection for government funding in 2021, instead being put into a 'reserve' group of projects. While an update on funding for these was expected in 2022, none has been forthcoming. The Scottish government's then energy secretary, Michael Matheson, warned that the investors might withdraw unless they received a decision from Westminster soon.

INEOS will spend about £1 billion on the hydrogen plant and other technology changes at Grangemouth. These should take CO_2 emissions down to below two million tonnes a year, about 60 per cent less than in 1999. It is also investigating whether the existing petroleum refinery could become a centre for biofuels – petrol and diesel made from crops rather than pumped out of oil wells.

One unknown is whether products made at Grangemouth will be able to compete on price once the investments are made and the new technologies bedded down. Companies that need bulk chemicals or plastics may simply choose to import from countries that do not have, or do not police, climate change targets. 'In UK manufacturing you are already facing a struggle to survive. If we pay for all this and no one cares, we will be swamped,' says Andrew Gardner, chairman of the INEOS businesses at Grangemouth.

Rising energy costs and extra regulation are already prompting some other big European players to reconsider where they base their plants. Martin Brudermüller, chief executive of BASF, the giant chemicals company that is a pillar of German industry, said in October that the company would become smaller in Europe 'permanently' and instead look to expand in China. A few weeks later Markus Steilemann, head of Verband der Chemischen Industrie, the German chemicals trade body, said the loss of cheap Russian gas and more government targets meant Germany risked 'turning from an industrial country into an industrial museum'.

Ratcliffe says the direction of travel is obvious.

'It [chemicals] is an enormous industry in Europe, but the lack of competitiveness gnaws away. If you compare the rate things are closing down to the rate things are opening up, it is clear where it is headed. The analogy is textiles, which was huge in Europe and in the UK, but the primary cost was labour. And eventually the lower labour costs in Asia just eroded textiles – the mills closed one by one.

'If you look at chemicals, the primary cost is energy. You can survive for a while. And if the difference is 10 per cent or 20 per cent, you can live with that. But not if your energy is two or three times the price of a competitor. You finish up with a set of assets in Europe that are old, and you won't build a new one. And so it will slowly die. In Italy and Spain it has largely gone, and there's not much left in the UK. With our new cracker in Antwerp [and other plants] we are trying to beat that trend by bringing US energy economics into Europe.'

EU and UK ministers are also waking up to the threat to their manufacturers from high carbon imports. In December the European Union agreed to bring in 'carbon adjustments' for imports in some carbon-intensive goods, including chemicals and steel. In essence importers will have to buy carbon permits to offset the carbon produced in the goods' manufacture. The aim is to level the playing field for European manufacturers, with more details expected before the new rules apply in October. Britain is expected to consult on its own version of a carbon border tax later this year.

Environmental concerns are also a big concern for investors, although for the moment more in equity markets than credit. Some large institutional investors now refuse to own shares in coal mining groups, and big oil and gas companies face increasing shareholder pressure to come up with concrete plans to wind down their exposure to hydrocarbons. Some analysts think companies involved in hydrocarbon production may eventually quit the stock market altogether and rely on private investors for their finance.

The same concerns have also begun to penetrate bond markets, where INEOS raises its money. Sustainalytics, a research firm that is part of the giant Morningstar business information group, rates bonds according to their environmental credentials. It recently judged INEOS 'low-risk', noting that while its production processes resulted in 'a significant amount of pollutants', its 'overall management of material ESG [environmental social governance] issues is strong'.

What next?

On 16 August 2022, President Joe Biden presided over a ceremony at the White House where he signed into law what he called 'one of the most important pieces of legislation this country has ever seen . . . The American people won, and the special interests lost,' he said.

This was the final step in bringing into force the Inflation Reduction Act, which began life as a post-pandemic economic stimulus plan, Build Back Better. As is the way with US legislation, it was substantially reworked as it wound its way through both chambers of Congress. While it includes tax reform and curbs on prescription drug prices, its main content is a giant package of subsidies for green energy – about $400 billion worth. Companies like INEOS are still digesting its full import, but many industrial groups believe it will substantially increase investment in green technology and shift this towards the United States. At the Davos meeting of business leaders in January, Jonathan Hausman, boss of the Ontario Teachers' Pension Plan, said there would be a 'sucking sound' of green energy investments flowing into the US. 'It's a very powerful signal to investors that this is where it's happening.'

European leaders obviously feel the same. They have complained that the act breaks World Trade Organization rules on unfair subsidies, and at the same time have begun work on their own package of tax breaks and grants to encourage industries not to flit across the Atlantic.

The US package adds an extra factor to INEOS's calculation of its plans for growth. With the exception of the planned spending on Project One, Europe and the UK seem much less attractive than other territories, notably China, where four big joint ventures are in train, the Middle East and the United States. Even without the new subsidies, the US has the great benefit of low feedstock prices thanks to shale gas. At the same time there are other opportunities for expansion in new business lines, notably INEOS Energy, which has moved quickly into not only oil and gas production, but also energy trading.

Ratcliffe says the US legislation is the subject of live debate within INEOS.

'We have talked about it quite a few times. It is quite radical. It makes a lot of these green projects economically viable – when normally they probably aren't. It might mean that many big projects go there.

'It also underlines the importance of energy policy. The Americans have an obvious energy policy – and Europe is just not in a good place. I mean – Germany is going back to digging up coal.'

Energy, and in particular oil and gas, is likely to be a big new business. INEOS Energy was set up as a separate division in 2020 under the chairmanship of Brian Gilvary, the former BP finance director. It grouped together INEOS's existing energy assets, including its North Sea fields, into a single group. Gilvary and Ratcliffe had got to know each other when the former was deputed to look after BP's relationship with INEOS, and they had a shared interest in triathlons.

'Some of the big oil and gas companies are now in transition – trying to work out how they get from hydrocarbons to whatever their new energy business is. They are under shareholder pressure to sell oil and gas assets – so if they are selling, why not to INEOS? They have seen what it has done in chemicals, and they do need these assets to go to a reputable bidder,' Gilvary says.

Ratcliffe says he has no particular target for how big the oil and gas business could be.

'I never had that for chemicals either. All we will do in oil and gas is look at the opportunities that come along. And if they appear profitable, then we'll take a serious look at them.'

The energy trading business has moved to take advantage of Europe's sudden thirst for sources of non-Russian gas. In December it signed a twenty-year deal with the US utility company Sempra to take 1.4 million tonnes a year of shale gas from a new export terminal being built at Port Arthur on the Texan coast of the Gulf of Mexico. At the same time it committed to supply part of that gas to a new import terminal being built in Germany in Brunsbüttel, at the western entrance to the Kiel canal.

Shale gas has completely changed the prospects of the US chemical industry, which two decades ago was in a slump.

'INEOS bought the BP assets in the US in 2005, and at that point the US was much less competitive. People thought the US would be downsizing, selling assets and offshoring. We were doing OK then, but after the 2008 downturn shale gas kicked in and really transformed everything. That's when we started to get more aggressive in our growth and expansion, and our profits have followed. So he [Ratcliffe] certainly bought at the right time,' says Mike Nagle, chief executive of Olefins & Polymers in the US.

And that competitive advantage remains.

'We are probably on a par with the Middle East now, and certainly ahead of Europe with everything that has happened to energy prices there,' he goes on. The Inflation Reduction Act will, Nagle says, speed the adoption of renewable energy. 'I think it is quite likely you will see more change in the next ten years than you have in the past ten.'

While the US is familiar territory, China is a new, large hunting ground that has increased rapidly in size in the space of a few years thanks to a burgeoning commercial relationship with Sinopec, the world's largest refining and petrochemicals company. In December INEOS completed two of four planned joint ventures with Sinopec, the first of which will see it take a 50 per cent share of the giant SECCO chemicals plant built in the late 1990s as a joint venture between the Chinese group and BP. SECCO sits inside the Shanghai Chemical Industry Park, a thirty square kilometre development zone south of Shanghai on the shore of the East China Sea.

The first contacts between the companies were not promising. In 2014, INEOS sued Sinopec for infringement of intellectual property rights, claiming it had used its acrylonitrile manufacturing technology without permission. The dispute was resolved, and when BP decided it would get out of chemicals completely in 2018, INEOS put in a bid for the SECCO stake.

'The rationale was that we didn't have much activity in China, and if we were going to get any larger in Europe or the United States there was a chance that we would bump into competition issues,' says David Thompson, chairman of INEOS Olefins & Polymers Asia.

INEOS beat off the competition, but then was frustrated when Sinopec decided to exercise pre-emption rights under the deal it had with BP, and buy the stake itself. In 2020 it decided it wanted a partner after all, and INEOS tried again. The negotiations started just as the COVID pandemic took hold, and nearly all the talks were held virtually.

'It must be one of the only large deals to have been negotiated on Teams – unusual, and very unusual for China, where trust and personal connections are so much part of the business culture,' Thompson says.

Sinopec originally proposed a joint venture where it would be the larger partner, owning 51 per cent to INEOS's 49 per cent. INEOS said it wanted fifty/fifty. Sinopec came back with a different idea. It would agree to fifty/fifty, but only if INEOS joined it in two other deals. INEOS agreed, and proposed a fourth. Sinopec accepted.

The three additional joint ventures will involve plants in Ningbo, south of Shanghai, and Tianjin, further to the north and close to Beijing. The first will make ABS (acrylonitrile butadiene styrene), a plastic commonly used in cars and computer and mobile phone cases; the second will make high-density polyethylene, and the third will share the ownership of a new plant in Tianjin. Together they will take INEOS's turnover in China to north of $10 billion.

'We have gone from not very much to a very significant player very quickly,' says Thompson. 'And of course, it is a very big market.'

Most Chinese plants use naphtha, a liquid distilled from oil, as their feedstock rather than natural gas. Thompson says INEOS is already investigating how it can ship shale gas from the US to the SECCO site to give it a cheaper option.

The other possibility for growth is more acquisitions. Industry analysts question whether another mega-deal, like the 2005 swoop on Innovene, could be possible, or whether the forces that drove that industry shakeout have run their course.

Bob Learman says there might now be new drivers for change.

'It is a difficult landscape for many companies in chemicals – rising energy costs, environmental pressures, the shift to renewable energy. For me the question is – do all the companies have the stomach for it? I think there will always be opportunities. And if we ever walked into the boardroom and told Jim we didn't think there were any potential targets for acquisitions, we would be on the next bus out.'

There is also the collection of businesses outside chemicals and oil and gas. The largest is automotive, with the Grenadier four-wheel-drive already on sale, and potentially football, if Ratcliffe succeeds with a bid for Manchester United.

How does the trio decide when to step outside their comfort zone, and when to keep their powder dry?

'Ideas come up, and we discuss them,' says Currie. 'It is normally Jim who has the idea, and if we like it then we find the money. In essence the three of us use our dividends from the main business, or part of them.'

'It's the three of us in the beginning,' says Reece. 'You have probably heard the story about the beginning of the car business – that it was Jim and some mates in the pub talking. But there was no rush back from the pub and great, we are going to build a car. We took time to put a plan together and it has gone on for a long time.

'The logic was that we were very successful generating a lot of cash. You need to have a bit of fun – you can't spend your whole life in chemicals.'

Manchester United would take the external investments to a whole new level – both in size and public profile. 'It would not be the kind of thing where you could have an executive committee meeting, and then say OK, see you in two months' time. You read about it every day in the paper!' says Reece.

Ownership of the famous club would bring a new level of scrutiny for Ratcliffe and for INEOS. One recent study suggested Manchester United had just short of seven hundred million active fans worldwide, although it is impossible to arrive at an exact number. Previous and present owners, the Glazer family, who bought it in 2005 for £790 million, found every detail of their finances pored over – not just by the press but by inquisitive supporters eager to divine the inner workings of the club.

Ratcliffe says he understands what comes with Manchester United, and while he is a fan of the team, he is not interested in throwing his money away on a passion project.

'It is in that box of challenges. I am not parsimonious, but I have never liked the concept of economic failure. There are very few things I have done where I have ended up losing. There are things we have tried at INEOS, some investments we have made, where we were not successful, and it is not enjoyable. So looking at Manchester United, my general view is that if we invest, even if the price tag is quite high, then in ten years' time, not two years' time, we would probably be in a good place. I don't think I am throwing my money away.

'A football club like United can operate successfully on its revenues. You don't need to keep tipping more money into the bucket. If you buy other clubs which are struggling and don't have so much revenue, you are continually topping it up. So I don't think Manchester United would be a bad investment for us, unless we were a dismal failure. And if we were, then we would expect to lose money.'

Pulling up the roots

At the height of the 2008–2009 battle with lenders for control of the company, Ratcliffe, Currie and Reece were looking at everything to try and cut spending. The right amount of savings might have made all the difference between keeping their heads above water or falling into serious default, with the possibility the banks would take over.

Paying less tax was one possibility. If INEOS moved its domicile from the UK to a lower tax country, it could save millions. It would mean a huge upheaval for staff with the relocation of the head office, but the amounts on offer were large. In the end, the trio chose Switzerland, which levied corporation tax at 10 per cent compared to the UK's (then) 28 per cent. It saved INEOS nearly £400 million. 'We had no option,' Ratcliffe told the *Sunday Times* in April 2010.

The move might not have happened if the government, then Labour under Gordon Brown, had agreed to a request from INEOS for breathing space on part of its tax bill. Ratcliffe asked civil servants for a one year deferral on VAT payments, worth £350 million. He was not given a meeting with ministers. 'If we were ICI, we would probably have got an audience,' he said at the time.

Ratcliffe is full of praise for the late Sir Jeremy Heywood, who was principal private secretary to Tony Blair and Gordon Brown, and went on to serve as cabinet secretary in the David Cameron and Theresa May administrations. 'He was a good egg. I really enjoyed his company and he did everything he could.'

But Heywood's support was not enough, and the refusal to give the tax relief was clearly a big moment.

'That changed my attitude to the UK. We looked at all the levers we could pull – capital expenditure, maintenance – and then we came up with the idea of a VAT deferral. They pumped £60 odd billion into the banks in 2008 and 2009. We were in the top three manufacturers in the UK, employed five thousand people, we asked for £350 million and they said no. They said it was all too difficult. And we weren't asking for them to give it to us – we just wanted a deferral for twelve months.

'Life isn't just all about banks. After that I was pissed off with the UK. And going to Switzerland saved us £400 million.'

After the shift, Heywood 'was always at me' to persuade INEOS to move back to Britain, and in 2016 he got his man. INEOS announced it would move back, with Ratcliffe then telling interviewers that the company had been naturally gravitating back to the UK. 'It's where we started and it's where our hearts lie,' he told *City A.M.* The move roughly coincided with David Cameron's enthusiastic support for the development of a shale gas industry in the UK. In 2014, Cameron vowed to go 'all out for shale', offering generous financial incentives to communities that allowed drilling. But the Conservatives' fervour gradually ebbed away, and fracking was banned in 2019 under Theresa May. The policy was briefly reversed under Liz Truss's short premiership, and reinstated by Rishi Sunak.

By 2018, Ratcliffe had decided he would move his personal tax domicile again, this time to Monaco. It was not the flip-flopping over shale gas that persuaded him to leave, but the possibility of Labour under Jeremy Corbyn winning an election.

'It kicked off with a conversation that I had with John [Reece] and subsequently Andy [Currie]. I was getting anxious about what would happen if Jeremy Corbyn won. He was quite popular, and there was a definite chance that he would win. I asked John, "How do we make ourself Corbyn-proof?" Because if he gets in, he will eviscerate people like us. We would be paying 90 per cent tax.

'Corbyn is a Marxist, in my view. People like us, who are very wealthy and have been very successful, would have got clobbered. That was the beginning of it. We looked at all sorts of alternatives, and one of them was to be based in Monaco.'

Ratcliffe's move to the principality may substantially be about money, but there are other reasons. He likes living there. He likes the sun, is close to the Alps for one of his favourite sports, skiing, and, as he told a *Financial Times* event last year, personal safety is less of an issue than in the UK. 'People think about Monaco for the wrong reasons. There is sun three hundred days a year. It is very like California – but you are in the middle of Europe.'

Perhaps, if Ratcliffe was successful in buying Manchester United, he would consider returning to the UK? 'No,' he says. 'I'm not leaving. I'm certain about that now.'

He thinks Britain is in a slump.

'I am depressed about the UK. I think whether you like it or not, it is
in a bit of a spiral, and I find it quite difficult to see how it comes out
of it. If you think about it like a company, it has a two trillion turnover. We are sixty-five billion. If you look at the depth and ability of
management in INEOS – it is quite complex, so we need and we have
good management. Then you step up to two trillion. The competence
of the people I meet in government ... let's just say there are not
many people I meet who would get a job at INEOS.

'The big ticket items for government spending are health, education, police, energy – areas like that. So you need to be really competent
in those areas. And we are appalling. The roads don't work, the hospitals don't work, the schools don't work. Just google how many police
stations have been sold recently – they are selling about fifty a year.
And if policing is all about presence on the streets, which it is in my
view, because it is preventative, then where does the policeman go to
the loo in the middle of the morning if there is no police station? It is
simple stuff. You can't go to McDonald's for a pee or a sandwich. You
can't expect the officers to walk around for five hours without a
sandwich.'

Ratcliffe is equally scathing about recent economic policy, saying the
pandemic furlough payments system, in which the government spent
£70 billion maintaining people's wages, was too generous.

'He [Rishi Sunak, then chancellor] just gave money away like confetti.
The payments were double any other country in Europe. Everybody
gets used to it, and nobody wanted to work. What do you think follows? It is the definition of inflation, because suddenly the currency
doesn't represent the same amount of value. You have diluted it with
all you have given away. Does he think it never has to be paid back?
Does he think about inflation?'

The government needs to tell the truth about the degradation of public services, he says. 'Tony Blair started with this concept of spin and it has continued. But if you are going to spend one trillion pounds on health and police and the rest of it, you have to start with the facts. You have to know what the true picture is and where the money is going. Otherwise you can't make it better. It is the same for us and safety. If we don't know that something fell off some scaffolding, then eventually someone will get killed.'

Ratcliffe has been portrayed as an ardent Brexiteer, but his support for the UK leaving the European Union has always been more nuanced. He wants a Brexit that includes free access to the single market.

'Britain is an island. We do have a slightly different mentality to the Europeans. It was called the Common Market, not the United States of Europe, which is what it became. That just doesn't work – you just get layers of legislation that makes everything very cumbersome. Switzerland makes it work, Norway is a halfway house. They make it work.'

Who comes after?

In 1919, the pioneering American carmaker Henry Ford handed control of his company to his son, Edsel. It was meant to be a smooth transition between generations, but turned out to be anything but. The pair disagreed on many issues, in particular whether to launch a new, more sophisticated car to replace the Model T. Edsel eventually won the battle and the Model A, which went on sale in 1928, was a huge success. Edsel died of stomach cancer in 1943 and Henry returned, nominally at least, to run the company, an unhappy period that led to him being forced out in favour of Edsel's oldest son, Henry Ford II.

That early turbulence over succession has now settled down, and Ford is one of the few global companies in which the founding family has a considerable degree of control. Professional managers from outside the clan have run the company since the late 1970s and its shares are publicly traded. A special class of shares, however, means that the family's 2 per cent ownership stake gives it 40 per cent of the votes. Bill Ford, Henry's great-grandson, is executive chairman.

Working out what happens when the founder moves on is a problem for any large company. It may not, however, be quite the nightmare many watchers of the HBO hit series *Succession* imagine. An oft-quoted book, *Keeping the Family Business Healthy*, by John Ward, founder of the Chicago-based Family Business Consulting Group, concluded that two-thirds of family companies fail to make it to the third generation, and only 15 per cent to a fourth. The findings, however, have been questioned, notably by the *Harvard Business Review*, which said they were based on a limited study and that in any event family-run companies tended to be much longer-lived than corporations with a wide spread of shareholders.

INEOS's three owners have just begun to consider what comes after them. Ratcliffe has always in public backed away from talking about succession, often joking that he found the subject morbid. Now, however, the three are confronting the issue.

'We have just started to think about it,' says Currie. Ratcliffe describes it as 'an interesting question. We don't have the answer just yet. There is no shareholders' agreement [a common corporate tool that sets out the rules to follow in case of any disruption or disagreement between owners]. So if one of us falls over, there is no document that says this is what will happen. Andy, John and I are forcing ourselves to sit down and talk about it. And it is odd, because two of the three – Andy and John – don't have any children. I think we should be more thoughtful than just leaving it to chance.'

Those who have had to deal with it say the issue can prove difficult and is therefore easy to avoid.

'It is very unusual for people to want to think about their own mortality,' says Sir James Wates, outgoing chairman of the Wates Group, the UK's largest privately owned construction and property development company, which was founded in 1897. 'There are many different ways to tackle it, and there are some obvious traps you can fall into – trying to make people do things they are not really cut out for, or one generation trying to cast things in stone for the next.' Sir James, who also chairs the Institute for Family Business, says it is worth engaging outside help. 'It takes some of the emotion out of it, and this can get very emotional. You are talking about someone's life's work.'

One answer would be to sell the company. That is Ratcliffe's least favourite idea.

'I'm not interested in selling it. I've got enough money. I mean, why am I still working today? I only do it because I enjoy it. What else would I do – sit around all day and drink lots of gin? That's not very satisfying. I do it because I enjoy the challenge.'

Reece says the founders would like to try and pass on the INEOS culture – that refrain of grit, rigour and humour. 'How do you pass it on? The people we work with day to day, who are closest to us – they fully understand it. But it has to get down beyond that level too.'

Executives at INEOS – and the owners – point out that there is a strong cadre of professional managers who would ensure the company kept running. 'It would be fine [without one of the founders],' says one experienced divisional chief executive. 'Jim doesn't do the day to day running of the company – it is handed to others, and they are very good at their jobs. What he and the other two do is steer it.'

Direction of travel is important, however, and Ratcliffe remains the dominant figure. 'He is 60 per cent of the shares, but 90 per cent of INEOS,' says another company executive.

Ratcliffe would also like the principles to continue.

'What we will leave is a philosophy that I hope people would adhere to. You can't chart the course exactly, but you can talk about philosophy. And I really want it to be a meritocracy, so the best people get to the top. Their surname shouldn't be relevant in that regard.'

Regardless of the name over the door, INEOS can be ranked as one of the most important private businesses to have emerged in Britain in the past three decades. While Sir Richard Branson is frequently named as the UK's greatest recent entrepreneur – he won a 2014 poll run by the *Sunday Times*, for example – Ratcliffe, Currie and Reece have created something much larger. The Virgin Group's annual sales (difficult to calculate exactly, as many of Branson's businesses are owned or part-owned by others and use the Virgin name) were about £17 billion pre-pandemic. INEOS has annual sales of £54 billion. It is also much larger than some other notable entrepreneurial success stories, such as Sir James Dyson's electrical goods empire (£5.7 billion in 2021) and JCB, the construction machinery business owned by the Bamford family (£4.2 billion pre-pandemic).

The rate of growth is all the more remarkable for coming in a sector on which Britain was assumed to have turned its back. The 1980s and 1990s were a period of rapid de-industrialization as one industry after another – mining, shipbuilding, textiles, machine tools – retreated under the weight of cheaper and higher quality competition. Bulk chemicals was on that list, but INEOS was able to keep some plants in the UK and Europe alive, and use them as a springboard for a global expansion. It did so using techniques borrowed from private equity investors, including high levels of debt, lean management teams with strong incentives to do well and a willingness to take unpopular decisions, and risks.

The next two decades will prove just as difficult to negotiate. The size of the company means that it will be expected to be at the forefront of the chemicals industry's response to demands for much better environmental performance, both in terms of plastics waste and greenhouse gas emissions. It is also well placed to take advantage if some of its competitors conclude that pressure is too much to handle and decide to sell up. There are big issues to be confronted on the future of its UK and European operations, some of which will continue to struggle as long as energy prices are high. An involvement with Manchester United would bring a whole new level of public scrutiny.

And while all that rages, Ratcliffe, Currie and Reece must decide how to pass on their ownership of the company, and the best way to achieve their aim of ensuring that the approach that made INEOS continues when they are gone.

3

Driving Ambition, Automotive

Quentin Willson

IT'S SOMETHING OF A COMMONPLACE among people who tell stories that you can't really tell a new one. Humans have been telling stories for too long. They've all been done. The best that you can hope to do is to put a new twist on an old story.

Well, the fact that the story of the Grenadier involves a vehicle with an engine obviously helps: technology has been moving along fast and combustion engines haven't been around that long. The task that INEOS has given itself also *is*, in key respects, new. A chemicals company making a car? There isn't a precedent for that, trust me.

Not just any car either. With zero experience of building cars, they set themselves to recreate one of the most renowned of all vehicles. They gave themselves a task that one Land Rover designer described to me once as '*the most difficult automotive redesign ever*'. So, you'll be bound to ask: how did that go?

You can take it from me that straight talking is what I do. *Top Gear* would not have wanted anything else. Like it and rave about it, hate it and be rude about it. So when I am impressed – even, perhaps, *enthusiastic* – you have my word for it that the feeling is perfectly genuine.

The last twenty-five years have seen INEOS expand rapidly into one of Britain's largest companies – into one of the *world's* largest companies: bigger than McDonald's, or Nike, much bigger than Rolls-Royce, or Marks & Spencer. Yet it seemed, somehow, to have remained beneath the radar. The largest company of which you've never heard: that was the oft-repeated line. But it's really not true anymore, such is their involvement with high achievement in a number of different sports as well as in consumer sectors. They are still large – very large – but most people now *have* heard of them.

The cliché is that INEOS has 'mushroomed'. But it really does seem to have grown, stealthily and almost overnight, without any razzmatazz or pompous declarations. Today its array of businesses encompasses not only the chemical and industrial sectors but also hygiene, sustainability, philanthropy – and now, almost incredibly (and of course this explains there being a chapter written by me in this book), cars.

INEOS's culture, it seems to me (and, it has to be said, to others too – as demonstrated in the title of this book) is defined by three core values – by grit, rigour and humour. 'Grit' might be defined as the determination to make things happen, riding out and seeing off any difficulties, 'rigour' as the focus and the concentration to see them through and the thoroughness to ensure that all i's are dotted and all t's crossed, and 'humour', self-evidently perhaps, as a unique playfulness that is refreshingly different from the sometimes sterile corporate fabric of most other big organizations. For many people, this is the side of life that they look for outside work – almost work's opposite. INEOS believes that the two can co-exist.

Talking to the key figures in INEOS Automotive has shown me that the way they do business is markedly different from the way that most other car companies do it. There is no hierarchy. It's a flat structure, with CEO Jim Ratcliffe at the helm. There are no complicated layers of management which might hinder progress and which swallow resources. *Simplicity* is a defining characteristic.

Effort is made to ensure that ideas can flow through fast track channels, and that creativity is given space to bloom. After all, what use is a good idea when it gets stuck halfway up the organization and is not acted upon? And – as you might guess from the fact that it has an auto-motive section at all – INEOS does not shy away from challenges which might emerge.

In many companies, the interchange of ideas can throw up chal-lenges which are then considered impossible. But – and this is a strand in the INEOS DNA which is absolutely central to the whole organism – everybody knows always to ask the question: 'Why *can* we do this?' rather than its negative opposite: 'Why *can't* we?' 'If we possibly can, let's do this' is the presumption. It's an ethos which one often sees in small companies and much more rarely in large ones. For one as large as INEOS, it's very impressive and a mindset that is fascinating to watch in action.

When I first heard that INEOS was going to build a new car, my reac-tion, just like that of plenty of others, was that this is sure to end in tears. Yes, it seemed a lovely idea. There is a romance about the Land Rover Defender which affects numerous car enthusiasts, myself included. The thought of it fading into history was a sad one indeed. But INEOS's plan also seemed shot through with very weighty commercial challenges.

Sir Jim, though, didn't make it as far as he has done by listening too much to people like me. Over the months that I have spent with the company, I have seen a resolve and a focus that I've never come across before in corporate life. And I really am not just saying that.

Sir Jim Ratcliffe, I have come to realize, is more than just an entrepre-neur. He starts with an instinct for an opportunity. And then he questions. Researches. Examines. Assesses that opportunity. At each stage, unless it is demonstrated, empirically, to be iron-clad, he won't move forward. It is, in the end, much more than simply a good feeling.

That rigour, coupled with a down-to-earth humility, means that he takes nothing for granted. He never bases important decisions upon somebody else's second-hand assumptions. Modestly, he describes his very considerable success in business as the result both of 'making consistently good decisions' (who could deny it?) and of 'surrounding myself with very talented people'.

It sounds easy enough. But in the massively complicated world of building cars – increasingly complicated with each year that passes, of course – are such simple philosophies enough? One thing's for sure: I've seen that INEOS Automotive does things differently from every other car company with which I've ever worked (quite a few, I assure you). And that, as it happens, is a very good thing.

The legacy automakers, as they're known – the huge behemoths of the automobile industry that everybody could name – have old habits, unwieldy processes and an insufficient customer focus. They have chains of command which are politically dominated. They also take simply ages to do stuff, which is increasingly impossible to defend. Nobody these days expects to be kept in the dark for weeks and weeks. Ashley Reed, chairman of INEOS Automotive, summed up the pace with which the company does things. 'Speed at INEOS is much faster than [at] other car makers. And Jim is even faster than that.' *Speed*, I should emphasize: not haste.

But will this alacrity, this good judgement, this obsession with quality and this humility be enough to propel INEOS's retro-styled off-roader to commercial success? Well, I'm no soothsayer, as you probably know. Only time will tell. But – and I'm not going to spoil this remarkable story for you – from what I've seen over the last few months, things are looking, well, rather promising.

The vision

First things first. Chemical companies have never made cars. They're not daft. They know that building a car from scratch is as easy as picking up spilt mercury with your bare hands. You need a completely different culture and you need a new set of skills, a new set of processes, new factories, new supply chains and new knowledge. There's no tradition of scientists in lab coats demonstrating car-building expertise.

Which is why the story of the INEOS Grenadier is so unprecedented. And let's not forget that automotive history is strewn with failed car companies, all with years of skills, knowledge, learning and experience. Yet they all still failed. DeLorean, Tucker, Kaiser, Studebaker, Alvis, AC, Gilbern, Jensen, Jowett, Marcos, Panther, DeSoto, Duesenberg, Cord – the casualty list stretches beyond the horizon, because the road to automotive profitability is long and hard.

We can presume that the clever people at INEOS were well aware of this fundamental truth before they started. Then again – perhaps not. Because here's the thing: INEOS didn't only set out to build a car from scratch. They identified one of the world's most famous and instantly recognizable automotive silhouettes and gave themselves the mission of redesigning it to look better. As mentioned, they gave themselves a task that one Land Rover designer once described to me as '*the most difficult automotive redesign ever*'.

If that wasn't enough, they also set themselves the job of making this brave new (but familiar-looking) 4x4 better built, more reliable, longer lasting and more refined to drive. What it adds up to is a miracle on the scale of feeding the five thousand. Impossible, surely? This then, is the unlikely story of how some crazy people in a chemical company designed and built a new 4x4 that has surprised everybody. But more on the surprising stuff later. We need to go back to the beginning. How on earth did this madness even begin?

Our tale begins on safari in Botswana, Africa, in 2015, when Jim, a serial Land Rover enthusiast, climbed aboard one of those converted Land Rovers which the safari tour guides use to drive their guests around the bush. If you're lucky enough to have been on safari in Africa, you'll have seen them too. Locally converted, long chassis, open-top Land Rovers with rows of not very comfortable seats, raised high enough to give passengers a good view of the terrain as well as protection from any hungry local wildlife.

Jim was no stranger to Botswana, or to those converted Land Rovers, and he'd chat to the drivers about their vehicles. It was during one of those chats that he heard that the fabled Defender was coming to the end of its sixty-eight-year production run. The cost of meeting the latest legislation regarding engine emissions and safety features meant that Jaguar Land Rover had been forced to end production.

That was the official line anyway. Another reason was the solemn commercial reality of hand-building the Defender in the old Solihull, Birmingham factory – a labour-intensive process that took fifty-six hours compared to forty-eight hours for the more complicated Discovery Sport. The Disco made money; the Defender did not.

The safari guide told Jim that this could be one of his last trips in Africa in a hallowed safari Land Rover and that he should enjoy it while he could. It was while processing the sad news that Jim had a thought: what if someone took over the rights to continue producing the Defender, but built it better? For most people this might have been the start of a short, idle daydream, and remained at that. Jim, though, is not 'most people'. And this was the moment when this very remarkable idea – the INEOS Grenadier – began its five-year gestation.

Let's be quite clear about one thing: the Grenadier was never meant to be a homage and it was emphatically not what is known as a 'vanity project'. Jim really did believe that the disappearance of the tough, ladder-framed off-roader was a significant loss to the world. Years spent in Africa had taught him that for many communities, Solihull's beast of burden was a lifesaver and an essential tool for work.

Without it there would only be a handful of entirely one-dimensional pick-up trucks available, all of which lacked the body versatility, the axle articulation or the gully climbing abilities of the ladder chassis Land Rover. Modern pick-ups are also less easy to fix in the field and (for the same reason) much more complicated by comparison with the Land Rover's rudimentary engineering.

This, for Jim, was a really important factor. Those communities and businesses in developing countries who, for decades, had relied on the Land Rover's simple mechanics would have no replacement. And since there simply wasn't any serious competitor left in the tough, durable, go-anywhere 4x4 sector, Jim sensed a commercial opportunity. This was a market that had been abandoned by every motor manufacturer in the world. In the vehicles' place was a slew of uptown SUVs that rarely, if ever, got muddy.

Jim reckoned that this gap in the market had the potential, on a low volume basis, to make money. As I've said, things happen quickly at INEOS. Within hours he had briefed the management team and agreed to meet in the now famous Grenadier pub, in London's Belgravia (which INEOS now owns). There he explained the reasons why he saw a definite commercial opportunity in the gridlock of faceless, luxury 4x4s.

Jim believed passionately – and he explained why – that the world did still need a pure 4x4, inspired by the great off-road legends. When he closed the meeting it was with a rousing 'let's do it!' Project Grenadier was born. And with that, the team went off to sketch out a plan and to begin research in earnest.

A year later I too was experiencing the same pangs of loss. The public announcement that a much-loved British icon, as familiar as red telephone kiosks and post boxes, was to disappear forever, hit the country hard.

It was 29 January 2016 and I was being interviewed by Chris Evans for BBC Radio 2 from the floor of the Solihull Land Rover factory. I was there with Vicki Butler-Henderson, one of my old *Top Gear* co-presenters, to act as hosts for a final farewell in front of seven hundred former and current employees – as the last Defender rolled off the production line. It felt like a funeral.

On his breakfast show, Evans summed up the Defender's place in history perfectly. 'This is the world's most famous car. Everybody, everywhere in all the corners of the globe knows what a Land Rover looks like.' For days previously I'd been doing misty-eyed media interviews and was honoured to have been asked, along with many other public figures, to help to bolt together the very last car. A pall of gloom had descended over the old factory.

Families who had worked on the production lines for three generations building Land Rovers felt this sadness very keenly. Tears were shed. And in my valedictory speech I felt my voice crack as I celebrated the tremendous influence and importance of this very special piece of British manufacturing history. Like Jim, I too had seen clear signs that the world's affection for this simple, utilitarian off-roader was undiminished.

As soon as word got out that the end was near, sales of the final Defenders boomed. Collectors laid them down like fine wine for the future, utility companies bought scores to mothball, governments around the world placed their final orders and wily opportunists offered new delivery mileage examples for twenty grand over list price. As a mad scramble broke out to own those last few thousand cars, prices went through the roof. And they have carried on rising.

Anyone who had any doubt about how admired the Land Rover was – and still is – needs only cast an eye on the appreciation in value of those final cars since production ended. The graph of achieved prices shows their value rising like those of old master paintings.

In 2022, a batch of thirteen of those last cars (delivery-mileage only) was offered for sale – six years after they were put into storage by a celebrated Land Rover modifier, Twisted Automotive. The company originally bought 240 units – a mix of ninety XS Hard Tops and 110 XS Station Wagons – from the final production run, but after selling two hundred decided to release the last few for public sale. With between ten and twenty miles on the clock, they really were in new condition.

Back in 2016 the official list prices were around £30,000 to £35,000 depending on spec, but these thirteen were up for rather more – £69,000 for the Hard Tops and £88,000 for the XS Station Wagons – which is more than 100 per cent appreciation over six years. And if you think that's a one-off price spike, rest assured that it's not. In September 2021 a Defender 90 XS with 107 miles on the clock fetched over £61,000 at auction. At the Goodwood Festival of Speed, a 110 XS Utility made £75,900. The highest price achieved at auction, and the current UK auction record for a low-mileage Defender, was set in November 2021 by an

Autobiography Edition 90 with 180 miles on the clock. It sold for an astonishing £77,063.

That some people are now willing to pay double the original 2016 list price does rather suggest that Land Rover might have been over-hasty in killing off the Defender. I remember talking to a senior figure at JLR during the final production ceremony, when he confided to me that, having seen the sudden rise in Defender orders: 'we could certainly have sold a lot more'. Jim's instinct that Land Rover had left a market vacuum for a utilitarian 4x4 workhorse just might prove to have been inspired. But to understand what all the fuss was about, and to get your head around the world's continuing obsession with a go-anywhere off-roader which boasts both presence and panache, you really need to have owned or spent some time behind the wheel of one.

When it comes to cars, I'm generally pretty level-headed. My check-list is short but consistent. My motors have to be reliable. They have to be smooth riding. They have to start instantly. They have to have good driving dynamics. And they have to be refined. But I'd be the very first to admit that, when it comes to Land Rovers, all of that wholesome good sense goes completely out of the window. They have an indefinable, almost mystical, appeal.

Over the years I've owned lots of different generations and have loved each one. So has my family. When my kids were little, we had a 110 Defender seven-seater, their default choice for school runs, holidays and even trips to France. It was fitted with a roof rack with an observation platform which my eight-year-old daughter would use as a vantage point whenever we parked, scuttling up the ladder to the roof with scary alacrity. The three rows of seats made it feel like a bus and the heavy, swinging, rear-opening door with its huge handle was the only way the kids would climb in. 'It was our magic door,' they explained, and they'd sit right at the back in their separate seats, whispering secrets to each other. Honestly, I have never seen them behave in the same way in a car, either before or since.

For me too, though, driving this noisy, heavy and hard-riding relic was also a wonderful, rather mystical experience. You feel like a buccaneering, non-conformist free spirit. You look down your nose at other SUV drivers in their predictable (if infinitely more comfortable) Nissans, Toyotas and BMWs. You're a lantern-jawed hero piloting a magical machine with broad-bladed bumpers, big wheels and high ground clearance that of course has no difficulty whatsoever in handling anything that the metropolitan marathon might throw at you.

An inexplicable emotional alchemy takes over when you drive these things. It's hard to explain or rationalize, unless you've felt that particular sense of all-conquering invulnerability. As the children grew older and I moved up to a Range Rover, the faithful 110 was driven less and sat unused in the drive for weeks at a time.

In an unguarded moment I accepted an offer from a friend and sold the family Landy. When the kids got back from school, I broke the news. I do not exaggerate when I say that they ran to their bedrooms, slammed the doors and wept. As adults they still regularly remind me of that cruel act of treachery, and admit that they were so devastated that they even talked about ringing Childline. Both say now that one day they too will own off-roaders of their own.

As a serious collector of Land Rovers, Jim understood all of this weird alchemy very well indeed, and distilling it into a new bottle was the basis of the founding of INEOS Automotive. But this was no sentimental flight of fancy. On the contrary: it was a clear-eyed project with a plan and a defined set of aims that could not be obscured by emotion.

The new Grenadier had to be excellent off road, much more refined than the Defender but conceptually familiar to 4x4 customers. Everything had to have a specific function, but the detailing had to be both cool and practical. The cabin had to be involving and special while the on road performance and ride quality had to exceed customers' expectations. Defined by the three core values of integrity, honesty and visual excitement, the Grenadier had to be true to its roots and to be a tool as much as a vehicle, with a design that was based around function.

Sensibly, INEOS knew that they needed a high calibre automotive team, a state-of-the-art factory, and a long list of trusted suppliers with proven track records. Industry heavyweights like BMW, Mercedes, ZF, Bosch and Magna were called in and work began to assemble a team of experts steeped in automotive engineering. It's a simple premise: work with the very best people and you do get a better product, designed and built to the highest standards. And to Jim, one of the country's most successful industrial entrepreneurs, engineering integrity was the very bedrock of the project.

Conversations about securing design rights to build the Grenadier began with Land Rover. Initially they were positive. But then they began to founder, both over the intellectual property of the Defender design and over whether ownership of the shape rested with Jaguar Land Rover or could be used by INEOS Automotive.

A court case ensued, followed by many more, along with representations to the UK Intellectual Property Office. After a great deal of legal wrangling, the case ended up in the High Court. To cut a very long story short (and one that is not perhaps completely gripping unless intellectual rights law is up your particular street), the UKIPO adjudged that while the Defender shape was very recognizable, it didn't have the 'distinctiveness' that would set it apart from other 4x4s and from many normal passenger cars. In essence, the simple two box shape – a box for the engine and a box for passengers or cargo – had been replicated in many other cars and 4x4 designs over the years.

Which technically, I have to say, was correct: look at a Nissan Patrol, a Mitsubishi Shogun, a Toyota Land Cruiser or a Jeep Cherokee. They have all used the familiar two box body architecture. And so have thousands of passenger car hatchback designs. As a result of this lack of definable distinctiveness, the court adjudged that the design and shape could not be trademarked.

JLR appealed on the grounds that the UKIPO had not considered expert evidence from a survey that JLR had commissioned or guidance from automotive experts. But the High Court rejected the grounds for appeal. Its ruling was that the Defender's shape could not be registered as a protected trademark.

All of which meant that any potential relationship with JLR did not look very promising, to say the least. Which was a shame. So, instead, INEOS decided to go it on their own and to build the Grenadier from scratch, their way. There was a lot of additional stress, and effort, and nobody wanted the relationship with JLR to break down to this extent. With hindsight, though, this decision was much the best outcome. This way INEOS could start with a clean design brief, unencumbered – by legacy tooling, by suppliers, by factories or by existing engineering. First, though, they needed a factory.

Jim was keen, for obvious reasons, to build the Grenadier in the UK. A new 4x4 with a very British name really *ought,* it seemed, to be built in Britain. But manufacturing, like life, is never simple. Every potential green- and brownfield site in the UK was considered and much thought was given to rooting the Grenadier in this country. Potential locations were considered in Teesside, Kent and South Wales. For a while Wales looked the favourite, but the numbers just wouldn't stack up.

Then there were other possible sites in Sweden, in Portugal and in Germany. But none of these ticked all of the necessary boxes either. This was when one of those moments occurred which seem, with hindsight, like they were meant to be – those moments which seem now to have followed the Grenadier project.

INEOS is a principal partner to the Mercedes F1 team, supporting them with key chemicals and compounds and working with their Applied Science Programme. In conversations, Mercedes had mentioned that their Smart EQ factory in Hambach in northeast France, close to the German border, would become available when production of the Smart finished. The pandemic had meant that a restructuring drive was necessary and as a result Hambach was surplus to requirements.

What is more, Mercedes had recently spent half a billion euros upgrading the paint and body shops. There was an existing and very talented local workforce, the site was close to the MB manufacturing centre in Stuttgart and all of its associated supply chains, and everything was already built, functioning and working, including hundreds of new, automated production 'Kuka' robots. Jim and the team visited the Hambach site and hesitated for an entire nanosecond.

Even more encouraging was the fact that Mercedes had widened some of the production lines to accommodate their planned electric EQB SUV, so the similarly sized Grenadier would fit on most of the tracks. Everybody agreed that Hambach was a massive opportunity – one that wouldn't just save close to a billion quid in building and formation costs but could also shave a couple of years off the project's lead time. While all the team genuinely regretted not being able to base the project in the UK, hard-nosed and unemotional accounting presented an irresistible case for building the Grenadier in one of the most modern automotive factories in Europe. So in December 2020 a deal was done. Everybody breathed a huge sigh of relief. All they needed to do now was to get cracking and make a car.

Having got to this stage, gentle reader, you'll be thinking that this is all sounding like a very bold endeavour indeed. And you'd be absolutely right. You might even be thinking that this is seeming a little reckless. Unhinged, even.

Which is why we must pause for a moment and consider whether this idea – the reimagining of a perpendicular utility 4x4 for the twenty-first century – has ever been done before. Was there an inspiration out there to justify what was ballooning into a very considerable investment?

Sure, there have been plenty of automotive heritage recreations: Mini, VW Beetle, Ford Thunderbird, Ford GT, Mercedes SLS, Fiat 500, Chevrolet Camaro, Ford Mustang. But these were all based around sports cars, coupes, and passenger cars (and built by major existing car manufacturers). Had anybody taken an elderly, two box, basic off-roader and made it sexy?

This is where INEOS's growing relationship with Mercedes

provided so much of an inspiration. Think hard and you'll get it. That's right. The Mercedes Benz G-Class, or G-Wagen to its fans. Here was a utility vehicle that had been completely reincarnated. Back in the seventies, the Shah of Iran (a large MB shareholder at the time) asked Mercedes to design a 4x4 for the military. Steyr-Daimler-Puch in Graz, Austria, did the design and testing and came up with a square-shouldered off-roader, featuring three locking differentials and a ladder chassis. As a military vehicle it was fine – basic, simple, tough, and accomplished – a lot like the Defender. But, also like the Land Rover, consumers liked the idea of owning a robust cross-country vehicle and the popularity of the G-Model steadily increased.

Over the years it became less military and more civilian, with refinements like fuel injection, automatic transmission, air conditioning, air bags, cruise control and even leather seats and walnut dashboards. Engines increased in size, there were continued facelifts and gradually the G-Model turned into the G-Class and became a much-admired member of the MB family. The word 'legend' wouldn't be misplaced here. In fact, it's become one of the longest produced vehicles in MB's history, spanning forty-three years, and it has plenty of parallels with the Defender story.

Like the Defender, the G-Wagen faced engineering challenges of its own with compromised emissions and safety features, and it needed updating to comply with new EU and American regulations. MB tried to replace it with a new GL-Class but there was a public outcry and in 2005 MB, wisely as it turned out, told its customers that the G-Class would continue to be built until at least 2017. They managed to do what Land Rover did not – to re-engineer their old icon so that it complied with modern safety and emissions regulations. That re-engineering certainly did cost many millions, but it gave the G-Class a completely new lease of life. Not to mention much improved profitability, which has even surprised Mercedes.

And here's the really interesting bit. As I write this in 2022, the G-Wagen isn't only still in production, but it's become a fiercely desirable designer icon in its own right. Go to London, New York, Dubai, Abu Dhabi, Berlin or Los Angeles and you'll see stridently coloured G-Wagens – many with jumbo 6.3 litre V8 engines (aka the G63) – rumbling around the high-end places where serious money comes to rest. Wrapped, jacked up, pimped up, gilded and even modified to have six wheels, the G-Wagen speaks with a different voice to a completely different and younger demographic. Utility can be sexy, and the G is proof.

What's more, it's done much to take the Mercedes brand into a new aspirational heartland of videos, movies, music, designer fashion and lifestyle. The G is now a brand in its own right. And with a price that *starts* at £130,000 and can rise to over £200,000, depending on spec, it's another indicator that the world's obsession with traditional, heritage-styled off-roaders can translate into very premium prices. Which for INEOS was very good news. Their business plan had a commercial precedent.

They weren't unhinged after all. Successfully reinventing and redesigning an old-school off-roader could be done – and most importantly – could be profitable. Given that INEOS's ambitions were always rather more modest than Mercedes', the team took the G-Wagen's sparkling success story as a huge inspiration. But who was going to be the Grenadier's target market?

Tom Crotty, communications director at INEOS, explained that the potential market has four levels. The largest consists of the lifestylists – around 65 per cent of the total – who will buy because they want something different. They see the Grenadier as a fresh, disrupter brand, radiating a progressive non-conformity, even though the styling is retro. This market segment approves of the quality, longevity and wholesomeness that's been engineered in. They're also likely to be physically adventurous, so the go-anywhere ability makes their buying choice a practical asset as well something cool to own.

Then come the 4x4 enthusiasts. This group regrets the passing of the Defender, is keen to crown a new off-roader as king and has shown that, if they're prepared to pay those very high prices for the last-off-the-line Land Rovers, they'll potentially buy something that's better engineered but also cheaper. There's a strange irony in the fact that the current starting price of a brand-new Grenadier of £49,000 is considerably less than the money being paid right now for the tiny-mileage 2016 Defenders which we talked about earlier.

Then comes the utilitarian market that needs a tough working tool that can carry loads, drive off road, tow and occasionally cross a stream or two. Think of all those outside jobs that need a workhorse that won't break – particularly one with a pick-up body – and you've got a sizeable customer base for the Grenadier Utility Wagon (that is, a commercial version, to you and me). The fourth segment is the corporate market: all those governments, militaries, NGOs, utility companies and construction firms that need 4x4s for specific jobs. That's a good-sized market as well. And having seen the Grenadier long wheelbase double cab pick-up in the metal, so to speak, I can tell you it's a very professional bit of kit, with broad appeal.

For the lifestylists, furthermore, INEOS created the Hard Way Home programme. Over a thousand people entered, hoping to be voted as one of the first three customers to pick up their pre-ordered Grenadiers from a remote location and then to drive them home a thousand miles, through some of the world's most challenging terrain, using only their wits, determination and navigational skills.

As car handovers go, it certainly beats driving your new car home from a showroom on the Coventry ring road. And building a Grenadier community is key to growing the lifestylist customer base. They won't be sold by dealers but bought directly from Grenadier, in order to keep the customer close to INEOS. INEOS doesn't care for middlemen. Indeed, Tom Crotty told me that he doesn't believe that most car buyers like the franchised dealer experience. And they hate haggling:

'The dealer showroom is usually the first experience buyers have of a car brand. And it's not always happy. We want to cherish and protect those first highly charged emotional moments – to make sure that all our customers begin their journey with us feeling joy, rather than sorrow.'

It's a business model that's been very successful for Tesla and which strips out a lot of unnecessary costs and risks to the brand. Only the American and UAE markets will have dealers, due to local sales laws. Warranties will be five years, with unlimited mileage for the mechanicals, three years for the body and twelve years for rust perforation.

The engineers I spoke to at Hambach talk of an uncompromising level of quality that could define a new industry-leading life span. Looking at the engineering of the mighty ladder-frame chassis – which took three years to create – with its thick box girder steel, heavy powder coating and cavity wax injection, I think that they might be on to something. And after more than a million miles of testing there's a feeling among the engineers that this is a vehicle that won't just last years, but possibly decades.

Jim's consistent ambition was to build the toughest 4x4 by far, defined by its pure engineering integrity. But before we talk about that engineering, we need to understand the design. Remember how earlier I said that reimagining a retro off-roader to be modern was one of the most difficult design jobs in the industry?

Well, here's another example of how INEOS thinks differently from other car makers. Jim gave this job – an absolutely critical one – to someone who usually sketches out yachts. Yes, seriously.

The design

Before the Grenadier, INEOS's head of design, Toby Ecuyer, had never designed a car.

An architect by training, he has spent twenty years drawing award-winning 100 metre long superyachts for what he calls 'extremely determined and powerful people' – as you can well imagine that those who are in the market for superyachts tend to be. Which is how he met Jim Ratcliffe.

With two of Jim's yacht designs already under his belt – and the pair remaining good friends – when Jim asked Toby if he would be interested in designing the Grenadier, he jumped at the chance. Drawing cars had always been a secret love. As an eleven-year-old, he had even sent some sketches to the Austin Rover design department from which, he tells me, he got a 'lovely' letter back.

He talks with passion and knowledge about a range of iconic car designs, without ever lapsing into pompous designer-speak. Like Jim, he's a very modest bloke. Within minutes of our first meeting, we were chatting like schoolboys about Jaguar E-types. (He owns one; I made the mistake of selling mine.) And then, before we knew it, we were exchanging car pictures on WhatsApp and discussing the flying buttresses on the seventies Jaguar XJS. Toby, like Jim, is a proper car guy.

As he freely admits, though, 'Jim didn't need a traditional car designer on a project like this because there would never be any sculpted bonnets or curvy wings. This', he says, 'is utility: pure and simple.' And you can see how Toby's simple approach to design can help solve technical problems.

On the early Grenadier prototypes, the bonnet was sitting too high to meet pedestrian safety regulations. Changing the front chassis, subframe or engine mounts would have been one solution, but a very expensive one. So Toby asked the question that nobody else had: 'What if we just remove the plastic cover on the top of the engine to free up more clearance?' That simple solution duly brought the bonnet down to the magical compliance height.

Toby freely admits that he's made a design career out of simply asking the questions that others won't. But you can well understand why this suits him perfectly for INEOS. Creating a fertile design environment that's open to criticism and to question is vital. There are plenty of cars out there that shouldn't have got past the sketch stage and look more like sudden slips of the designer's pencil – that were crying out for an awkward question or two.

In some countries, there are corporate cultures where it is considered rude to disagree or to suggest changes. I've sat in styling studios with designers of major automakers offering feedback which you know isn't really welcome. On the contrary, it's a sort of unspoken rule that the design that's presented in a clinic is not really open to an alternative view. In general, boardrooms, accountants and liability lawyers have too much influence on the way cars look these days. And that's broadly why so many cars look the same – or just plain bland.

Sure, there will always be regulatory issues that dictate things like lights, bumper heights and external safety dimensions. But that doesn't mean that the fundamental design vernacular has always to be compromised by compliance. It is both patronizing and simply wrong always to style cars so that they follow a homogeneous look – one that automakers believe is *what the customer wants*. Pure automotive design should take risks. It should challenge the accepted norms. And it should offer consumers something genuinely fresh and different.

Which explains Jim's hatred of gratuitous curves, and the fact that so many cars are now hard to tell apart. He cites the Porsche 911 as a brilliant original design which then, over the years, was skilfully updated and refined, managing always to keep its unique identity. And he was determined that the Grenadier needed its own distinctive design language and separate visual identity.

Early in the project Jim became frustrated at being told why his design ideas wouldn't work and in fact he very nearly pulled the plug. 'I'd argue with the engineers', he recalls, 'and get tired of being told why something won't work, rather than how it can.' Then eventually the engineers would come back, and say that actually, 'if we just do this, we *can* make the design work'. It was a pivotal moment: this was when design began to lead technology, and to become unfettered.

Fundamentally (and quite rightly), Jim believes that car buyers demand visual individuality. If you look at the most admired classics of car design in the world – the Jaguar E-type, the Ferrari 250 California Spyder, the Lamborghini Miura, the Ferrari Dino or the Mercedes 300SL Gullwing – they all have an independence of spirit and a timeless individuality which you know came originally from pure design impulses.

And they all have faces. The most successful car designs don't present anger or aggression: they radiate approachability, like the original Mini or the Citroën 2CV. Toby calls this the 'Family Pet School of Design'. And that's also why the Grenadier doesn't look angry. But most important of all, both Jim and Toby believe that cars should clearly describe their function through their looks. There should never be any confusion over what they're meant to do. Hence the Grenadier's friendly front and commodious rear, a bit like the prow and stern of a boat.

You can see too how Toby's experience of styling boats has influenced the Grenadier. It's all in the functionality of the details. Hard-core off-roaders like to carry stuff on the roofs. But why fit something which is an aerodynamic and an aesthetic compromise, like a roof rack? They whistle as you drive. They create turbulence. And they look ugly. Why not just reinforce the roof panel and provide tie off points around the perimeter, so that the entire roof area becomes the rack?

Look around the Grenadier's lower roof and you can see two handy tie off locations sculpted into the panels on each side. Lower down on the flanks, meanwhile, there's a sort of tool belt running along either side, to which you can attach whatever you want. 'We didn't want owners drilling holes for clamps, lights or accessories. So we built in all these location points for mounting and tying things off. A lot like a boat.'

Toby's brief from Jim was to design the ultimate utility 4x4 that shows no ambiguity about its role in life and radiates utility from its core. Nothing should be for show, nothing should be flash – or 'poncy and fluffy', as Jim puts it. There should be a simple no-nonsense logic to the design. And starting with a completely new chassis and new power-trains meant that the shape of the Grenadier would be design-led. No poncyness. Just an old-school, hardcore off-roader that spoke to customers in a normal voice.

When I asked Toby whether he was worried that some have said that the Grenadier looks too much like the Defender, he was unapologetic. 'There's a basic design vernacular to all off-roaders', he insists. 'You have an engine, a front cab and a passenger area.' As a kid he admired the angular lines of the Nissan Patrol, the Ford Bronco, the Jeep and the Unimog, so he wanted to create something that was as cute as a Bronco, as determined as a Unimog and as tough as a Patrol:

'Try designing a utility off-roader and you always end up with that same perpendicular outline. You need flat surfaces, wide arches for wheel articulation and lots of passenger or cargo area. In fact, you always arrive back at the two-box silhouette.'

For Toby, one of the joys of the project was Jim's constant involvement. There were no focus groups or design committees. Just the two of them in the design studio, poring over paper sketches, or prowling round clay models. 'Jim was totally involved with the design process from day one,' he tells me. 'He would literally take a scalpel to the clays and slice bits off or smooth away curves. Jim', he says – telling me what I already know – 'has a hatred of gratuitous curves.'

The pair worked together, regularly refining and smoothing the outlines, until they'd reached what they both considered to be the shape of an uncompromising, dual-purpose vehicle. At first Jim would give Toby an abstract idea. Toby would sketch it out. And then they'd both work on realizing the design. In fact this partnership was so close that they effectively designed the car together. 'Jim has this reductive view of design', Toby tells me. 'Remove the unnecessary and make the necessary simple.'

For instance: why have painted bumpers when they cost more, add an extra stage to the manufacturing process and get damaged easily? Rather than painting them, simply make them out of the hardest and lightest material possible so that they never degrade, or scratch, or need respraying. The same logic was applied to the door mirrors. Make them safe, simple, clear and almost indestructible. Where is it written that car door mirrors must always look like over-designed, tear-shaped chalices?

Keeping the design dialogue simple, and communicating only within a tight group, helped speed things up considerably. 'Of course,' Toby says, 'we asked for inputs from enthusiasts, and lots of people offered suggestions as to what's important in their ideal 4x4. We considered all the good stuff,' he assures me, 'incorporated some of it, but since Jim and I own and drive Land Rovers regularly, we had strong internal instincts of our own. We were,' he tells me, 'a design team of two.'

Following those instincts, furthermore, created genuinely new elements for the design. For instance: they wanted a fold-out table onto which you could put drinks, food, maps, tools or whatever, to keep items separate from a usually fully-packed load area on trips. On the inside of the station wagon rear door they mounted a strong metal folding table that took up minimal space when flat, but which became a very useful small shelf, platform or table when folded out. And then they reduced the weight by cutting out sectional apertures in the metal pressing. It's perfect for everything from champagne bottles to shotguns. See it work and you can't fail to be impressed by the sheer blinding simplicity of both the idea and its realization.

The split rear door is another example of the Grenadier's simple, customer-focused minimalism. On most 4x4s a single swinging rear door, with a spare wheel attached, can feel like opening a vault – heavy and unwieldy. Split the door in two, though, with a smaller opening on the left, and you can use the lighter, easier door for most of your routine access to the rear load area. It's convenient. It's easy to use. And it's so simple you wonder why nobody's thought of it before.

The electric wiring harness which is built into the roof is also a case of design leading function. The idea began with the experience of owning 4x4s, and understanding that many enthusiasts wire up accessories like spotlights, winches and roof lights. Those accessories all need separate switches on separate circuits. So instead of leaving customers to splice into the main wiring harness and to fit multiple switches to the dash – which often looks rather like a toddler has thrown a bag of sticky boiled sweets (not, it goes without saying, a terribly pretty sight) – why not, they thought, provide a dedicated roof panel for extra toggle switches, connected up to a special accessory harness which runs along the roof?

This is when design-led function throws up opportunities for visual theatre. Why not make that roof panel a toy? Jim wanted the panel to look like the roof controls of a plane or a helicopter and Toby agreed that owners should be granted a little moment of fantasy – allowed to feel 'that they were flying an aeroplane or steering a ship.'

Look up at the roof panel and you see how it takes design towards that fantasy. The switches are old-school chunky, with clear white legends, but each one is protected by two small metal hoops which reference fifties and sixties aeronautical, marine and aerospace control panels. Yes, there's a definite moment of emotional indulgence here. But the hoops do have a serious function, of helping to locate the switches if you're wearing gloves or trying to operate them on challenging terrain.

Once you start looking around the interior and interrogating the pair's joint design decisions, everywhere you can see very distinct trains of thought. And the pre-eminent thought is that customers should never have to suffer to own a 4x4. You might think that that's a truism, but far too many off-roaders feel like they are designed to keep an army of osteopaths in work for years.

The splash-proof seats are made by Recaro, experts at sitting comfortably in cars. To both Jim and Toby, having supportive, comfortable and durable seats for long distances was massively important and formed part of the original design brief for the Grenadier to be an accomplished performer both off road and on.

Cryptically, Toby remarks that designing the interior was 'an intense period', with scores of difficult decisions. Like why follow the trend for having a starter button on the dash? It's fake and bogus and supposed to remind us of cars of the forties and fifties that didn't use ignition keys. Toby thought it was frivolous and preferred a conventional ignition lock and key. Another design trend that he didn't follow was an electric handbrake. On a utility off-roader, an electronic parking brake system would be both unnecessary and vulnerable to mud and water from off-roading. Far better to have a stylish leather-clad lever as another tactile control point.

And do you build sat nav into the design? Since most of us have smart phone navigational connectivity, there seemed little reason to incorporate an operating system which would be dated by the car's launch and which would need regular updates anyway. Electric seats were another unnecessary complication. Motors, relays and switches for powered seat adjustment eventually fail, and if the Grenadier's interior was to be, as Jim had always hoped that it would be, 'hose-able' enough to clean down, the last thing you'd want would be a bunch of electric seat motors getting wet. Much better to have good, old-fashioned, lever-worked-by-hand technology.

Not getting wet is also the reason why the car's USB ports face downwards, so that they don't fill up with water. There are also removable plugs in the floor to drain water (like a boat). Making the interior special and a place for escapism, meanwhile, was very important. Toby posed the question to me: 'When was the last time you got excited by a car interior?' And he's right. Making the cabin adventurous enough to be enjoyed by both driver and passenger is very rare in modern automotive design.

The Grenadier's control stack is sited centrally so that it involves everybody. Buttons and switches are clear, analogue, logical and visible to rear passengers, and the operating system touch screen is accessible to both occupants in the front. The thinking here is that if the driver is manhandling the car with both hands on the wheel over rough and uneven terrain, the passenger is close enough to both the controls and information systems to lend a hand – and also to be positively engaged with the car's progress.

This need for tactile engagement runs all the way through the interior, with plenty of grab handles, grip bars and textured surfaces. The steering wheel is a focal point that the owner will handle, caress, move and make constant contact with over thousands of hours and miles. That intimacy of touch is why Toby wanted the option of covering it in saddle leather, a material that accumulates patina and texture and 'grows with the owner'. He hopes that over years of use, each Grenadier saddle leather steering wheel will have its owner's individual imprint, embedded in the wear on the leather.

These are the tiny touches that mean so much and that are never even considered by the big automakers. One of Toby's proudest design ideas is the 'toot' button on the steering wheel. He explained that when you want to make a non-threatening use of a car's horn to warn a cyclist or pedestrian that you're near, even a brief blast of the horn always sounds confrontational and aggressive. He wanted the motoring equivalent of a bicycle bell and designed a small red button on the wheel with the logo of a bike, with the word 'toot' above it, and gave it a comical, cartoon-like sound.

I can say with complete confidence this has never been done before by any car maker and is a metaphor for not just how differently INEOS sees the art of car design but how playfulness and humour should always be core elements. There aren't many car companies who build a self-deprecating charm into their designs. More's the pity.

But how do you marry unorthodox design with lean, cost-effective manufacturing which is underpinned by a culture of quality? It's here that the wisdom of not using another manufacturer's chassis, drive train, tooling or processes is obvious. Just because you can run chemical factories doesn't mean you can build a car. But there are cross-learnings in manufacturing that can apply to both disciplines.

Walking round the huge Hambach factory, I was struck by the forensic cleanliness. It may have been very recently fitted out by Mercedes, but the ovens, paint baths, pressurized sprayers, pipework and robots are almost surgically immaculate.

Jim is a great believer in reindustrialization and in getting society back to making things. The flat white service economy doesn't, he reckons, advance the human condition. Rather, he believes that we need to use science, technology, engineering and mathematics to increase our manufacturing base. The UK used to have over 20 per cent of its GDP generated by manufacturing. Now it's less than 10 per cent. That, he believes, has got to improve and for companies like INEOS to transfer their manufacturing talents into other sectors is an obvious industrial shift which benefits the wider economy.

While there's a definite culture of humility in INEOS, they're rather pleased to know that even the Mercedes engineers at Hambach now admire their safety culture. Accidents at chemical plants are immense events, with often tragic repercussions. Before INEOS put their safety protocols into Hambach, the US Occupational Safety and Health Administration accident rate there was 5.0, meaning staff would likely have five injuries in their working lives. Now it's 0.16 – one accident for every 625 working years – and just one of the reasons why INEOS leads the world in chemical safety.

They're also quietly pleased that major players like Mercedes, BMW and Magna are asking Hambach to do other projects for them, and that the demanding German automotive supply chain is also reaching out. Mercedes has asked INEOS to keep making the Smart range until 2024 and also to produce body parts for their GLE model. The quality that they've so far delivered is actually better than Mercedes.

The partnership with Magna – which has been instrumental in helping bring the Grenadier to production reality – has been so successful that Magna is looking to devote 30 per cent of their capacity to future INEOS models. Other suppliers and car makers are also talking about setting up similar partnerships.

The Grenadier and the way that it's designed and built has raised automotive eyebrows. The mighty steel chassis is heavily corrosion-protected, ancillary running gear is attached and then fitted with six BMW in line 3.0 litre petrol or diesel turbo engines, coupled to ZF's well-proven eight-speed automatic gearbox. The steel body frame is also thoroughly rust-protected and dipped, and then the hanging aluminium panels, like the doors, bonnet and tailgate, are attached. The roof is the only outer panel that is made of steel.

There's a surprising amount of manual intervention on the line and I watched one man spend ten minutes hanging a single front door, repeatedly measuring the shut lines so that they were perfect to the millimetre. He then tightened the hinge bolts with a special electronic tool that measures the torque applied – and (here's the fascinating bit) those torque measurements are then recorded in a central database for fifteen years, so that refitting a door after an accident can be done with exactly the same factory precision. That level of design process detail simply isn't something that is normally associated with an automotive start-up. But at Hambach, it's everywhere.

Watching the scores of welding robots is mesmerizing. It reminded me of the line in Charles Dickens's *Hard Times*, where he describes the steam engines of the northern industrial towns of the eighteen fifties as 'melancholy mad elephants'. Obedient, industrious and uncomplaining, the robots swing, bob and peck at the steel pressings. The geometric positioning of each spot weld has a production accuracy target of 99.7 per cent, and looking at a freshly welded pick-up load bed, the rows of welds seemed as perfectly aligned as the stitching on a Hermès handbag.

The paint shop is more like a science lab. A series of chemical baths, immersions, E-coats and cathodic coats build up the rust protection and paint base and after every stage an army of people hand finishes the surfaces. I watched seven people flat, buff and polish a shell before it headed down the line for its final atomized spray clear coat. And after electric-fired curing, it is polished and buffed yet again. There's a Rolls-Royce vibe to each process, a mix of cutting-edge robotics and of engineering that is precise to the nearest millimetre, all overseen by old-fashioned expert human intervention.

I'm not surprised that it took four long years just to get to the first prototype stage. In the General Assembly area, there's a huge flow chart on the wall, detailing the dozen different processes which are needed to complete each Grenadier. Laid out with logic and simplicity, it deconstructs the entire process, from the 'marriage' of chassis, engines, gearbox, axles, diffs, and body through to fitting harnesses, seats, wheels, bumpers, interior trim, centre console, windows, roller testing and the final visual control.

Even so early in the full production process, the need for minor rectifications at the end of the line is running at around 20 per cent, a figure that the Hambach engineers hope eventually to reduce to 10 per cent. Much of that achieved quality is a credit to the original simplicity of the car's design, coupled with the design logic of the manufacturing journey. Like just eight attachment points to mount the body onto the chassis. Or using half the number of electric control units that are usually fitted to cars.

The factory is buzzing and after reaching the Prototype 1 stage, it's taken a little over a year to start the first customer builds. The site is now filling up with the first batch of orders, parked in neat rows and finished in the ten different colours available. Seventeen thousand potential buyers have expressed an interest and while not all will convert to actual sales, there's now a six month order bank built up, with utility companies and fire services ordering the pick-up version entirely unseen. Jim hopes that production will reach twenty-five thousand to thirty thousand units a year, at which point the Grenadier would become a financial success and begin to pay back some of his brave £1.7 billion investment.

Jim is pleasantly surprised at how well the project has progressed:

'Apart from Tesla, we're the first large company to build a totally new car for several decades. And that's not usually an enterprise that's crowned with commercial success.'

But there's not much, with the benefit of hindsight, that he'd do differently. Making Grenadiers in ten different colours he regards as overly ambitious. It has created a lot of extra work and cost:

'We would have been far more sensible to have just four available colours, like Tesla uses, but looking at the baby blue Grenadiers now rolling off the line I feel that we were right to follow our instincts and offer more consumer choice as well as strengthening the car's individuality.'

He's also keen to offer a range of factory options, so that personalizing the car can be done directly by the factory, rather than by the after-market. There are optional Smooth Packs and Rough Packs, featuring a mix of diff locks, raised air intakes, rear view cameras, puddle lamps, heated seats and eighteen-inch wheels along with pre-configured models called Fieldmaster and Trialmaster for lifestyle adventurers and hard-core off-roaders. There are other options like engine snorkels for wading, rock sliders for harder terrains and a heavy duty winch. Jim smiles when he talks about the winch. On a recent test drive with Grenadiers in Namibia, they were constantly used to winch Toyota Land Cruisers out of trouble:

'Imagine the picture. This new 4x4 that nobody's heard of yet regularly pulling the supposed King Kong of desert off-roaders out of the sand. The locals couldn't believe it.'

He's clearly enjoyed his Grenadier journey, because he and Toby are now working on another model, the Grenadier E, a scaled down off-roader with a battery only drive train:

'The E will be slightly smaller than a Land Rover Discovery with a flat battery pack that can be safely immersed in water and is strong enough to withstand off-road knocks. This will be the world's first proper off-road EV that can tow two tonnes and have a wading depth.'

A clay model of the E sits in the Hambach styling studio, showing the now familiar Grenadier design grammar. It's lower and more compact than its bigger sibling, but uses the same boxy shape. Magna will work to bring the E model to production and Jim hopes to have it ready well before the UK cutoff date of 2030 for the end of sales of new combustion cars and vans.

It's an obvious progression for a company which has ambitions to become a car maker in its own right. There are plans for yet another, even smaller electric model which, right now, Jim is keeping very close to his chest. 'Sustainability is very important to INEOS. Hambach is powered by renewable energy and we're one of the largest electrolysis providers in Europe.' When we talk about hydrogen, he becomes animated:

'As a chemical company, we're very good at making green hydrogen through electrolysis with water so there are no carbon emissions. Last year we announced that we will build a low carbon hydrogen plant at Grangemouth. If you make hydrogen as a byproduct of methane gas it won't be green, and you will always need to get rid of the carbon somehow. We're working hard to prove carbon capture – pumping the CO_2 into shafts in the ground. Making green hydrogen is more expensive but if we can make it at scale and lower the costs, we will have created a promising new zero emission energy source.'

The chemist in Jim comes alive as he draws out molecular structures with his fingers and talks about direct-burn hydrogen engines:

'We could build a hydrogen car with a direct-burn power train rather than a fuel cell. JCB is working on direct-burn engines now for their plant machinery. You could convert the combustion Grenadier to hydrogen relatively easily. We could make the cars and engines and supply the green hydrogen at scale but then you'd need the infrastructure. But that wouldn't be our job – that's down to governments.'

At which point he sighs and observes ruefully: 'I just wish politicians and parliamentarians knew more about this emerging energy technology and would think beyond short electoral cycles.'

At which point you suddenly realize the reasons why a chemical company would want to build a range of cars. Think beyond piston engines, and all that chemical expertise becomes an inspired platform for developing battery packs and hydrogen engines – it's an obvious manufacturing circle, and one that the legacy automakers don't yet occupy. INEOS is working on energy transition and alternative power sources, but Jim reckons the world will need to burn hydrocarbons for a while yet:

'Sustainable energy is an important goal but if you look at all the projections, the world will actually increase its use of hydrocarbons up to the 2050 net zero target, simply because there won't be enough renewables produced to replace gas and liquid fuels completely. Our energy strategies need to encompass the need for a mix of wind, solar, hydro, tidal, nuclear and oil and gas to keep the world's economies turning.'

And when it comes to chemical energy, Jim and INEOS are global thought leaders. INEOS bought BP Chemicals in 2005 and has been steadily buying up not just more of BP's unwanted chemical operations but other energy assets from the USA, China and Europe.

How we power and fuel our cars in the future will always involve chemical reactions, be they moving electrons between anodes and cathodes in batteries or burning hydrogen atoms that don't emit carbon dioxide but only water. Making those processes as clean and as low carbon as possible will be one of the major industrial challenges of the twenty-first century. As one of the world's most successful chemical and manufacturing companies, INEOS seems ideally placed to help take that transition forward.

The triumph

I'm on an autoroute in Northeastern France and Dominic, the PR guy, is looking anxious. 'You must reduce your speed. There are many police on this road.' He keeps lowering his head to check the side mirror for cops behind.

I'm pulling 160km/h at the wheel of a pre-production Grenadier. It's the petrol 3.0 six-cylinder turbo – the BMW X5 B58 unit – coupled to a ZF eight speeder auto, as used by Aston Martin, Rolls-Royce, Jaguar, Bentley and many others. It's a fluent powertrain combo with lots of torque and smooth shift sensitivity. I poke the throttle and the box changes smartly down from eighth to sixth and we spool forward.

Dominic jumps. 'No, no, no. Too fast.' To avoid an argument, I lift off back to 110km/h and admire the view. Like most French roads, the surface of the A4 is super-smooth and I'm struck by how the Grenadier rides. Shod with seventeen-inch all-terrain Bridgestones, the lack of tyre noise is good, even on the silken tarmac. I've spent years thundering up and down these French toll roads, mostly in Range Rovers, and right now the sensations coming through the pedals, seat and steering feel very similar. Secure, stable with very little NVH – a car industry acronym for noise, vibration, and harshness. The Grenadier definitely doesn't feel agricultural. I've also done Birmingham to Bordeaux in a Defender several times and that really *was* wearing. My speed creeps back up to 150 and Dominic gives me a pained look. The willingness of the power delivery means I have to concentrate hard on the speedo needle to keep myself from inadvertently straying over the legal limit.

Dominic had apologized that the car wasn't final production quality, and so was not representative of customer builds. It is true that the electric power steering is over-sensitive and needs too much correction, and there's a numbness at the straight-ahead position. He assures me that the Hambach engineers are programming in more weight and feel.

In the rear is Tom Crotty, INEOS's communications director, and we're talking at normal volume without having to shout. I'm one of the few journalists so far to have driven a prototype Grenadier on tarmac rather than off road and I ask him how much effort has been put in by the engineering team to tune the on road refinement: 'We've been really conscious that this must be a dual-purpose vehicle, capable of crossing both fields and continents. So we've done years of work tuning the chassis, suspension and body to ride as smoothly and quietly as possible'.

With proper off-roaders, there's always a compromise between on and off road, and the work on ride quality shows. The long-travel, progressive-rate Eibach coil spring and Bilstein damper suspension display little roll or pitch and feel very planted. 'If you're spending £59,000 plus on an off-roader, it needs to be your only car. That's why big SUVs have become so luxury-focused.' But that duality of purpose is what sets the Grenadier apart. Posh 4x4s are normally much better on road than off, while gully-climbing off-roaders get tiring on tarmac. The Grenadier may just have bridged this gap.

As I talk to Tom, I miss my exit and Dominic shoots me another anxious look. I apologize, but the prospect of another stretch of arrow-straight autoroute isn't exactly unwelcome. Settling back into the Recaro seat, the cockpit feels wide and open with plenty of light from the long side windows and optional twin glass roof panels. The thin screen and door pillars give good visibility and there's a handy ledge on the driver's door to pivot your elbow while you squeeze the steering wheel between forefinger and thumb. The Defender by contrast was always short on elbow room, so you tended to cling onto the wheel with both hands.

The Grenadier's relaxed driving position feels like a Jag. I'm doing my best to keep to the speed limit but the eagerness of the BMW turbo six is surprisingly tempting. There's 210 kW of power at peak torque of 4,750 rpm – that's 280 bhp in old money. The same as a Lotus Exige or Subaru BRZ turbo. Having so much torque at low revs suits the car well and the engine's emissions have already been tested for all global markets by BMW, so choosing this unit rather than building one from scratch was definitely a wise decision.

The much-acclaimed ZF automatic with its bespoke heavy duty torque converter is another reason why progress feels so lively. 'Both the gearbox and engine are tuned to our specification and aren't standard,' Tom explains. 'We've spent two years and 1.8 million kilometres doing recalibration, to make both units exactly right for the Grenadier's character.' There's no perceptible lag from the turbo and the clever gearbox shifts up and down crisply, giving a seamless smoothness. I catch Tom in the mirror and he's tapping away on his phone, serenely writing emails as we move equally serenely down the A4. When everybody goes quiet, I'm able to appreciate quite how quiet the cabin is at speed.

Missing my exit means that I've had to drive an extra fifty kilometres to the next one. We reach the toll, Dominic pays, and after the barrier lifts I peel off, taking the very tight exit curve on the off ramp a little too briskly. The brakes feel modular and progressive, scrubbing off my speed without squat or dive. The car stays level round the bend, the well-bushed anti-roll bars doing their job keeping the body and chassis firmly controlled against the cornering forces. The grip feels strong.

On the stretch back to the factory I think about doing some quick lane changes, to see how the chassis will cope with fast shifting of mass. But I know that, if I did that, Dominic would have apoplexy. So I resist the urge. Instead, the last stretch of the A4 passes in silence. Dominic sees that I'm not misbehaving and Tom is engrossed in his emails. I pass the time gently fiddling with buttons and switches.

If you want to really get a feel for a car's build quality, what you should do is to test the interior switchgear and air vents for lateral movement. All car companies cut corners, or use cheapo parts. Bin switchgear and you can quickly feel how well things have been crafted. There have been some good decisions here – everything feels sturdy, with little play.

The gearbox shifter is BMW and so is the iDrive control on the centre console. Both feel robust. The column stalks click firmly, the air vents glide smoothly and there's a tactile solidity to the minor controls. Seeing what I am doing, Tom volunteers:

> 'We spent a lot of time choosing the right suppliers. We told them that our parts had to be defined by durability and that we expected them to last decades. We think the quality now matches BMW and Mercedes.'

I'm on the last stretch, approaching the exit to the factory, and on our right is the glass tower that used to be stacked with little Smart cars when the site was known as Smartville. The factory was opened by Jacques Chirac and Helmut Kohl in 1997, a Franco-German partnership which was partly bankrolled by the EU. From the road it certainly looks impressive and it now sports INEOS branding on the sides of the white modernist buildings.

Dominic wants to turn the glass tower into a totemic icon, with a neon light show inside and a floodlit Grenadier perched on the top. 'Tens of thousands of cars pass here every day so it's a great promotional opportunity.' I like his ambition and creativity. The major car makers usually delegate that sort of thing to big (and expensive) design agencies, who tend to dilute the really edgy ideas. That Dominic – who has worked at Hambach for years – has been empowered to make important artistic choices for the factory branding says a lot for the company's culture. I discuss this point with Tom, and he says:

> 'We see ourselves as the plucky underdog that does things fast, with humour and attitude. We will never be a huge behemoth that outsources its decision making to others. We've got some world class talent at Hambach.'

As I drive through the factory gates, I order my thoughts. The most immediate reference point is my 21 plate Range Rover Sport TDV6, parked back at the airport. I'm surprised to be thinking that the

Grenadier feels extremely similar on road. It may not be quite as softly cossetting or as leather-lined, but the ride quality, the interior NVH, the drive train smoothness, the road noise and the body control all feel eerily similar. This is, you must understand, a strong statement. But it's an overwhelming sensation that won't leave me. It's certainly much more refined on tarmac than I expected.

As a result of my navigational blunder there is no time in the tightly packed schedule to go off road, but from what I've already read and seen from the motoring media the Grenadier's mud-plugging talents have been well received by road testers and by the off-roading community. Its talent on tarmac won't be widely judged until later in the year but for me, the drive has been a revelation.

So, here's my feedback: the petrol Grenadier's refinement on road is up there with the current crop of luxury SUVs. No question. It's a very well-rounded machine. I'll drive the diesel later, but the BMW oil burner is well known for being a smooth unit so I wouldn't expect the overall feeling of on road composure to be much different. My senses now peeled, I pick up as we drive through the site a very slight rotational tyre rumble at low speed. It's really tiny. Most people would never feel it. But because everything else is so polished, it would be worth ironing out.

I tell Tom that I think it's probably a tyre compound/road surface compatibility issue, and he duly notes this down. My only other criticisms are that the glove box lid could feel a little bit more substantial, there are some sealing finish issues around the insides of the doors and a block of foam insulating rubber is visible between the front inner and outer wings. And I'd like more information about fuel economy and average consumption on the main display screen.

But that's it. I'm genuinely impressed. With time now pressing, I ask whether I can possibly have a look at a finished Grenadier from underneath? An unusual request I know – and call me old-fashioned – but that is where you see the real engineering. The way that pipes, hoses, roll bars, axles and subframes are mounted and attached shows how focused the build quality really is. My request doesn't faze Dominic at all, and he leads Tom and me into the factory, to the General Assembly area where finished cars are suspended on the production tracks above.

Here I look up and see an essay in old-school engineering: box frame ladder chassis, Carraro beam axles, heavy top and bottom links, thick Panhard rods and a specially designed, manually operated transfer case, all bolted together like a battleship. No electronics or air springs, just heavy duty, multilink suspension, tough differentials, braided hoses, copper brake lines and a stainless steel exhaust system. All easily access-ible, using the general INEOS philosophy of 'Hard to break. Easy to fix.'

I'm reminded of a ship's engine room or the landing gear of a jet. Big bolts and meaty shafts and rods. This is how real, rufty-tufty off-roaders should be built. Monocoque bodies, ECUs and air suspension are for passenger cars. You won't be able to plug in a franchised dealer's diag-nostic computer in Botswana or in the Sahara. There, you mend things with chunky sockets and spanners.

We've been conditioned in the UK to think of 4x4s as a largely sub-urban vogue. But we forget that there are dozens of remote markets where engineering integrity and ease of repair are the sole buying pri-orities. In Zambia or the Kalahari, they won't be buying Grenadiers for the school run. Jim has been resolute from the beginning regarding the importance of *quality* to him: 'I don't want to build a car that breaks down. I want one that's unbreakable.'

Maybe the now mythic Grenadier obsession with engineering, at which I am staring up, has become a much more valuable USP than the legacy automakers had previously thought. According to online data analysts Sitecore, web sales of Grenadiers have hit 110 per cent of target in just two months – and that's with no consumer test drives yet avail-able. Reservations are running at around twelve Grenadiers every minute, or 260 per cent of target. When I've spoken to Jim Ratcliffe, I could sense that he's breathing a mighty internal sigh of relief that inter-est and reaction has thus far been so positive. But he is also adamant that, for such a young car brand, there won't be any complacency. 'The customer will judge us, and until we know what owners think after several years of hard use, we won't be popping any champagne'. I can tell you that in the auto industry such humility is rare indeed.

What's also very rare is the openness that we've seen since the project began. Car companies can be very secretive. Prototypes are wrapped in camouflage, tested at night and on private tracks with high walls and barbed wire fences. Journalists test hand-built press cars on carefully selected roads which flatter ride quality and handling. There's a story of one big car maker (who shall of course remain nameless) flying motoring hacks to a European resort where the test route roads had been freshly resurfaced, specifically for the press launch.

The INEOS Automotive PR team took the decision to remove camouflage and let the early prototypes out onto public roads undisguised. Jim was unequivocal about this. 'Why would we want to hide anything? We want people to follow the Grenadier story and watch the progress we're making'. And when early prototypes were taken on tour for journalists and off-road enthusiasts to try out, it was all done without glamour or glitz. Just muddy quarries and fields, driven in well-used prototypes which often had dashboards which still wore the engineers' test labels on switches and controls.

Journalists like authenticity. They like to see behind the magic curtain. And that's one of the reasons why the reaction to the early prototypes has been so positive, with so much goodwill. I noticed that one famous motoring media website has written on their YouTube Grenadier road test thumbnail: 'The *Real* Defender'. You can't get more fulsome praise than that.

Mind you, it was very brave to let an Australian off-road pundit who is known for his 'technical' approach to the hobby loose with a prototype. Slightly predictably, he suggested that the Grenadier needed double the fuel tank capacity, much higher ground clearance and thirty-five inch wheels and tyres. But not everybody needs to cross the Australian outback, or drive everywhere with 180 litres of fuel swilling about. Nevertheless, INEOS graciously welcomed his feedback.

This internal culture of openness is important when you're a disrupter. If you're genuinely claiming to do things differently then there's nowhere to hide. You can't be ambiguous. INEOS has loads of people working for it who are incredibly clever and incredibly skilled. So you need to listen to what they've got to say. And there needs to be a culture deeply embedded in the company that criticism is welcomed – that there is absolutely no blame, or shame, attached. On the contrary – this is how progress is made.

In all of my conversations with the INEOS Automotive teams, there has been an honesty. They've told me how difficult this journey has been, how getting the software working properly has been a nightmare, how raising the quality of components made by outside suppliers has caused tensions and how manufacturing a car at scale has been one of the greatest industrial challenges that the organization has ever faced. Of course it has. How could it not be? But this transparency about the back stories makes the achievement all the more remarkable. And it means that you believe what they tell you, because you know that when it's not all rosy, they will tell you that too.

As I wait in the factory reception for my ride back to the airport, there's a bustle of activity pushing Grenadiers into a hall for an evening event where Jim will be talking to the factory teams. The now famous prototype Number One is on display. There are several chassis fitted with drive trains. There are a couple of engines on stands. And there are some highly polished black Grenadiers that look a lot like G-Wagens.

One chassis is painted bright red, which I'm told is an option for customers who want to highlight the underneath engineering of their Grenadiers. Who knew? At this event I guess that there's unlikely to be any hoopla or razzmatazz, and I suspect a lot of talk will be about INEOS's culture of quality, which to me has been ever-present, visible everywhere during my time at Hambach. On the flight back to London I talk to Fran Millar, the CEO of Belstaff clothing, another undervalued brand that Jim has recently snapped up.

Fran was previously CEO of the INEOS Grenadiers cycling team, and before that head of winning behaviours at Team Sky. Along with reinventing Belstaff, she's also working closely with Jim, burnishing the expanding portfolio of INEOS consumer brands:

'Working with Jim is like nothing I've ever done before. You get pushed very hard but supported to really do your best work and to stretch yourself and your teams beyond what you thought you were capable of – it's inspiring and, without doubt, that drive comes from Jim. INEOS's discipline of expecting a yes, rather than a no, is infectious. Once you see it working you push harder to embed it in the culture of your business. You learn to develop it as a skill to improve outcomes. For me personally, it's been transformational.'

Everybody with whom I've spoken at INEOS tells the same inspirational story: don't tell us why we can't do this, tell us how we *can*.

If we are looking for answers as to why on earth a chemicals company would want to build a car, the reasons are the same as for why they've taken on an award-winning cycling team, why they are principal partners with Mercedes Formula One, why they have built a ten factory health hygienics brand, why they have given traditionally motoring Belstaff clothing a sexy new identity and why they have built the Britannia sailing team to compete in the America's Cup. It's down to a very singular leadership and vision.

A vision that's also donated £100 million to Oxford University to research resistance to antibiotics, that's built a green hydrogen plant in Grangemouth and made record-breaking contract purchases of wind energy for heavy industry. If you have the personal drive, the financial resources and the manufacturing scale to build things differently, to improve society and to help save lives, why wouldn't you? For Jim Ratcliffe, being a force for positive change appears to be a moral duty, an obligation to put something back and enable others to do the same.

The fact that he's been so incredibly successful in reindustrialization and in manufacturing ought to be an example to governments and industries all over the world: single-minded determination delivers results. And let's not forget the other major reason why he's built a new 4x4 from scratch – and looks set to create a multi-model automotive brand: he's a car guy. A proper one. Anybody with a Ferrari 250 California Spyder, a Jaguar D-type and a genuine AC Cobra 7 litre has got the car bug really bad – along with exquisite automotive tastes.

I titled this section of the Grenadier story *The triumph*, because that's exactly what's happened here. It might sound like flattery. But really it isn't. You have to understand that so much could have gone wrong – and so much nearly did. The many court cases with JLR, the twelve month supply chain delays, the COVID constraints of having all the teams working from home, the complications of getting the car homologated, trying to build a completely new greenfield factory in South Wales just as the pandemic struck. Any one of these could have caused impossible challenges and set the project back years.

And then, as if by magic, being suddenly presented with the opportunity to use a newly refurbished, purpose-built Mercedes factory, surrounded by world class suppliers and with a fully trained one thousand four hundred strong workforce already in place. This is fairy-tale stuff. It is a triumph of old-fashioned tenacity. Along, yes, with some very large helpings of luck – but luck which you feel has always been made. One is reminded of that old Gary Player saying that funnily enough, the harder he practised, the luckier he seemed to get.

To create a credible car and a respected automotive brand from a blank sheet of paper, and build it component by component, usually takes several billions and many years. That's why only the incredibly brave, with very deep pockets, need apply, and why disrupters and new entrants are rare indeed. Apple and Dyson have both tried it and both have walked away. These, of course, *are* people or companies with deep pockets. Tesla has been one rare success story. But they began their journey back in 2008. And they depended upon a major shift in the automotive industry – the move to electric – to assist the massive shake-up that was felt by all of the existing brands. To pull off what INEOS has done, in five years, for less than £2 billion, and to have earned already the clear admiration of the auto industry and of car enthusiasts (a crowd which, trust me, is one that is hard to please) is unprecedented.

Jim shrugs off this view. As a manufacturer, after all, he has always done things this way – has always done things differently. He bought chemical companies from the majors, like BP, who of course had their own way of doing things. And he challenged those systems and processes in order to make those acquisitions more successful. This is the model upon which INEOS is built. One thinks of Amazon taking on the major supermarkets – moving into their area, groceries – because it believes that they are a cosy cartel, ripe to be taken down by an unbelieving disrupter. It is hard to think of any other convincing comparison, and it is certainly too early to say whether this particular strategy will be successful (I am thinking of Amazon's, although I suppose that INEOS might say that this applies to them too, promising as the early signs certainly are).

Jim believes that the automotive industry has the same problem as the old-school oil companies: of doing things too traditionally, of reaching a stage where design groupthink, commonality of parts and similar build processes have made all cars look the same. By applying the simple Ratcliffe business logic of making consistently good decisions, of not respecting, and not adopting, the manner in which things have always been done simply because this is the way in which they have always been done, he's shown that you can build cars in a different way. So that the end product is better designed and better engineered.

The takeaways from this tale of triumph are myriad, but there are a couple that stand out. The first is that Jim and INEOS have proved that disrupters *can* succeed in the auto sector. So far, anyway. Car making isn't a closed shop anymore. What accepted wisdom deemed to be virtually impossible has in fact been achieved, in a very short time frame, by a new entrant who has improved build quality, shortened manufacturing cycles and created a design grammar all of its own. In future years, automotive historians just may cite this achievement as the moment when CEOs of the big autos looked at Tesla and at INEOS Automotive and realized that a wind of change was coming. Take a peak at the past: massive behemoths do fall, as times change and their models, or products, cease to be relevant. History is littered with the carcasses of such dead elephants.

This is a change that could – hopefully – put more industry focus upon quality, creativity, individuality of design and transparency to consumers. I also have a suspicion that the Grenadier could change our perceptions about vehicle life expectancies. The traditional twelve years, one hundred and twenty thousand miles useful life may be reassessed when we see Grenadiers still performing perfectly after twenty years and over a million miles – that's twenty years and over a million miles of very tough life, of course. We've known before now that really well-made cars last much longer than a dozen years. Well, the Grenadier *is* a really well-made car. It goes without saying that, ultimately, only time will tell on that one. But the engineering that I've looked at does suggest that the vehicle's service life could be much longer than we normally expect.

The second takeaway is that the Grenadier story will significantly increase global consumer awareness of the INEOS brand. As one of the world's largest privately owned chemicals companies, it has a strong visibility but not enough in consumer sectors. Obviously, INEOS's involvement in sports sponsorship, as well as in the hygienics and clothing sectors, has of late been changing that. But the Grenadier may well become the group's halo brand: one that is mobile, highly visible and easy to understand.

This, I reckon, will illuminate the whole organization with a new sparkle. There's nothing like a new car brand to catch people's imaginations. Polymers and macromolecules just don't do it. And it won't be hard for consumers to decode the intrinsic culture of quality and integrity in their vehicles, and to make the imaginative leap into how other INEOS products and services are built, created and delivered using precisely the same demanding doctrine of excellence.

So when you think about building the Grenadier as a floodlight upon the entire INEOS brand, illuminating all of it in a new light, it really doesn't seem such a daft idea after all. In fact, accidental or intentional, this is all beginning to look rather inspired. And if I was a betting man – which, I hasten to say, I am not – I'd wager that there might be the potential to use INEOS's considerable chemical and energy expertise to create an entirely new energy ecosystem.

The proposed electric Grenadier E and the hydrogen prototypes that have already been built will of course be heavily dependent upon electro-chemistries, something at which the organization excels. Looking at the vaulting ambition that has characterized this project from the very beginning, I wouldn't be at all surprised if this very unorthodox new automotive brand did start to do some very new and very unorthodox things.

I have said this already, I know, but in automotive history, the Grenadier story really has no precedent. Just consider the sheer, jaw-dropping complexity of what INEOS has pulled off: for an organization with no car manufacturing background whatsoever to move into the sector, to design a completely new product, to assemble the supply chain, to create tens of thousands of unique parts, to rigorously test them, to build prototypes, to rigorously test those, to buy a factory, to train the workforce, to create and build the assembly processes and the parts supply, to reach the final prototype stage, to homologate the car, to build thousands of finished vehicles, and then to build brand awareness, media goodwill and sales channels – it is all a truly breathtaking achievement.

And, if all of the early indictors are accurate, INEOS has captured the public's imagination too. Generated sales that are running over target, with a six month order book – all done while forging partnerships with major automakers and suppliers, creating tens of thousands of jobs and making the rest of the auto industry sigh with admiration. I have of course grossly oversimplified and underplayed the amount of work involved, but you get the idea. For an established car company this would be hard, but for a chemicals company with no previous experience to do this – and through a global pandemic and the worst economic downturn since the Second World War – is frankly, a manufacturing triumph without equal.

Reading between the lines of this achievement, moreover, you see something else that's remarkable. While the judgement, skills, knowledge, talent and speed of delivery which are the foundations of the INEOS mothership are unquestionably formidable, they have proved – and here perhaps is the most interesting thing – to be very transferable. The way that INEOS does things in the abstract – their cultural bedrock, their business cultures, their emphasis on swift, safe delivery and on positive outcomes – these skills and learnings can be applied to other sectors.

We're back to Jim's aphorism about success and consistently good decisions. Surround yourself with enough talented, experienced and intelligent people, and decision-making excellence becomes your USP, your competitive edge. As a principle it sounds disarmingly simple, but every day, in every industry and sector, we see that good decision-making skills are in enormously short supply. In business, far too many ill-considered decisions get made, and as consumers we're too often on the receiving end of mediocre products and services, as a direct result of rubbish decision making.

If you apply your core skill of making well researched, farsighted, and carefully balanced decisions in other sectors, you can succeed at almost anything – even making cars. What's been demonstrated here is decision making *as a science, not an art.* That, for me, is the most powerful insight to come out of the Grenadier story, *one that is not really about cars at all, but about business in general, even about life in general.* It is the realization that success in anything is a cerebral process, requiring the steady application of intelligence and considered judgement.

Real success will never be driven by instinctive, impulsive or impatient decisions. The measured, careful, considered culture of making chemicals safely – which at the start of this chapter, and at the start of my relationship with INEOS, I thought seemed such an odd bedfellow with car making – is in fact precisely what defines the Grenadier project. And having now demonstrated what was generally considered impossible, INEOS has the opportunity to transfer all of their significant and hard-won learnings from Grenadier to a raft of other sectors, industries and products. I have a strong feeling that successfully building this plucky, defiant off-roader with attitude will not prove the end of the story. It will prove to be just the beginning.

4

Sporting Gold, Sports

Patrick Barclay

To PINPOINT THE ORIGIN OF sports sponsorship would be an impossible task. Might a Roman noble's admiration for the courage of gladiators have funded the stonework of the Colosseum? Might medieval jousters have enjoyed endless supplies of a particular brand of chain mail? When Christians decided to celebrate Shrove Tuesday with a ball game, did they appoint an official supplier of pancakes? Might there have been a message on the original Eton Wall?

Who knows? Those who have studied such things tend to date this form of patronage from the years immediately before and after the turn of the twentieth century, which saw the modern Olympic Games thrive in tandem with American sports such as baseball: pictures of the major league stars were allowed to appear on cards slipped into cigarette packets. (These cards were often collected by the smokers' children and, all in all, the tobacco business was done no harm.)

This era featured the rise to transatlantic prominence of Sir Thomas Lipton. No individual had previously been able to harness the power of sport as effectively as this Scot of humble beginnings who became extremely rich through tea and almost as famous by virtue of his persistent strivings to win the America's Cup. Vainly he yearned to bring the trophy – carried across the ocean by the members of the New York Yacht Club after the first race around the Isle of Wight in 1851 – back to its founding land for the first time.

After his fifth and final endeavour, Lipton was honoured by the city of New York, whose mayor joked that he was 'possibly the world's worst yacht builder but absolutely the world's most cheerful loser'. By now Sir Thomas, whose sailing friends included King Edward VII and his son, the future George V, had plenty to be genuinely cheerful about: his tea, once sold in small packets to the poor of Glasgow, was hugely popular among the Americans, who usually took it iced – and often out of caddies bearing the smiling image of Lipton in a sailor's cap.

It would be facile to draw much comparison between Lipton and Sir Jim Ratcliffe, whose second attempt to help Sir Ben Ainslie to win the Cup will culminate in 2024; for one thing, Lipton revelled in personal publicity while the ambivalence of Ratcliffe's attitude to the limelight might be illustrated by his almost bashful acknowledgement of the hordes of OGC Nice football fans hailing the INEOS takeover of their club in 2019. But Ratcliffe likewise yearns to change the history of a sport of kings; the boat to be used in Barcelona next year bears the same name – *Britannia* – as the beloved vessel of Edward, and George, whose dying wish saw it scuttled in 1936.

The contrast between the kings' boat and Ainslie's reflects a century of technology. And INEOS is determined to find the cutting edge at last. Ratcliffe, asked about Lipton, replied that he knew of his efforts but had a simple attitude:

'We have never arrived at an America's Cup with a boat capable of winning. Clearly I don't know about every boat over 170-odd years. But if you look at the America's Cup in the context of Formula One, you see marriages of technology and sporting ability. They're inextricably linked. If you put Lewis Hamilton in a Williams car, he cannot win. Absolutely cannot. So, if we've always pitched up at the America's Cup with an inferior boat, it doesn't matter how good our sailors have been. Technologically we've always been behind the Americans – sort of happy amateurs.'

Ratcliffe believes the inter-sport approach developed by INEOS over the past few years, and embodied by Sir Dave Brailsford in his role as director of sport, can change this. Brailsford presided over British Cycling's ascent from obscurity to world dominance, and INEOS, as well as having acquired the Brailsford-managed cycling Team Sky, now INEOS Grenadiers, is involved in running (Eliud Kipchoge's team and the 1:59 Challenge), sailing (Ainslie's America's Cup challenge), motor-racing (Toto Wolff's Mercedes team in Formula One), football (as this book went to press Ratcliffe was negotiating to add Manchester United to OGC Nice in France's Ligue 1 and the Swiss club Lausanne-Sport) and rugby union (the All Blacks). The strategy is for the sports to learn from and to feed off each other.

It is not just an idea; it has been happening since 2019, when Kipchoge was assisted by aerodynamic advice from sailing and motor-racing in running his historic marathon, and it intensified two years later when Ainslie's boat designers moved to the Mercedes headquarters at Brackley, Northamptonshire, and came jointly under the technical directorship of James Allison, already a serial winner with Hamilton on the track and somebody who is greatly respected by Ratcliffe.

Ainslie was in his office at Brackley, surrounded by designers and engineers roughly split between the aquatic and motorized disciplines, when he recalled that, after the failure to win the 2021 America's Cup in Auckland, Ratcliffe had long pondered whether to persevere. 'In the end it was accepted that to succeed we had to be the best technically,' Ainslie said, 'and we decided to achieve this through the tie-up with Mercedes. It was very much driven by INEOS.'

Every six or eight weeks Ainslie, his colleague Dave Endean and Allison report to Ratcliffe and his co-owners Andy Currie and John Reece. 'We go through everything,' Ainslie said, adding, 'as team principal, I have to justify my decisions and the INEOS guys – particularly

Jim – have an amazing ability to sniff out bullshit. The moment they sense you might be winging it a bit on some technical detail, they get straight to the point. Which I guess is why they have been so incredibly successful in business.'

The INEOS headquarters in London is just yards from the baroque grandeur of the Harrods building but a million miles away in style. The facade, bland to the point of anonymity, speaks of the company as it used to be ('the biggest you've never heard of') before the sports division started to burgeon in 2018 with the first investment in the America's Cup. On a wall of the lift that carries you from the lobby to the floor on which Ratcliffe works is a giant compass, its many points denoting 'things we like' in a northward direction, and 'don't like', southward.

Among the likes is sport – and one of Ratcliffe's favourite dislikes pertains to the quest with Ainslie. As he explained to me:

'What it says is that we don't mind you making mistakes – but try not to make them twice. In a lot of companies people never put their heads above the parapet because, if they make a mistake, they get shot. In INEOS we don't mind mistakes – I've made them in my life – as long as you learn from them. So I hope I'm not about to make a fool of myself in the America's Cup, frankly, by repeating things we got wrong last time.'

Those shortcomings were observed at close quarters by Ratcliffe, who moved to New Zealand for three months. 'There was no way that boat was going to win, however good Ben was.'

He referred back to Hamilton and the relinquishing of the Formula One championship after six driver's titles in the seven years to 2020. 'Without question, Lewis is the best driver in the world – better than Max [Verstappen]. But he couldn't keep winning because his car wasn't quick enough.' Hence the integration at Brackley. 'James Allison is the most successful technical director in Formula One ever,' Ratcliffe said (a claim hard to deny in the light of eleven constructor's titles with

Ferrari, Renault and latterly Mercedes) 'and, if you look at a boat and a Formula One car, they have much in common – they're built out of carbon fibre, you've got lots of special alloys, sophisticated control systems . . . stuff like that.' When they came together in 2021, the philosophy of INEOS Sport was defined.

Late in the same year, Dave Brailsford took charge of coordination. In truth he had already been working zealously across the sports – Ratcliffe recalled his being 'all over' Kipchoge's marathon in 2019 – and was soon throwing himself into football with the revamp of Nice. Brailsford replaced the director of football Julien Fournier with Florent Ghisolfi, who had made a bright start to his post-playing career at RC Lens, and sanctioned the arrival of mainly British-reared players – Aaron Ramsey, Ross Barkley, Joe Bryan, Kasper Schmeichel – on the advice of the former Cardiff City and Crystal Palace sporting director, Iain Moody.

OGC Nice was certainly different from INEOS's other major sporting buys – the only one which could not be described as world-class. Under Brailsford's guidance British Cycling became the most successful on the planet; Ainslie is the leading sailor in Olympic history; Kipchoge is considered the greatest marathon runner of all time; Hamilton and Mercedes have repeatedly topped the Formula One rankings; New Zealand has more world rugby union titles than any other country. And there, gazing enviously through the windows of this hall of fame, is Nice.

Nice did reach the Coupe de France final in 2022, losing to Nantes, but they were last national champions at the end of their glorious 1950s, when international competition was in its infancy. The ambition now is to make them Champions League habitués and, although their European campaign this season has been two tiers down in the Conference League, it is hardly fanciful given that their neighbour, Monaco, with the backing of the principality's royal family (and a friendly tax regime), reached the Champions League final in 2004. Nice has yet to appear even in the group stages. They did earn a playoff in 2017–18, under Lucien Favre, but lost to Napoli. Favre then left for Borussia Dortmund. His successor, Patrick Vieira, achieved fifth place in Ligue 1 in the first season after the INEOS takeover but was eventually replaced by Christophe Galtier, who in turn gave way to the returning Favre. An air of instability has persisted and, when Favre in turn went, he was replaced from within by Didier Digard on a caretaker basis.

Results nevertheless improved and by the spring Nice were both respectably placed in Ligue 1 and in the last eight of the Conference League. But along the way Brailsford had felt the sting of criticism. Did the task remind him of his early years with British Cycling? 'It's similar in that you're taking over something that has not performed at the highest level.' At the Manchester Velodrome, he had been visited by Sir Alex Ferguson; they got on well and years later, at Ferguson's house, were discussing the art of having everyone committed to a common cause when the medal-bedecked Manchester United veteran leant over and said, 'Dave, it's simple – just get rid of the c***s.' Brailsford blinked but came to accept the need to watch for egos that obscured the message. (The All Blacks have a similar 'no dickheads' dictum.)

Brailsford clapped. 'That's the point where you have to make clear there is one person in charge.' Then 'you have to get people believing they can reach the top of the mountain. You get your three, four or five people. As you progress, some leave or get pushed out – those who think it's chaos or bullshit – and you start to build a new team with energy, to perform, find a rhythm – and then you get a period of acceleration. Everything I've done has gone through that cycle.'

Both Brailsford and Ratcliffe are friendly with Ferguson, who often advised aspiring managers to choose their clubs on potential. Nice can put a massive tick in that box according to Ratcliffe, who swept a metaphorical arm towards the Mediterranean and declared that, of all the cities on its coast, only two had 'big brands'. One was Barcelona, the other Nice. Both had glamour.

'Marseilles – industrial. Naples and Valencia – a bit industrial. But the big brands are Nice and Barcelona. And Barcelona's got an iconic football club and Nice doesn't. Why should that be?'

Actually Ratcliffe tried to buy Barcelona as well, but he continued:

'France produces fantastic footballers who have won the World Cup twice in the last twenty-five years [and oh-so-nearly three times, of course], while England hasn't won it at all in that time. England's got several top clubs – three in the north and three in London. France has one, in Paris. That's the simple logic. It's feasible. If you look at Paris St-Germain and Manchester City, they have only become major forces in Europe relatively recently. So it would be very satisfying to build a decent club in Nice.'

Especially as he lived round the corner at Cap Ferrat.

It is startling to reflect, given the now-global remit of INEOS Sport, on the speed of its growth. Things accelerated around the start of 2019. Ratcliffe was with friends on a motorcycle trek in Argentina, from the Atacama Desert near the Chilean border to southerly Ushuaia on the Beagle Channel. It was then that a casual conversation prompted something rather momentous:

'All off road, crossing the Andes five times on these big BMW 1200 bikes. We were halfway down, in the hotel bar one night and I think it was after the third beer, while we were discussing the last barriers in sport, that Leen Heemskerk [an INEOS executive now running Lausanne-Sport football club] came up with the sub-two-hour marathon. It all happened very quickly after that – Leen was straight on the phone back to England.'

Soon John Mayock, the former Olympic middle-distance runner now with INEOS, was in touch with the London Marathon organizers. Believing that only one man could break this barrier, they spoke to Kipchoge's manager, Valentijn Trouw. Was Eliud interested? He certainly was. In fact he had tried once, at the culmination of a Nike programme at Monza in 2017, and narrowly failed; his heart remained set on it.

All the parties met at the Laureus awards ceremony in Monaco, where Kipchoge was shortlisted along with Lewis Hamilton for the main men's prize. Trouw remembered:

'So Eliud was there, and Jim Ratcliffe, and Dave Brailsford. I was there, the London Marathon people were there – it was our first face-to-face meeting and we said, "We go for this." We didn't know the location, or the timing, and we didn't speak about any finance. We just shook hands and that was it.'

Brailsford had not known Ratcliffe for long. He had approached INEOS because Team Sky was losing their sponsor after much controversy in the cycling world about drugs – and he had been referred initially to the man who was Ratcliffe's chief aide in dealing with the outside world, Tom Crotty. I spoke to Tom about it, and he recalled events well:

'I'd known Dave would be knocking on doors, so it was no surprise. I tend to be the first person guys speak to – a sort-of filter. If I think it's a dead end, I'll close it off. If I think it has value, I'll take it on. In this case, I said to Jim, "Look, there are two big issues. One is they've just won the Tour de France six years out of the last seven – the only way is down. And there's the hangover from the drugs taint. You can write the headline yourself – 'chemical company . . .'." Anyway, I took these issues back to Dave and his responses were solid. So I said I'd try to fix a meeting with Jim. And very cleverly Dave suggested he come to Monaco and have a ride.'

When Ratcliffe arrived with his sons Sam and George, Brailsford had been called away, and in his place were a few of the Team Sky riders including Geraint Thomas, the most recent Tour de France winner. They all got on their bikes together. 'I could feel myself being reeled in', Ratcliffe later told Crotty. Not that he minded, in spite of the rigours of the day. In Thomas's memory it was certainly not a rigorous workout. He remembers now:

> 'A nice little cruise but maybe [he admits] we went a little bit too hard because we turned round and discovered it was just ourselves – Jim and the others were nowhere to be seen. For a brief spell anyway. It was very up and down with no real flat. Not the easiest route. But obviously it was a very productive ride in the end.'

The next day Brailsford returned to the Côte d'Azur and met Ratcliffe for breakfast. 'We chatted about background, where we came from, stuff like that,' Brailsford said. 'At the next meeting, we discussed a sports group. And, at the meeting after that, we talked about how it might be structured.'

Brailsford, known for his advocacy of the theory of marginal gains, seemed already to have embraced the notion of mutual gains because at the Laureus awards he had invited Valentijn Trouw to a cyclists' meeting in Tenerife. 'He said it was nice to build a relationship between the sports', Trouw said. And a few years later, in the Kenyan mountains where Eliud Kipchoge trains, he and his runners began to share their camp with a cycling academy dedicated to applying the endurance attributes of the East African highlanders to a new sport. Perhaps, in time, some will be found who are good enough to join the INEOS Grenadiers.

It was the 1:59 Challenge, Trouw said, that 'opened my eyes' to the potential of cross-fertilization. The Dutchman remembered his experience of the insights that other sports could provide:

> 'In our own small worlds, we are the top. And, when we are challenged, it can be uncomfortable. But, at times during the challenge of running a marathon in under two hours, knowledge came in from sailing – we had the weather reports, advice on where to go for less wind and the right temperature and humidity levels – and from cycling and Formula One in terms of aerodynamics.

'For example, on the use of pacemakers. When the first advice came in from the cycling and Formula One programmes, we told them they were crazy. In athletics we were used to running in a kind of pyramid formation, with one in front and two behind and so on. And they are used to running shoulder by shoulder like that.'

The advice was to invert the pyramid, with Kipchoge at the back, to funnel the wind and create a sort of vacuum in which Kipchoge could avoid wind resistance.

'But to run in that position feels extremely uncomfortable for any athlete. Mine told me "Valentijn, go back and tell them it doesn't work." But we did it – and broke two hours! We did it by just under twenty seconds, but margins are small and this was definitely one of the critical points.'

Leading athletes out of what were their 'own small worlds' was not easy, Brailsford conceded. 'You're so busy trying to survive and do what you do. So we are trying to develop this opportunity to share in a collegiate way.' And to do so safely, added Mark Robinson, the chief executive of New Zealand Rugby.

He wasn't talking about security guards and dogs. No, Robinson explained, the INEOS umbrella was unique in offering protection to those who sought 'to share openly in a spirit of trust'. So had sport become a den of industrial espionage? 'Well,' Robinson said, 'the margins are incredibly small. The way I'd put it is that in most high-performance sports there's a certain amount of intellectual property on which they'd wish to maintain a degree of confidentiality.'

It had been through Ainslie and his sailors, indirectly, that the All Blacks joined up. Robinson recalled:

'Jim met some of our people when he was over for the America's Cup. New Zealand is a small place and we have a close relationship with the yachting community. During our conversations we kicked around what might be possible and found shared cultures of a commitment to excellence, humility and hard work. We are very excited to be working with the world's best. We see them coming together, driven by getting better and Jim's overarching commitment to take on the big challenges in sport and, I guess, answer some big questions about the performance side of sport.'

And so the great oak of INEOS Sport continued to spread.

The little acorn from which that great oak grew was planted in a forest. Jim Ratcliffe lived in the New Forest, a National Park whose northeasterly border is a few miles from Southampton, when he formed INEOS in 1998. Since he preferred not to commute into the City of London, it was decided to build the headquarters near his home in the substantial village of Lyndhurst. His son George played for the local boys' football club and Ratcliffe said that INEOS would buy them a new kit. The team's coach, he recalled:

'. . . was called Paul – a very nice chap – and, when he asked if I'd like to choose the colour, I said, "No, Paul, you choose". So I go to watch them in the first match and he's bought a green kit! You can't see any of our players – they're all camouflaged! But not only that – he's put the team in the wrong year group. So they're all aged eleven and playing against twelve-year-olds. They lost 28–0. So it wasn't an auspicious beginning to our sports operation.'

But certainly it was cheaper than buying Nice, or than funding an America's Cup challenge. Or even than when INEOS branched out into rugby union, by helping the Tottonians club with kit, training equipment and fees for coaches to work, mainly with youngsters.

'It was very little money in those days', recalled David Thompson, who was later to take charge of INEOS's relationship with ice hockey and football clubs in Lausanne. Sport, however, already formed part of its identity, as it had been for Ratcliffe since a boyhood spent playing football on a council estate in Failsworth, where Manchester sprawls northeast into Oldham. Sometimes he had been taken by his father to Old Trafford, to watch the United of Denis Law, George Best and Bobby Charlton, and now he was able to indulge his passion with a trip to Barcelona in 1999 to see the club complete a historic treble by overcoming Bayern Munich in the most thrilling of all climaxes to a Champions League final.

In 2007 and 2008, however, came the crash: the global financial crisis. Personally, in his business career, Ratcliffe had known worse times. In 1992, for instance, approaching his fortieth birthday, he had first taken the scary step into entrepreneurship with his initial venture, Inspec. It was a 'huge risk', which involved mortgaging his house. And then the Chancellor, Norman Lamont, 'got himself into a mess' with the European Exchange Rate Mechanism (ERM).

'Interest rates shot up to 15 per cent and the Bank of Scotland rang me and said it was all off because I couldn't afford the interest. And the following day we came out of the ERM, interest rates came back down again and the deal was back on. That was a personal low moment of my life.'

Much later, in 2008, the economy was once again in shock. The crash fell into the lap of a Labour Chancellor, Gordon Brown, and Tom Crotty admitted that the aftermath was so tough for INEOS that he went to the government. 'We said, "You're giving all this money away to the car industry etc. – we need a break. Can you give us a quarter's ease on the VAT bill?" That was all.' The reply was short and sharp. So INEOS went to Switzerland for five years. And that, as Crotty explains now, was the beginning of the company's involvement with sports teams:

'When you go out there, it's a horse trade. Which canton is going to give you the best deal on tax? And the canton of Vaud, which includes Lausanne, said that we needed to do something for the community. They suggested the Lausanne Hockey Club, which was on its knees. So we sponsored them, got them promoted and everyone thought we were wonderful. And later we were asked if we wanted the football club for a song. So we owned a football club. Those were our first forays into professional sport.'

The association with Lausanne-Sport began in 2017 and it has been far from smooth; the club has suffered two relegations. But INEOS's sporting involvement in Switzerland has always looked towards the grass roots, according to David Thompson, who said that the original hockey sponsorship was accompanied by relatively modest outlays on youth development in various sports – including not only hockey but rugby and even cricket. Ice skating and gymnastics have followed. In football the Team Vaud project was about helping young players to get into professional clubs' academies. As Thompson said,

'In terms of investment, it was a quantum leap – but very successful. Even then, in stepping back from the ice hockey club, we continued to sponsor their juniors. That reflects our philosophy.'

This approach is also evident in The Daily Mile – much more about which you can read in the chapter here on the Next Generation, but whose approach, in short, was to ensure that the children at all partici-pating schools benefitted, not simply those with any aptitude for running. Regular exercise was a benefit to everyone, something about which Ratcliffe (himself a keen runner) was passionate.

Ben Ainslie had read about Jim Ratcliffe in the business pages of news-papers. But, despite suggestions from a mutual friend, the yachtsman and adventurer, Chris Cecil-Wright, they had never actually met until the three got together at a members' club in Mayfair, soon after the 2017 America's Cup in Bermuda.

When they did, Ainslie quickly realized that his own hunger for the trophy had met its match. More time-consuming was the process of INEOS becoming his team's sole backer. It was treated, as he recalled, from the INEOS perspective, like any other M&A (mergers and acquisitions) proposal: 'I found myself in a room with a dozen lawyers and some quite difficult discussions.' But progress was made and, in the spring of 2018 came the announcement of INEOS Team UK, known now as INEOS Britannia.

For Ratcliffe the challenge, then and now, is to go where no Briton has been before. From Ainslie's point of view:

'Coming from a maritime background, I see a part of our maritime history that is missing. We've won pretty much everything else in world sport. We've never won the America's Cup. So there's a common drive. Yes, we're deriving core technical expertise from Mercedes. But we're pulling it across to INEOS Britannia – and Britannia says it all. It's about the heritage of the team. *Britannia* was George V's racing yacht – the one that was scuttled when he passed away. And we also race for the Royal Yacht Squadron, which is probably one of the oldest sporting clubs in the world [founded in 1815] and based on the Isle of Wight, where the America's Cup was initiated. The Americans took the trophy off [originally the RYS £100 Cup, and still informally the Auld Mug] and renamed it and we've never seen it since! So we're taking expertise from wherever we can find it in this national effort to win this oldest international sporting trophy. That's how I'd put it.'

For Ainslie, sailing is in his genes. Like Ratcliffe, he was brought up in Manchester, but in its leafy southern reaches. His parents, Roddy and Sue, sailed a twenty-eight-foot boat around Anglesey. One rainy Sunday afternoon, a few years before Ben was born, they were in the yacht club at Holyhead, when they saw an advert for the first, crewed, round the world yacht race, sponsored by Whitbread. As Ainslie remarks now:

'They'd obviously had too many pints of Guinness and decided to sign up. My father cobbled together a crew with some mates and they all took out loans or mortgages to charter a seventy-one-foot yacht. The only professional was a navigator from the Royal Navy. So they set off from Portsmouth in September 1973. And came seventh out of twenty-four – not bad for rank amateurs who'd never done more than cross the Irish Sea.'

Ben was privately educated in Cheshire and, after Roddy had sold his manufacturing business, Cornwall. At first sailing was purely recreational, but Ben became keener when he started racing.

'When it got to qualifying for the Olympic Games it was really serious! And when somebody offered me a job to sail for an America's Cup team for what, at the age of twenty-one, seemed an obscene amount of money, I had to pinch myself.'

He won silver at the 1996 Olympics, then gold in 2000, 2004, 2008 and 2012 – a haul which makes him one of the very greatest British Olympians. His America's Cup record features victory in 2013 as a tactician for Oracle Team USA in San Francisco. In that year he was knighted for services to a sport that has changed so radically since he started. 'Looking back,' he says now, 'we'd have laughed at the idea of the boats of today, multihulls or monohulls reaching a hundred kilometres an hour.'

Almost as he spoke, in October 2022, Britannia's test boat was launched in Palma, Majorca, where sailing operations are based before the move to Barcelona. The management and technical teams remained in Brackley, but a lot of their preparatory work had been done after Team New Zealand triumphantly crossed the line on 17 March 2021.

Bertie Bicket, chairman of Royal Yacht Squadron Racing, handed a letter to his New Zealand counterpart, who accepted it.

This ensured that Ainslie's team would be the Challenger of Record in 2024. Asked why this was so important, he replied:

'We negotiate the rules with the holders. So straight away we were in strategic discussions in terms of what would best suit our set-up. Then we could decide our programme of design and manufacturing. Then get on the water and start the testing programme.'

But how did he secure Challenger of Record status?

'By having a strong relationship with Team New Zealand. I used to sail for them and introduced Jim to the CEO, Grant Dalton – he's a quite similar no-nonsense character.'

The enactment of the collegiate approach could really be dated from Ainslie and Dave Brailsford 'kicking around ideas, talking through different challenges' in the early part of 2019 while Brailsford was inviting Trouw to Tenerife and becoming immersed in Kipchoge's marathon. Now it is visible in all sorts of minor details: in, for example, the 'cyclors' on Ainslie's boats.

Cyclors use pedal power to replace the traditional manual method used by 'grinders' – crew members operating manual winches reminiscent of coffee grinders – to generate the power necessary to control the yacht's sails and boom. Pedal power, significantly greater of course, legs being much stronger than arms, was due to be banned from the America's Cup in 2024. But the rules have reprieved it. So, with Brailsford and his cyclists on board, at least metaphorically, INEOS Britannia should be superbly prepared in terms of both technology and training routines.

'Not necessarily rocket science, is it?' Ainslie remarked, referring to the theory of marginal gains. Even Brailsford believes that it has been over-discussed, occasionally to the point of mockery, as in the case of

Sir Bradley Wiggins, in a knockabout speech given for the benefit of businessmen. 'But I think', Ainslie continued, that:

'... it's the implementation of marginal gains that Dave is really talking about. And I think Dave works particularly well with INEOS because one of their favourite expressions is "rigour" and Dave's rigour is phenomenal.'

Could he mean that Dave is slightly obsessive? 'I think any sports person is obsessive,' he replies. 'You need that for success.' So what about Jim Ratcliffe? Has he been obsessive, as a patron?

'I would say so, yes. I don't think I've met anyone who wants to get into detail like Jim, who wants to understand, wants to learn. It's amazing. It's also quite inspiring when you think of what he's achieved that he still wants to talk to people like me, or designers on a boat or whatever, about things that others might find insanely boring.'

Perish the thought that these might include the difference between cyclors and grinders!

In Dave Brailsford, as in Ben Ainslie, it is easy to detect parental influence. In Jim Ratcliffe too, as it happens, for it was from Jim's father, a joiner who ended up running Britain's biggest laboratory furniture business, that Ratcliffe may have inherited entrepreneurial flair, as well as an undying passion for Manchester United.

Brailsford, asked if he had a strict or inspiring childhood, replied: 'both'. His father, John Brailsford, was orphaned when very young, being sent then, alone, to a foster family. It was a difficult start. 'But he found his way into the Boy Scouts,' Brailsford recounts, 'which led him into mountaineering and rock climbing.' He became a blacksmith in a Sheffield steel factory. 'And then, when I was six months old or something, he moved the family to Wales so he could climb with Joe Brown and Chris Bonington and all that gang in the Llanberis Pass.' He also became a mountain guide:

'At my school I spoke Welsh, did all my exams in Welsh. I wanted to be part of the Welsh community with all my mates. And I had this crazy dad who was English and did all this climbing thing.'

Cycling too: on summer holidays the family would be taken to the French Alps – where a couple of times they glimpsed the Tour – and John pedalled off for days on end. John showed a technical flair in inventing climbing equipment such as the curved ice axe. He was, Brailsford said:

'A very driven guy. Do it yourself, he'd say, and make sure you're professional in everything you do. However, when I was nineteen and said I had to leave and become a professional cyclist – I wanted to win the Tour de France! – my mum was horrified, saying I should stay, get married and make a career and the rest of it. My dad disagreed strongly. So I have a lot to thank him for.'

Brailsford left his job as an apprentice draughtsman to travel to France, where he learned the language and much else, becoming a lonely but voracious reader of books about psychology, including sports psychology, while racing as a sponsored amateur for a team based in St Étienne. Eventually he accepted that he would never make it as a fully professional cyclist, let alone win the Tour, and returned to Britain to embark on studies that were to lead indirectly to fame and fortune, obtaining a degree in sport and exercise sciences at Chester College of Higher Education (now the University of Chester) then an MBA at Sheffield Hallam University. He worked for a company selling high performance bikes, before in 1998 being hired by British Cycling, becoming their performance director in 2003 and of course overseeing a boom in the sport that not only brought unprecedented honours but changed the face of urban Britain. Before Brailsford, the British were hardly a nation of cyclists like the Dutch, Danes or Chinese. Now our roads teem with piston-pumping Lycra and streamlined helmets.

The concept of marginal gains was about breaking a sport into its components and improving each by 1 per cent. Then, when these were added together, the overall performance would improve significantly. This was the theory and it involved constant monitoring of the cyclists' statistics. While it was being implemented, alongside more orthodox coaching, Britain won two golds at the 2004 Olympics and eight each in 2008 and 2012, plus fifty-nine world championships across various disciplines in the decade that ended with Brailsford's resignation to focus on Team Sky. Brailsford had assisted Bradley Wiggins's 2012 victory in the Tour de France – Britain's first ever – and then continued that with Chris Froome in 2013, 2015, 2016 and 2017, Geraint Thomas in 2018 and, under the banner of Team INEOS, Colombia's Egan Bernal in 2019.

Asked, though, whether he would swap all this achievement for the fulfilment of his youth's vain dream for personal cycling glory, he went silent and pondered. At length he said:

'Maybe one of the drives of my career was the fact that I wasn't a first-class cyclist. I was gutted. I'd figured that, as long as you give it all you've got, as long as you work harder than everybody else, you'll get there. But when I look back, I realize I wasn't eating the right things, training in the right way. If I'd known then what I know now, maybe it would have been a different story. I was tired all the time – maybe under-fuelled. Having said that, I went back home and got interested in the new courses just emerging in sports science. Remember I'd left school at sixteen – I'd hated it. But now I'd found my calling. And so I concentrated on enabling others to do what I hadn't been able to do.'

Just like José Mourinho, Arsène Wenger, Arrigo Sacchi and countless other football coaches? 'Yes!'

He was speaking in the office of the sport operation: one room in INEOS's unpretentious Monaco base, off a side street with no distracting view of the superyachts in the bay. Tapping on a laptop was Ratcliffe's son Sam, who generally works from the London headquarters. The adjacent waiting room might have been that of a suburban dentist, except that the magazine placed slightly apart from the rest on a low table happened to contain a review (a glowing one) of INEOS's newly marketed Grenadier off-road vehicle. Brailsford hailed an aspect of INEOS that the Grenadier represented: a refusal to accept that something couldn't be done. 'Build a 4x4 – let's do that. I love people who won't accept no.' And the absence of bureaucratic barriers:

> 'The agility to go fast, to avoid the massive structure. There's no big HQ, no middle management. It's a federated model and you're in charge of making your business work.'

Living in Monaco seems to have done Brailsford no harm – even if, by his own count, he has worked from 'seven in the morning until eleven at night, every day, including weekends', to make the 2022–23 season one of pivotal progress for OGC Nice. He is lightly tanned in the way that used to be associated with southern California and manages to look extra lean and well fed at the same time: not bad for a 59-year-old who keeps gambling with his reputation. Switching disciplines, he said, entails hard work.

> 'My approach has been to go narrow and deep. So with the cycling team at the Olympics I pretty much lived in the Velodrome and the Lowry [a Manchester hotel] for many years. Then I went into professional cycling and bought myself a big motorhome. I was the only manager to do all of the races, every year, rather than be back at base. You get a sense of what's going on and the vibe in your team – these things are really important.'

Geraint Thomas remembers that Dave breakfasted with the riders every single day. 'He loves it and is probably more professional than some of the guys in the team!' Brailsford went on:

'As I've switched into the marathon and put a foot in the football world, I've totally absorbed myself in those things in order to learn fast. I care so much. It's the way I do it. It's as if . . . here's my career and I'm taking the chips I've won along the way and I'm putting them all on red or black. It's been a pattern. Every time I go to a new competition.'

Did football give him butterflies? 'A hundred per cent, yes!' Was it his biggest gamble? 'At the start of the 1:59, I was going into a different world – didn't know anything about it.' Yet was football not even more daunting – an inexact science compared with running, in which Kipchoge could be assisted by aeronautical advice?

'In some respects, that's true. But to be successful a football team must get the chemistry right – its recruitment must be spot on, it must have an identity. The various leadership roles – manager, CEO, captain, certain players, backroom staff – must be in synch. It doesn't have to be harmonious – I think a lot of the best teams are not that harmonious – but that chemistry . . . it's like a great rock band. As more and more people analyse it, as there's more and more data and scientific input, it should be possible to narrow down the probability of success.'

Asked if sport was not becoming more – and by implication excessively – scientific, he replied:

'Oh, I don't know. Certainly, when we started out, we wanted to use the application of data, insights, in developing human performance. And before you knew it everyone was on to the Big Data and *Moneyball* [the book and film about ultra-statistical strategy in US baseball] and trying to be too clever for their own good. I've been round all that and come back to the idea that you are dealing with human endeavour – what's between the ears. Sport is not PlayStation.'

But wouldn't the best boat, rather than the best sailor, win the America's Cup? 'Yes, but the engineers who built that boat will still be human beings.' And the Formula One title will go to the best car? 'Exactly, and if you have the best engineers, they still have to collaborate, to perform.' So why wouldn't they be on the same salary as Lewis Hamilton? 'You still need the driver to make the decisions.'

The chemistry he spoke about in football was, of course, metaphorical. 'I'll never be an expert in football. Wouldn't pretend to be.' Hence his hiring of Florent Ghisolfi. The clue was in the title; Ghisolfi would direct the football at Nice. 'But I do know how to apply certain principles to human beings that give them a better chance of performing.' And there were common factors. Cycling, for example, was 'about supporting people in their self-sacrifice,' and there was a parallel in football in the process of selection, in which players were judged all the time.

'For a human being, that's quite a big deal. To be able to roll with that, and manage it, and keep everybody engaged . . . Alex Ferguson was the greatest at that.'

In explaining why Brailsford was given his wider role, Ratcliffe pointed to 'our bread and butter, the chemicals business, the biggest part of INEOS by far'. It was very well-organized.

'In our federal model we have extremely capable groups of people running each business, with full responsibility, and they meet with Andy [Currie] and me once a month. If you look at INEOS, the one thing that stands us out from the pack is the people we pick. Nobody ever leaves INEOS. There's no turnover at all. But finding equivalent people [in relatively new ventures such as the automotive and fashion fields as well as sport] is not easy.

'It takes time to get to know people and recognize their competences. And to appreciate the depths of people. Dave's history is in cycling – he transformed the British Olympics team and then won the Tour de France, which we'd never won before, seven times with four different riders. So there was a simple conclusion. I don't believe in coincidences. Dave is 24/7, very thoughtful, and very focused on performance, as we saw during the 1:59 [Brailsford was chief executive, working closely with Valentijn Trouw and Hugh Brasher from the London Marathon]. Then, with him being based in Monaco, we saw more of each other and I realized the breadth of his capability.

'Also, Dave has a charming personality. If you're in these central roles, you need a personality – you can't just dictate. You can't have Dave Brailsford telling Ben Ainslie what to do. It just wouldn't work. So personality is important.'

And trust? I asked Tom Crotty why it was that he got on so well with Ratcliffe. He replied that loyalty, in both directions, was a 'big deal' with him. So was trust essential? 'Correct. One hundred per cent.'

Geraint Thomas, who has worked with Brailsford since 2003, said:

'I think Dave's great strength is getting the right people around him, in the right areas. He'd be the first to admit he's not an expert in all aspects of all of the sports. But he's always been able to command the troops, get the best out of people and keep pushing them.'

The late and lamented journalist Richard Moore, a specialist in cycling, wrote a book about Brailsford which likewise concluded that he was less a coach than a manager, excellent at delegation. He hired coaches and other experts, and he oversaw them. He had, Moore noted, compared himself with an orchestral conductor.

Others had compared him with Sir Clive Woodward, whose

reputation as coach of England's victorious Rugby World Cup team in 2003 took something of a knock when two years later he became performance director at Southampton Football Club. After three tense months the manager, Harry Redknapp, left and Woodward became director of football, supposedly to work with the new head coach, George Burley. But when the next season began Woodward had departed, never to return to a game that he had loved since boyhood.

There is an element of intensity which Brailsford accepts:

'I get obsessive about things because I want to win. I don't accept that we can't win Olympic medals just because we haven't won them in that sport before. I like the idea of finding the biggest thing you can win in a sport and going for it. It's just a question of application, and of mentality. I'm not a big fan of coming fourth to eighth.'

What?

'In the Olympics, most finals are eight people. So you can make the podium or be fourth to eighth. And I really don't like fourth to eighth. Maybe it's a bit crass. But, when I was younger, I could see the difference between the people making the podium and the others and I didn't want the fourth to eighth mentality. I don't like losing. I really don't like losing. And so, yes, I do sometimes feel like "I wanna be the boss" in following that obsession. But you've got to know how to delegate in the end. And to do that you must empower people.'

Which brought us to marginal gains. Brailsford, resisting any temptation to sigh at the subject's familiarity, said:

'The whole premise – and I think it's lost its way a bit – is that, when we started with the Olympic programme, we were so far away from the podium – we looked at it but didn't believe we could get there.

Rather than try to wave a magic wand, it was, like, "What are we going to do today? And next week? Can we, by next week, improve a little in some of the key areas?" The cyclists agreed. So we decided to take it day by day, week by week, month by month, and see how we got on. And we began to see a recognition that, boy, it does matter.'

The cyclists were asked to keep their dressing room tidy – not to leave towels on the floor and so on – and to be friendly to each other.

'OK, alone it was not going to make us the best in the world, but it signified that we cared. And the enthusiasm was contagious. In any sport there are basics. If you're not world-class at the basics, you can do all the marginal gains you want. It's a combination.'

With Team Sky there were special pillows and mattresses to aid sleep, hypoallergenic sheets, a washing machine on the team coach – and a habit that was to prove years ahead of its time:

'One of the problems in a three-week race is that the team is together and, if one gets sick on the bus, if you're not careful everybody gets sick. So we researched how to minimize avoidable illness and somebody said we should use hand gel – after all, surgeons did it. And then we decided not to shake hands and do fist bumps instead. And everyone thought we were w*****s because we were walking around fist-bumping each other. Now I don't think COVID was funny in any way, but I must admit we did have a chuckle five or six years later when everyone started doing those things.'

Chris Haynes, former director of external affairs for Sky Sports and Team Sky, described Brailsford as 'a brilliant adaptor of ideas'. The marginal gains theory may not have originated with him, but he could see how to apply it. Nor did he ever stop listening and learning.

'And he and INEOS are a marriage made in heaven because he's been learning from business for many years. Once, en route to Corsica for the first stages of a Tour de France, he bought three business books from a shop at the airport. We changed planes at Paris and, as we got up, I noticed he had left the books on his seat. Dave, I said, pointing at them, you've forgotten … He said it was OK, he'd finished with them. In the time it took to fly from London to Paris.'

Brailsford smiled in half-recollection but said it wasn't unusual:

'I tend to scan some books. A lot of it's the same stuff, written in a different way. But every now and again you find a little nugget – something that triggers a thought in your mind. Because management, or performance, is not a game that stands still. It's something that's running away all the time. It's not just about how you're progressing with your own team. If you can't keep up, you get left behind.'

As the spring of 2019 approached, a telephone rang in the headquarters of Global Sports Communication in Nijmegen, the Netherlands.

The call was from the London Marathon executive Spencer Barden, who in turn had been contacted by INEOS's John Mayock. Yes, said Valentijn Trouw, his client Eliud Kipchoge would very much like to be the first man to run a marathon in less than two hours. The project hatched in the Andes had, quite literally, gained legs.

Trouw, born in Nijmegen, was never much more than an enthusiastic amateur sportsman. He studied law and worked for two years in speedskating before joining the agency. Specializing in the management of long- and middle-distance runners, he has looked after Kipchoge and other distinguished East Africans since 2003, spending much of his time at Global's training camp in the spectacularly beautiful Highlands of Kenya.

When the 1:59 Challenge was taken up, it was already March and the marathon had to be run in October, because of Kipchoge's programme for the Tokyo Olympics [he had won at the previous Games and was to triumph again]. 'A lot changed,' Trouw recalled:

'The first idea was to have it in London so we looked at places there and, because they were not ideal, outside London, desolate airfields and so on. But in the end, mainly for weather reasons – October in Britain is too great a risk – it came down to Eastern Germany or Austria and we eventually chose Prater Park in Vienna.'

Throughout the seven months of preparation, Brailsford, Hugh Brasher and Trouw spoke constantly. Kipchoge had his long-time coach, Patrick Sang, but the need for extensive back-up – including a sports doctor, physiotherapist and nutritionist – was met by INEOS. When the day of destiny, 12 October, arrived, Trouw mounted a bicycle and was at Kipchoge's side throughout the run, offering advice and delivering hydration. Such help, supplemented by a leading car and the now-inverted pyramid of pacemakers, meant that the time of 1 hour 59 minutes and 40.2 seconds was not recognized by the athletics world body, which stipulates that the drinks, for example, must be collected from a table by the athlete. 'The way Eliud looks at it', said Trouw, 'is that he has two records.' He already held the record and in September 2022, at the Berlin Marathon, he broke it by thirty seconds, completing the 26.219 miles in two hours one minute and nine seconds.

'Now his focus is on the Olympic Games in Paris and the major marathons. There are six of them – London, Tokyo, Berlin, Chicago, Boston and New York – and never in history has anyone won them all.'

To date Kipchoge has won Berlin five times, London four times, and Tokyo and Chicago once each. Only Boston and New York remain unconquered. 'This', Trouw affirms, 'is also a goal.'

At the age of thirty-eight – he was born on 5 November 1984, in a village not far from where he lives and works now – Kipchoge might appear to be running out of time. Trouw, however, is unsure. Or rather, he is sure – sure that the general view is mistaken:

'It's very understandable that people should think that way, but what I see with Eliud, and more and more athletes, is something different. Most athletes, when they stop, do so for mental reasons, not physical. Yes, they get small injuries but also people keep telling them they are getting old and their motivation drops. I'm totally convinced that, in an endurance sport – maybe in football, at speed, it's not quite the same – you can still achieve at forty-two or forty-three. As long as the mind is there.'

Might family pressures also contribute to an athlete's decision to retire?

'Absolutely. But, if you take the case of Eliud, he spends every weekend at home. From Monday to Saturday, he is in the training camp. But the family home is in Eldoret, less than an hour away. So on Saturday he comes home and stays until Monday afternoon. It's different from a cyclist, who might be away two hundred days a year, because in general Eliud runs two marathons a year. All other months, he is at home or close to home.'

On the edge of the village of Kaptagat, some eight thousand feet above the Rift Valley, stands the camp that Kipchoge shares with a few dozen fellow athletes. Surrounded by farms where cows and sheep graze, it is fairly basic: a place of work. There are two main buildings. In one the men sleep, two to a room. The other houses the women's dormitory, a television room and a physiotherapy room. Behind is a small kitchen and dining area. Here athletic greatness is forged in conditions which are perfect for endurance running.

Kipchoge is determined to use his relationship with Ratcliffe, who has visited Kaptagat with Brailsford, to develop the potential of his young compatriots there. As Trouw says:

'When we built the camp, it was intended to be for junior athletes who didn't have the financial means to live by themselves and dedicate themselves to training. But when Eliud became successful, and the money started to come in and he got his house and comfort in life, he was one of those who wanted to stay, not just because he felt the mindset had helped him but because he felt responsibility to inspire others and show them what is possible when you are serious about your profession.'

A performance partnership between the Kaptagat-based NN Running Team, which contains several world record holders, and INEOS, was announced in January 2022, but it was the friendship that had grown between Kipchoge and Ratcliffe during the 1:59 Challenge that led to an intriguing development five months later. Kaptagat was also to become the home of the Eliud Kipchoge Cycling Academy, as Trouw recounts:

'INEOS wanted to build something for the future and we thought, "Why not try something new? We already have a camp for running – why not add cycling and give an opportunity there, to see if in the future there can be a cyclist from East Africa in the INEOS team?" We first started to speak about it when Richard Carapaz was winning the Giro d'Italia and Egan Bernal the Tour de France. Carapaz was from Ecuador, Bernal from Colombia – each was from Latin America but, more significantly, from altitude. Well, we have athletes from altitude – it's just that they don't have bikes yet!'

As Brailsford noted on the day the Academy's formation became known, Eritrea's Biniam Girmay had just become, at the 2022 Giro d'Italia, the first black African to win a stage of a Grand Tour race. Girmay was from Asmara, the second highest capital in Africa, after Addis Ababa in neighbouring Ethiopia.

'So we know the talent is there,' Brailsford said. 'And they certainly should have that talent for cycling's gruelling road-races,' Ratcliffe added: 'They've got the best endurance DNA on the planet'. And, given that talent thrives on role-models, Tom Crotty made the point: 'We've got a whole stable of them.'

Toto Wolff grew up wanting to be where Ayrton Senna was: at the pinnacle of motor-racing. He left school at eighteen and raised some sponsorship. 'I was basically a one man show,' he said, 'without a parent or someone else supporting me. I raced for a few years.' And had some success. But after Senna's death at the San Marino Grand Prix in 1994, a key sponsor abandoned the sport and Wolff took stock.

'I realized I wasn't going to be a Formula One world champion – and I always aim to be the best.' So he went into banking, then sold steel and at twenty-six became a venture capitalist, riding the internet wave very profitably while staying in touch with motor sport through investments, including the acquisition of a share in the Williams Formula One team. This was in 2009. Four years later he left for Mercedes, and there his ambition to be the best was realized with a record seven consecutive double championships – plus the 2021 constructors' title – as team principal.

A couple of hundred medals were displayed opposite Wolff's desk in the sleek and spacious Mercedes headquarters at Brackley, eight miles from the Silverstone circuit. Through the glass wall of his office was a vast open plan design area in which the technicians worked at their computers, some in mixed groups: Mercedes and INEOS Britannia employees were distinguishable only by the team tops some wore. Wolff smiled. 'At first it must have been a little bit odd for the Britannia people, because there is no sea around us.'

Although for Wolff home is now by the waters off Monaco – Ratcliffe and Brailsford are near-neighbours – he did not have the easiest of teenage years. Born in Vienna in January 1972, Torger Christian Wolff was a pupil at the renowned Lycée Français, and remained there after the death of his father had left his mother struggling to pay the fees:

'Every semester it was a question of whether they were paid or not. For me it was the worst and – considering my later life – best thing. When you are a poor child in a poor environment, it's pretty much the same for everyone. But I was a poor child in a rich environment – and every day confronted with it. You are not the same. It was very important in my development. It made me more resilient, and more determined.'

Because his mother was from Poland and he knew the language, Wolff was able to sell enough steel there to begin his venture capital company, which is roughly the same age as INEOS and looked after by his business partner, Rene Berger, a fellow alumnus of the Lycée, letting him focus on Formula One.

He is a charismatic figure in the sport, sensitive enough to the world outside to have stood alongside Lewis Hamilton and ordered the repainting of the Mercedes cars after the death of George Floyd and the Black Lives Matter campaign. The Silver Arrows became black for two years and, although they regained their traditional colour last season, Wolff said during the winter break that he was pushing for black again: 'We haven't got all the stakeholders over the line yet. But we're trying.' Wolff has a mischievous side. 'We get more of a return on investment', he explained, 'with white stickers on black cars.'

The failure to regain the title from Red Bull was ascribed in some quarters to 'zero pods': almost non-existent pods on the sides of the car. Wolff dismissed this, saying: 'We don't believe it had any influence. Many other things we got completely wrong.' Such as?

'We developed the car with maximum downforce at relatively low ride heights. So we have a car that is basically being sucked to the ground. That was the theory. We were the most radical in running the car close to the ground. But it was smashing the floor. And when we started to lift it to prevent that we got aero-porpoising [the car rose and fell as it travelled]. It was zero to do with the pods.'

The rivalry with Red Bull was ostensibly exacerbated by disclosure that Alinghi Red Bull Racing would compete in the next America's Cup. The Alinghi team, formed in 1994 by the Swiss biotechnology billionaire and philanthropist Ernesto Bertarelli, brought the trophy to Europe for the first time in 2003 and successfully defended it in 2007. Now they had joined forces with Red Bull, promising mutual gains. Wolff doubted that the relationship between track and sea would be comparable to that around him; INEOS, after all, was a shareholder in Mercedes:

'We're not selling them our engineering capability. We're not making a margin. We have just taken on the challenge and want it to be successful. It's very different to how the others are set up.'

In describing how the INEOS relationship began, Wolff explained that he was always studying 'the universe of competitive companies' to see if there was 'some kind of synchronization'. Did it make sense to look at a partnership? 'We are looking at a thousand companies every year and, although Jim Ratcliffe was obviously known to us, and I had personally admired him for being bold in building his business, it never got to the stage of getting in touch because it was such a long shot.'

After every Grand Prix race, Wolff is handed a list of the people who have attended. In this case it was a comparatively minor event: pre-season testing in Barcelona.

'UBS [the investment bank is a Mercedes partner] always brings along a group of wealthy clients to look at the cars and follow our testing. So a week later I get a list of the people and I see Sir Jim Ratcliffe. So I asked who looked after Sir Jim Ratcliffe and why the hell hadn't I known he was coming? Because I was there. And I was told Sir Jim had been looked after by our reserve driver, Esteban Gutiérrez, and met Valtteri Bottas, our race driver at the time, and that was it. So I sent him an email saying it was a shame we did not meet. And he responded. We met soon afterwards and were immediately on a wavelength. It happens. The moment I met him, I knew he was going to be a part of my journey with Mercedes – and probably I was going to be part of his journey in building an ecosystem of sports teams.'

At first they agreed a sponsorship, but then Ola Källenius, chief executive of Mercedes-Benz, suggested that INEOS take shares. At the time Mercedes-Benz owned 70 per cent and Wolff 30 per cent. Ratcliffe was open to the idea:

'So we had a dinner in Stuttgart, in a place called the Center of Excellence, where we show the most exclusive cars, and within ninety minutes of dinner – maybe it was sixty minutes because we are all not chatterers! – we arrived at one third each. And that was it.

'And for INEOS it was a great investment. Because they were bold, they came in when COVID struck, they bought a third of a Formula One team that made no profit. Two years ago, we were not set up to make profits – we were set up to reflect the brands that we partnered. We were always around break-even because we were successful and got a lot of TV income and good sponsorships.'

But they generated no money. And then Formula One introduced a cost cap, with all teams agreeing to limit their spending.

'Our business has turned into a profitable enterprise, a bit like the American sports franchises. And INEOS is reaping the benefits. We have a much higher valuation than when they started. We are very profitable. So, like in their core business, INEOS invested when nobody else would have done.'

If elite football could cap its costs – overwhelmingly made up of players' salaries – it could become ultra-profitable and, although Wolff is not a passionate follower of the game, having been to watch OGC Nice only twice, he did see the potential of Ratcliffe and Brailsford's quest there, declaring:

'At Nice, as at Marseilles, with all the Arab communities, football brings hope. If the team can be sustainably successful, this would be a fantastic story for the city.'

A difficulty was that they would 'come up against nations'. He referred, of course, to the Qatar-owned Paris St-Germain and, farther afield, Abu Dhabi's Manchester City. 'I know and admire them. But if only the owners were able finally to agree on something we have implemented, a cost cap, or a salary cap as in the United States . . .'

In Formula One there is a comparatively small group of owners. In football, this threatened to happen only when a self-appointed elite of twenty clubs announced a European Super League in April 2021. It was opposed not only by FIFA and UEFA but by governments, players and coaches and, perhaps most fiercely, by the audience and media. Nine of the clubs withdrew and, within a matter of days, the organizers beat a retreat.

'The concept was wrong,' Wolff said. 'You have to allow Brackley Football Club to dream of winning the Champions League.' But a salary cap would actually increase opportunity, he argued, and help to prevent the sort of wage race that has led to PSG, who make big losses, paying Kylian Mbappé more than twice as much as the profitable Mercedes team gives Lewis Hamilton. UEFA seemed to be taking a step down that path with their new Cost Control Rule, but it is likely to be a gradual development.

During the winter World Cup of 2022, Dave Brailsford kept an eye on the refurbishment of OGC Nice's training ground on the outskirts of the city, near the Allianz Riviera stadium. It had been hailed as 'state of the art' when a squad featuring Mario Balotelli took possession as recently as 2017, but INEOS's ambition had outgrown it and this was only phase one; Brailsford had the enthusiastic approval of the city's mayor, the former Grand Prix motorcyclist Christian Estrosi, for a complete redesign incorporating a multi-team performance facility for the cycling, sailing and Formula One contingents as well as for the footballers and academy aspirants hoping one day to step into their boots. It would, he said, be 'a consolidation of the sports' in Europe.

There had been less of a long-term air about the summer intake of players. Of five who came with English Premier League experience, all were on free or loan transfers apart from the former Leicester City goalkeeper Kasper Schmeichel, a then 35-year-old whose final contracted year was said to have cost £1 million. But the group contained big names who, as Brailsford put it, 'know what good looks like'. None fitted this description better than Aaron Ramsey. He was at Arsenal under Arsène Wenger, alongside Cesc Fàbregas and Robin van Persie, and at Juventus under Andrea Pirlo, with Leonardo Bonucci and Giorgio Chiellini in defence; with Wales, he was Gareth Bale's co-star.

Neither Ramsey, released by Juventus in his thirty-second year after a loan spell with Rangers in Scotland, nor Schmeichel, was in the first flush of youth. Ross Barkley was coming up to twenty-eight, Joe Bryan twenty-nine. Only the 27-year-old Nicolas Pépé could have been called full of potential, and even then only because he had never quite fulfilled it in the three years after Arsenal had paid Lille a record fee of £72 million; Mikel

Arteta had given his shirt to Bukayo Saka. Pépé, perhaps because he had history of playing well in France, settled quickest, but Ramsey returned from Wales's World Cup anticlimax optimistic that his latest club adventure might be career-enhancing. After speaking to Brailsford and Iain Moody a few times, he had found himself being drawn into the project:

'By how ambitious they were, by how Jim wants to back Nice to become one of the best clubs in France, if not the best, and compete in the Champions League. Although it always takes a bit of time, I have no doubt that this club will be able to achieve it, because of the way Jim and Dave and all the people behind the scenes are committed. These are people who have proved they can get to the top in whatever they've gone into. Hopefully I'll be here when it happens. Nice has everything. It's a lovely part of the world, the stadium's great, the fan base . . .'

As he spoke, league attendances at the Allianz were averaging 22,000 – comparable with the healthiest figures since the stadium opened in 2013. Although misbehaviour had led to partial closures for some matches in the past two seasons, generally the atmosphere created by the ultras of the Populaire Sud was an inspiration, causing visitors to wonder how the place would rock to the sound of a genuinely full house.

And the training ground would be up with the best, said Ramsey. 'At Arsenal, everything was amazing – the pitches, the detail – and what they've done here is bring in people who have worked on top Premier League projects.' Ramsey shared Brailsford's belief in detail. Asked what was expected of him, he said:

'The team generally is quite young. I was asked to give my experiences. They didn't say it, but to be a leader as well. To behave with discipline. A footballer must behave in the right way. Clean up after himself, for instance. If you leave the dressing room in a mess for others to clear up, how are you going to be on the pitch? Are you going to leave something on the pitch for others to clear up as well?'

An international at seventeen, just before leaving Cardiff City for Arsenal, Ramsey was captain of his country at twenty. The Arsenal ethos under Wenger suited him:

'Things were spot-on. You had the kit men on at you if any towels were left on the floor, or water bottles not put in the bin. At Juventus as well, they believed in getting the little details right.'

Nor had football evaded the advance of data and science. Around the time Ramsey was born, and perhaps especially in Britain, a lot of players thought rehydration meant a few pints over a game of snooker after training. Ramsey smiled:

'Don't get me wrong. There's still a right time for a team to get together over a few beers. But, the way the game is now, there's no hiding place. Everything is monitored. Teams at the top are there for a reason. And you can see it. They have the top players – but those players work their socks off.

'Data's huge now. Everything is analysed and data-driven. I think we've been left behind a little bit in this respect, which is why it's good for this club to have the crossover with other sports. INEOS is involved at the top in a lot of them, so there's that knowledge of what it takes. Of course football is a different animal. But the principles are the same. It's how disciplined they are, how driven they are, every small detail of what they do just to give themselves that 1 per cent extra to get their body in the best possible shape to compete. These little things get them where they are. So this is interesting. It's unique for a set of footballers to be able to chat to the top cyclists, or sailors, or the Formula One guys.'

Among those offering insights were the running coaches from the Kenyan Highlands, with tips on how to be faster over the first ten to twenty yards, and on strength and nutrition. You might think the last player to need advice on endurance was Nice's captain, Dante, for the tall and lean Brazilian will be forty this autumn. Nor would Dante be short of experience of how to deal with sport's highs and lows. In 2013 he collected a Champions League winner's medal as part of the Bayern Munich side which completed a treble by beating Borussia Dortmund at Wembley. Bayern set record lows for goals conceded that season and Dante was described by the club captain, Philipp Lahm, as 'one of the best defenders I've ever played with'. Little over a year later, Dante, deputizing for the suspended Thiago Silva, featured in Brazil's 7–1 defeat by Germany in an infamous – from the home nation's point of view – World Cup semi-final in Belo Horizonte.

According to Dante, the main improvement that INEOS had brought to Nice was 'mentality'. He had been at the club for three years before the takeover and said: 'We now know where we want to go and what we have to do to get there.' Since Brailsford became more hands-on, a familiar message appears to have resonated:

'We have to reflect on what we do every day. Is it enough? Or not? That is why to hear the values of successful people from other sports, to share experiences and to learn about their behaviours in terms of food, for example, or recovery, is so very, very important.'

The cyclists and footballers mingled in October 2022, when the INEOS Grenadiers held their end of season get-together and testing session at the Nice training ground. There are around thirty riders in the team, of fourteen nationalities. One of the nine Britons was Geraint Thomas and he remembered it fondly:

'Oh, it was quality, that day. It was great to see how excited grown adults can get when there's a football around. It felt like we were back on the school playground. Everyone was loving it. It's putting a ball in the net, isn't it?'

Thomas especially enjoyed meeting Ramsey. He had first encountered his fellow Welshman in 2014. Arsenal, Thomas's favourite club, had won the FA Cup with Ramsey man of the match after scoring the crucial goal against Hull City in extra time. Amid the whirlwind of celebrations, Ramsey had attended the Monaco Grand Prix the following weekend and Thomas was there. 'I was star-struck, for sure', he recalled; even though Thomas already numbered two Olympic team golds among his achievements, his Tour de France glory was yet to come:

'I met him a couple of times again, so it was good to see him at OGC Nice. The only trouble was that there were stations for the various skills and he was on keep-ups – I was a bit rusty, to be honest! Obviously Nicolas Pépé used to be an Arsenal player as well. So it was a great day.'

Ramsey revelled in it too:

'Just being around some great athletes and interacting with them. Also the mechanics – we had up to 150 people here. We put on a session and had a bit of a laugh. Then we went into the trucks afterwards and saw how the mechanics do things.'

Thomas agreed that the INEOS concept could help everyone:

'Being selfish with the cycling, I think the aerodynamics side of Formula One is particularly interesting. Also as a Welshman I'm a massive rugby fan so the Kiwis' knowledge of strength and conditioning is a key advantage.'

From July 2021, when INEOS entered a performance partnership with New Zealand Rugby and the teams in black, the All Blacks lost seven matches out of twenty-one. Most rugby nations would be happy enough with that, but for the pride of New Zealand it verged on under-achievement.

True, their female counterparts, the Black Ferns, retained the world women's title in the autumn of 2022, but they were run close on home soil by England, winning only through a thrilling late try. Which served to emphasize Mark Robinson's contention that the 'margins are small' principle applies to the traditional leaders of rugby as much as to anyone.

Robinson was an All Black. Mainly a centre, he made nine appearances. It should have been more, but he had terrible luck with injuries. When at Cambridge University, doing postgraduate studies in politics and philosophy, Robinson had half a season with Bristol and his playing career ended in Japan before he moved into the sport's administrative circles in 2007, as chief executive of the Taranaki union in New Plymouth, near his birthplace of Stratford.

He was appointed to the board of New Zealand Rugby in 2014 and, after also serving on the World Rugby executive committee, became chief executive in 2020. The following year the America's Cup came to Auckland and conversations with Ratcliffe there led to the six-year pact with INEOS. 'I think Jim has a wider appreciation for the Kiwi way,' said Robinson, 'and INEOS's connection with that ethos is really important to us.'

Last year at Twickenham, Ratcliffe led an INEOS contingent at the autumn international which ended in a thrilling – at least for the English hosts – draw with the All Blacks. Up to then the All Blacks had won six matches in a row. It might have been seven but for the yellow card that left them with fourteen men for the closing stages. At the end of a tour, they seemed to tire.

Any lessons will be applied during the build-up to the World Cup in France and the Brailsford-coordinated INEOS link will be involved. Robinson said that there had been various approaches from prospective partners around the world. In this case there were shared values which included humility and hard work, plus a belief in the benefits of sharing:

'It's in our interests to share! We want to reach a stage where we are incredibly open [in the conversation with other sports]. Some of our greatest All Blacks coaches have had a view that it forces you to re-invent yourself, in order to stay ahead of the pack.'

Robinson discounted the notion that the All Blacks had a winning formula and, therefore, more to lose than gain from the sharing pro-cess. As he said:

'The top end of international rugby is hugely competitive. The world is getting smaller and smaller, information transference is getting faster and faster and the need to improve, even by small margins, is critical. Also some nations have greater resources than us, bigger populations. As a country of five million people, we have restrictions on the size of our market and size of resource. So we are constantly looking for every small advantage.'

Times had changed since he played:

'Sometimes when I see the equipment, nutrition, mental skills – the whole approach is vastly different. I'd offer an observation that we can benefit more from what you might call the harder edge of high perfor-mance, the data analysis, the technology side. I think we've done a reasonable job, over time, of establishing an extremely strong personal meaning – a culture, aligned with legacy, that is very powerful.'

Few would deny that the pre-match haka, a Maori tradition which has been observed by the All Blacks since 1905, remains one of the won-ders of the sporting world:

'And we'll continue to work really hard at that. Teams feeling highly motivated and connected with their environment is very important. But maybe this [the new approach, these new areas] are where we haven't been quite as strong as other unions with more resource.'

*

Sir Jim Ratcliffe is lean, still likes a daily hour of running or cycling and has stopped doing marathons only because of 'a football injury suffered when I was sixty-two'. He's very tall, with floppy hair and a preference for casual clothes: to find a rare photograph of him in a suit and tie, you might check the official record of his being knighted (for services to business and investment) by Prince William in 2018.

He speaks with similar informality, and Geraint Thomas recalled being pleasantly surprised upon meeting him before the Brailsford-arranged bike ride on the Côte d'Azur:

> 'When you hear he's the richest man in the UK, you get an image in your head. But he wasn't like that at all – just a normal friendly bloke who loved his sport. He talked about various sports including football – and being a United fan gave me a bit of ammunition!'

Manchester United had just sacked José Mourinho and made Ole Gunnar Solskjær caretaker. They would finish sixth that season, one place below Thomas's Arsenal, who also reached the Europa League final under Unai Emery.

Ratcliffe's passion for United had already been stirred by his father when, in 1958, Manchester was stunned by the tragedy at Munich in which a plane carrying Matt Busby's great 'Babes' crashed at the end of a sleet-covered runway. Eight players were among the twenty-three who died. Busby survived but spent months in hospital before resuming his managerial duties with a vow to honour those lost by rebuilding the team.

This he did with the help of three outstanding players: Bobby Charlton, who had likewise emerged from the Munich wreckage, Denis Law, for whom United paid the Italian club Torino a British record fee of £115,000, and a skinny boy spotted by the club's Northern Ireland scout called George Best. In 1968, a decade after Munich, United became the first English champions of Europe by defeating Benfica at Wembley.

Ratcliffe senior was there, explaining to an outraged fifteen-year-old

Jim on his return that he'd been able to get only one ticket. By now the family had moved to Hull, where Jim attended Beverley Grammar School, so father and son, the former building his business, watched United more sporadically. They tended to favour away matches in York-shire rather than the 'schlep' across the Pennines. One was at Leeds, Ratcliffe recalled:

'When we got to Elland Road, the ground was overcrowded. We didn't have tickets so it was me, my brother and my father, standing outside, locked out. There were a couple of youngsters trying to scale the wall so I asked my father if he'd mind if I had a crack. There were a few more now so I joined them and got to the top of the wall. And two of the others got over. As soon as they landed they were nailed by the coppers but, while they were being detained, I managed to drop over. The crowd was solid, all standing, but I wriggled in. Within five minutes they were carrying out women, over our heads, because of the crush. I can remember helping to get these women out. I can't remember the score.'

Football was Ratcliffe's only sport then:

'You could play cricket in the summer. But I got bored with cricket. So it was still football, three times a day.'

Although this was the time of Law, Best and Charlton, 'and Paddy Crerand, and Nobby Stiles . . .', his football hero – 'if I ever had one' – came later in the shape of Eric Cantona. So his seventieth birthday, in October 2022, was all the happier for a video of best wishes from sports people who included three with United connections:

'David Beckham, who I know a little bit . . . Alex Ferguson . . . but the real surprise for me was Eric. I've never met him. Eric transformed the club. He changed the fortunes of Alex Ferguson. When Eric came,

United hadn't won the League for twenty-six years. He'd just been at Leeds, where they won the League for the first time in eighteen years. Then he comes to United and they win the League. He's at the club five years – and one of those is the kung-fu kick [Cantona served a long suspension for assaulting a spectator at Crystal Palace] so he's really only there four full seasons. And we win the League in all those seasons. Oh, and he brought the class of ninety-two along [the generation which included Beckham, Paul Scholes and Gary Neville]. Because he had presence. He was the figurehead of Manchester United.'

Cantona swapped football for film around the time that Ratcliffe was taking his first steps as an entrepreneur, honing the skills (Ratcliffe, that is) that would eventually make his vast fortune, paying for homes on the Côte d'Azur, the Hampshire waterside and elsewhere, not to mention a seventy-eight-metre yacht. What an astonishing step-change for the boy from the council house who scaled the Elland Road wall and who can now take part in, not just view, a panoply of great sporting events all over the world! Asked to describe it, he lapsed into the second person:

'I think what happens is that your roots are in football, because it's the only thing, but you really enjoy sports and, as your life moves on, you try cross-country running and all the others you keep bumping into. And, if you like a bit of a challenge in life, and somebody invites you to have a go on a racing boat, or climb a mountain, you try it. Some people in our sort of position, they enjoy going to the theatre, or reading books, or studying history. I happen to like physical challenges and [they] keep me sane, really. Because we work quite hard.'

Was he not, though, now doing increasingly extraordinary things for fun?

'Hundred per cent. You get to an age. When I left university, you didn't have a year off. I didn't even have a summer off – my job started the following week! And you get to a point when you've wrestled with this business for twenty-five years, got great people running it, you sort of deserve to enjoy yourself and take up a few new challenges. You can afford it. So, if the opportunity comes along to get involved with the Mercedes Formula One team, why wouldn't you?'

Equally it was enjoyable to take on challenges like the 1:59. But he added: 'We've always said the fun was only one of two reasons for getting into sport.'

The other involved the car venture: the INEOS Grenadier 4x4, named after the Grenadier pub near the company's London headquarters, in which Ratcliffe and colleagues resolved to find an alternative to the recently discontinued (but now revived) Land Rover Defender – about which, of course, you can read in the Automotive chapter.

Tom Crotty took up the story:

'It's really important for us, as we become more of a customer-facing organization, to see the brand associated with positive sporting outputs and imagery. We can no longer call ourselves the biggest company you've never heard of. At the last count, we had 25 per cent recall. If you ask people in the street, a quarter will have heard of INEOS. They'll say "Oh, they're in Formula One," or mention Nice football club. It's a transformation for us. And it becomes hugely important when you're trying to flog people a car, because buying a car from someone who's never made one before might seem a bit of a risk. It becomes less of one when you think "Oh, INEOS – I've seen their name on Formula One cars."'

Or, he might have added, on sleek yachts, or on the vests of leading cyclists. The Grenadier apart, the company will become more and more widely known due to hygienic products such as sanitizer gel and handwash and the Belstaff clothing brand. There is also a planned expansion of trade with China, which according to Ratcliffe makes brand and image more and more important.

'So you can spend your money on advertising – or you can do it in a completely different way, which is to invest in sport. If I put money into a Formula One team and in consequence get a lot of publicity, it isn't money that's disappeared. It's money that's invested. And my investment in Formula One will be worth more in five years' time. So all that brand exposure won't have cost me anything.'

Asked to estimate how much INEOS spent on sport in a year, Ratcliffe said it varied but averaged about £300 million. How big an impact football will make on that going forward remains to be seen, but Ratcliffe mentioned an instructive chat with Khaldoon Al Mubarak, the chairman of Manchester City since the Abu Dhabi takeover in 2008.

Mubarak estimated that he had spent $1.6 billion on the City group of clubs (there are others in New York, Melbourne, Mumbai and elsewhere) and now had an asset worth maybe twice as much. If Manchester City, whose initial cost to the Emiratis was not a great deal more than the hundred million euros that Nice cost INEOS, were now worth billions, football might indeed no longer be as risky a business as people used to think, before Americans such as the Glazers at Manchester United realized the potential in the English game for making easy money – and others from Russia and the Middle East took their opportunities to wash and brush up their images at relatively little cost.

Which brought us to Ratcliffe's interests in the high end. Once a season ticket holder at Chelsea (because it was too much of a 'schlep' from Hampshire or the Côte d'Azur to Old Trafford), he tried there:

'We came in late, so we were culpable in that regard. There's always stuff going on at INEOS so, if I am buying, say, a business in China,

Chelsea coming up does not automatically go to the top of my list of priorities. Also it's going to be three or four billion, you're going to put yourself on the front page of the newspapers every week. If you're a venture capitalist in America, it's quite an easy decision to have a quick look, but people like me, and Andy and John, we need to think about it.'

By the time that they did make an offer, Chelsea were 'all wrapped up' for Todd Boehly and his American consortium:

'An American mergers and acquisitions house was running the sale [for Roman Abramovich]. The only three parties they were talking to were private equity houses in America. They didn't want us involved at all. We did have a word with the government, and with the supporters' club, because football clubs are community assets, but Boris [Johnson] and company didn't want to know.'

Another rebuff was more gentle. This was at Barcelona. 'We had an extremely interesting conversation.' The former MP Joan Laporta had been returned to the presidency of the seriously indebted Catalan club and he and Ratcliffe got on well before 'it became too political' due to Barcelona's obligation to the membership. The club is owned by its 144,000 socios. They elect the president who becomes, in effect, a minority owner, a steward. Upon hearing that Laporta and his fellow directors planned to sell a proportion of the club's television rights, Ratcliffe said, he was horrified:

'We told them, "Don't do it, guys – we'll put in two or three billion, renovate the Nou Camp and have 50 per cent ownership – and sign a deed to say we'd never sell." Our interest was in football alone, not making money. I think it would have worked well. We talked about it but, in the end, they didn't think they could go to the fans with it.

'The road they are going down is a disaster. We tried to point that out and they said, "We know, but . . ." They are all short-termers [Barcelona regimes] because the president comes in, does it for five years and hands the mess over to someone else. They have now sold a chunk of the TV rights, and merchandizing rights, for the next twenty-five years. They've sold them to American hedge funds. So they've got this big slug of cash, which they can now . . . waste.'

But if you looked at top football clubs – Real Madrid, Barcelona, Manchester United, Manchester City and so on – they had roughly similar budgets: say £800 million for the sake of argument. Because of what Barcelona had done, theirs would be more like £500 million.

'That's why we told them not to do it. But they said no, and now we've got that out of our system, we can concentrate on Nice.'

Getting Manchester United out of his system, though, was always going to be more difficult. When the word – however vague – was that the Glazers might consider selling, Ratcliffe and colleagues of his flew straight across the Atlantic. 'We went to see them and they were charming.' INEOS looked at the books, did the analysis.

'They are all very nice [Avram, Joel, Kevin, Bryan, Darcie and Edward, children of the late Malcolm Glazer], despite the press they get. Josh was really hospitable. But the club is owned equally by siblings and you can't talk to that many siblings, really.'

At least that was Ratcliffe's view until in November 2022 the possibility of a full sale became official and talks resumed. A serious competitor emerged in Sheikh Jassim bin Hamad Al Thani, son of a former prime minister of Qatar. The Glazers were said to be seeking more than £6 billion but as Easter approached Ratcliffe was still in the game.

The stakes were high because, as Ratcliffe pointed out, the Glazers had been 'fairly insulated from the publicity side of it' [despite some serious public demonstrations of fan fury about the Glazers' ownership model, which had seen United take on substantial debt while paying interest and fees to the Florida family].

There would be no ocean barrier to protect Ratcliffe from any unrest or impatience were he to take over – and it was now clear that, for the love of his footballing life, he would set aside his reservations about being a constant target for media attention, and about having to spend a lot more than the basic £2.5 billion Boehly and partners paid for Chelsea. And not only that, but take on an obsolescent (if impressive) stadium, and the United training ground, with no guarantee of being thanked for any of it unless the team's fortunes continued to take a distinct turn for the better. In spite of all of these factors, it was obvious that the pull of sentiment, mixed with the view that world-leading Premier League clubs were hardly a high-risk investment any more, made him a formidable rival even for the apparently limitless financial muscle of Qatar.

Meanwhile he remained committed to Nice. Indeed he had sounded more like a fan than an ice-cool international tycoon as he bantered with Tom Crotty in his Knightsbridge office about the travails of some of the club's British acquisitions – and a couple of other players of whom, it might fairly have been said, he was less enamoured.

'It's driving me mad,' he mock-fulminated. 'I keep saying, "Brailsford – tell him". It was in midwinter, when Favre was still head coach. And Dave says, "I can't tell Favre who to pick – he's the coach." So I say, "Well, I'm paying the wages." Seriously, I don't want to interfere but there comes a point . . .'

What he was serious about was the philosophy – short term, by Brailsford's admission – behind the summer 2022 intake. It was that Ligue 1 was equivalent more to the Championship in England than to the Premier League and that, since the likes of Ramsey and Barkley would be in every Championship team every week, the same should apply to them at Nice.

'There's clearly a good reservoir of Premier League players we can tap into. Because Nice is a nice place to be, even on loan. But if you start to get a rumour in the UK that it's fine but you don't get picked, it's quite difficult to scotch. Look at Ramsey. He's the best footballer we've got. He should be playing every week because, with game time, you settle down and confidence grows. It's similar with Ross Barkley. I saw him at Chelsea and he's a really good footballer. If his mind's in the right place and he's in really good shape, you could play him twice a week because he's built like a tank, really strong. You have to give a guy a chance to settle. And he gets one game every three or four. It's ridiculous.'

In football, wise owls tend to be suspicious of players who have been repeatedly unable to meet high expectations – and of clubs who take them on, believing that they can succeed where others have failed. It would perhaps be harsh to call Barkley such a player, given that he made thirty-three appearances for England between the ages of nineteen and twenty-five. Hailed as a prodigy at Everton, he was blighted by injuries and yet Chelsea paid £15 million for him. From there, though he figured in around half of the club's matches, he was allowed to go on loan to Aston Villa and was then released by mutual consent. Brailsford understood the gamble but liked the odds:

'He has unbelievable ability. If you can unlock it – what a footballer! That's the challenge.'

Football sucks people in and that it should permeate INEOS is no surprise given the owners' childhood experiences growing up in northern parts of England. Each of the three supports a hometown club. For Ratcliffe, Manchester United. For Andy Currie, Doncaster Rovers. And for John Reece, Sunderland. Tom Crotty also follows United, although he is a rugby man. 'More you than me, Tom,' said Ratcliffe teasingly. 'I admire the All Blacks – but remember I'm not public school!'

Perhaps the most poignant allegiance among the sports stars is that of Ben Ainslie. As a youngster in the Manchester area, he favoured red and slept under a United duvet cover:

'After the family moved to Cornwall I forgot about football, but in my late teens one of my best mates was a massive Spurs fan. So I thought, "Which team can I support that's really going to piss him off? Chelsea!"'

Ainslie's friend was a fellow sailor, Andrew Simpson, affectionately known as Bart. In 2008 he won a gold medal at the Beijing Olympics – shortly after Spurs had beaten Chelsea in the League Cup final. Thereafter, bragging rights reverted to Ainslie and to Chelsea. Until in 2013, when training for the America's Cup with the Swedish Artemis team, Simpson was trapped under a capsized catamaran in San Francisco Bay. Doctors were unable to revive him. He was thirty-six. Sometimes even sport is put in perspective.

But sport is, and probably always will be, a fun side of INEOS. You listen to the banter between Ratcliffe and Crotty and are reminded of the old saying, perhaps with its origins in *Alice in Wonderland* but since adapted in a million framed notices behind bar counters or on office walls: 'You don't have to be mad to work here – but it helps.' To paraphrase slightly: you don't have to be sports-mad to work for INEOS – but it does seem to help. And, if it helps the brand along, so much the better.

Such a philosophy certainly served Sir Thomas Lipton well. Except that he never did win the America's Cup. So it is tempting to imagine that, when the thirty-seventh race for the Auld Mug gets under way in 2024, Sir Thomas will be raising a celestial glass – or a mug, perhaps – of tea, and wishing the very best of luck to Sir Jim and to the INEOS *Britannia*.

5

Going Green, Energy Transition

Sean Keach

THE FUTURE OF ENERGY IS the future of humanity. Getting it right isn't just important, it's existential.

A very great deal of our advancement as a civilization can be linked directly to the energy we produce and consume. It is both a macro and a micro issue. Energy controls the way we heat our homes, the transportation of goods locally and globally, the cost of products on shop shelves and so much more. Almost nothing we do as a species can be separated much from energy.

The challenge is that we only have one planet – at least until we make several more of those 'giant leaps for mankind'. There is one finite Earth, from which everything we do, know and love must come. We've built a staggeringly complex and fruitful world courtesy of fossil fuels, but we know now that their extraction and use have exacted a heavy toll on our planet. We all know that for the sake of future generations, we must clean up our act. Collectively we need to develop greener energy systems and more sustainable forms of production, and we need drastically to reduce emissions. No small ask.

At the same time, we need to strike a balance. It's clear that we must shift away from fossil fuels, but the taps of oil and gas cannot be switched off overnight. Government, science and industry need to move with blistering pace, but there is no obviously simple solution to swapping out global energy supplies for greener alternatives. It takes unprecedented collaboration, huge amounts of capital and – above all else – time. Recent conflict in Europe has demonstrated exactly how devastating disruption to the flow of energy can be. The systems we have today aren't fit for the future. We must rebuild the house, but we can't do it in the dark. The lights must stay on.

In many ways, that's the INEOS mantra. It's a company with its eyes keenly on 2050 and beyond, but still focused on keeping those essential lights on. The picture of Earth's future is so often painted bleakly, but the story of energy transition – and INEOS's part in it – is really a tale of hope. It's the hope that with enough grit and determination (and some very clever minds), we can develop the energy solutions we need to keep our planet healthy and our fellow humans happy.

It's clear that INEOS is aggressively (and successfully) investing in critical areas like hydrogen, carbon capture and storage, and the sustainability of chemicals and polymers. Sometimes that work is very tangible: INEOS is repurposing huge sites for carbon capture and storage, and building vast solar panel arrays. The business is already producing hundreds of thousands of tonnes of hydrogen today, which will only become cleaner. Creating more sustainable polymers that work their way into myriad supply chains around the world is a harder win to grasp – but it's a win nonetheless.

But sadly, going green is no easy task. The demand for energy globally has never been higher. Likewise the pressure to produce energy in better ways is at its greatest. The world is racing to replace old systems with new. How do you balance those desires in a globalized economy where every action has a reaction?

Take hydrogen: an extremely clean and abundant fuel, for example. Even if you massively scale up hydrogen production (and make it green or clean), you still need new and effective means of transporting it. You need buyers who have the means and desire to process it in a meaningful way. An entire economy needs to be built up around it, so that it can receive investment in kind – and then ultimately scale up with supply and demand.

Even though hydrogen is a fairly safe bet in the long run (it's the most abundant element in the universe, after all), these things take time. INEOS is laying the groundwork for the future, but it won't come cheaply or easily. It also won't come in isolation. INEOS is already working with partners around the world, and that must continue. Industries and governments need to get on board and collaborate to make a success of the great energy transition. Everything depends on it.

Making hard commitments will be part of that. In the enduring words of Coldplay, nobody said it was easy. INEOS has committed to achieving net zero emissions by 2050. When you recognize the scale of INEOS – with a score of business units and over twenty-five thousand staff – you understand that this will be a staggering feat. To realize that dream, INEOS will need to minimize emissions and capture carbon. When hard limits of reduction are reached, INEOS will need to offset. Plans are underway and it's increasingly easy to imagine the reality of a net zero INEOS. Countless businesses around the world will make the same journey over the coming decades. These specific and measurable goals are an essential part of the energy transition.

It's impossible to ignore the fact that there is huge public interest in this energy transition. All eyes are on major energy producers to meet their goals. This chapter will explore some of the fantastic INEOS projects that will have a real impact on global energy production, emissions and sustainability. Naysayers will always find something to criticize – and INEOS is by no means perfect right now, as its leaders will admit – but we can't let perfect be the enemy of good.

That's why this chapter is called Going Green. It's the big global movement that is seeing the world's energy industry shifting away from systems based on fossil fuels: coal, oil and natural gas. In their place will come renewable energy sources like wind and solar, clean hydrogen as a fuel, and lithium batteries packed with electricity. As investment pours in, the costs of these alternatives will drop. Just take this excerpt from a report by the analysts at S&P Global:

> 'After years of depending on regulation for growth in the sector, renewable energy sources have become a powerful and cost-effective source of electricity. The costs of both solar and wind have fallen so drastically that in some regions of the US, as well as in the UK and Europe, wind power has become cheaper than traditional high-carbon energy resources. As costs continue to fall and wind and solar become mainstream, the renewable energy sector will only keep growing and solidify as a strong investment opportunity.'

INEOS is working on several efforts to bring about this low carbon future. Abandoning the fuels that have brought so much wealth might seem like a step backwards for civilization – but it needn't be. It can be a period of opportunity and ingenuity. Moving from wood to coal was a key driver for the industrial revolution. Since then, we've learned to maximize our use of oil, and more recently of natural gas. There will be new gains, expanding industries and opportunities for innovation during the energy transition. We're really only at the beginning and it's impossible to say exactly what the world of energy will look like in twenty or thirty or forty years – and even far beyond. It will drive science and engineering forward. The World Economic Forum even suggests that the clean energy transition will generate as many as 13.3 million new jobs around the world by 2030, with just three million lost – a net gain of 10.3 million roles. A 2022 report notes:

> 'In order to properly utilize the new sources of energy, the largest expected job gains are in electrical efficiency, power generation and the automotive sector. Combined with modernizing the grid, they make up 75 per cent of the 13.3 million in new job gains expected.

Comparatively, new energy sources like bioenergy, end-use renewables and supply chain resources like innovative technologies and critical minerals combine for 3.3 million jobs.'

Where are we now?

So INEOS is now striving towards its net zero greenhouse gas (GHG) emissions future, with a view to hit that target by 2050. To make sure it's on track, INEOS will aim to reduce 33 per cent of its emissions by 2030, against a 2019 baseline. It monitors its operational GHG emissions each year, and then publishes them in an annual sustainability report. That way we can all see how far INEOS has come – and what's left to sort out.

This analysis process is largely led by Greet Van Eetvelde, a highly accomplished professor at Ghent University with engineering degrees in bioscience and chemistry, a Master's in environmental sciences and a PhD to boot. She also happens to be the global head of climate, energy and innovation at the INEOS Group. 'Globally we set out a strategy for climate and energy, we set strategy for sustainability, we set out strategy for what we do with current and new feedstocks,' Greet explains.

'I've got a few people who work for me. If you asked them what they were doing, they would say: "we're the data machine". So anything you see in the sustainability report – the data intelligence behind it is what my group does. The basic idea of adding innovation to all of the challenges that we have is coming from there. All the green tech, clean tech – it always has a link with new processes, new products. Making sure the products that we put on the market and the processes we use not only help us move forward, but also help our value chain partners, suppliers and customers. Not only driving our own climate agenda, but also the climate and circularity agenda of all those who are working with us. That's exactly what we do. This is done at a group level, because we need to be consistent in recording across all the groups and businesses. But still, they need to feel that it's their action. We come in – and it's a very thin line – and set out a strategy, and we play *Inception*, like the movie.'

The typical way to follow carbon on a mega-industrial scale is with a headscratcher of a measurement unit: Mt CO2-eq. That stands for a million tonnes of carbon dioxide 'equivalent'. A tonne is a thousand kilos, which is easy enough. But what about the equivalent bit? Thankfully it's quite simple: 'equivalent' relates to the fact that carbon dioxide is not the only greenhouse gas. Different greenhouse gases – like methane or nitrous oxide – each have their own GWP, or global warming potential. For instance, a million metric tonnes of methane is equivalent in emissions to twenty-five million tonnes of carbon dioxide, at least in terms of its GWP. By using carbon dioxide 'equivalence' as a measurement, therefore, you can track greenhouse gases with a simple standardized unit.

For its 2019 baseline, INEOS had a global greenhouse gas footprint of 24 Mt CO2-eq. In 2021, this footprint had fallen to 22.8 Mt CO2-eq. That's a reduction of 1.2 Mt CO2-eq compared to the baseline – or about 5 per cent. Roughly 0.15 Mt CO2-eq is linked to INEOS agreements for purchasing power. Since January 2021, several INEOS sites across Europe began receiving wind power supply. Ultimately by 2050, the total figure will need to drop to zero Mt CO2-eq.

INEOS's greenhouse gas reporting is actually split into two different categories. These are called Scope 1 and Scope 2 emissions – common terms when it comes to carbon 'accounting'. Scope 1 is everything that is emitted from an owned or controlled asset. If an INEOS furnace is emitting carbon then that's a Scope 1 emission. A Scope 2 emission is more indirect, and comes from the generation of the energy you've purchased to power your systems. If you suddenly started using renewable energy to power everything, therefore, you would wipe out those Scope 2 emissions. That's certainly getting easier and cheaper, but it's still not possible to power the entire INEOS operation with renewables just yet. The bulk of INEOS's greenhouse gas emissions are Scope 1, at around 71 per cent (and the vast majority of that is in the form of carbon dioxide). High Scope 1 emissions offers an opportunity: for instance, it means INEOS has significant control over that chunk of emissions. For instance, INEOS can make its plants more efficient to reduce greenhouse gas emissions – or work to capture carbon emitted at a site. To reduce Scope 2 emissions, you need the energy market to keep developing so that carbon-free renewable energy becomes cheaper and more widely available.

There's also another emission grouping that is a little harder to measure, called Scope 3. These are the indirect greenhouse gas emissions. There are two types of Scope 3: upstream and downstream. Downstream are the emissions from using any products sold by INEOS. Where does an INEOS plastic end up, and does its final product form lead to greenhouse gas emissions? Upstream is the reverse: what are the emissions of your suppliers? Think third party transportation of the goods you've bought, or how they were warehoused. INEOS is currently working on a scientific method to track all of these emissions. It's not easy, but it'll give INEOS a much better picture of its overall emissions globally.

There's already some progress in INEOS businesses when it comes to Scope 3 emissions. INEOS's giant subsidiary, Inovyn – which makes chlorvinyls that end up in industries like construction, automotive and healthcare – has already made good headway. It has completed environmental product declarations (or EPDs) that detail the carbon footprint for all of its chloralkali and PVC products. This is essential to the reduction process. The INEOS Mercedes-AMG Petronas Formula One team has also committed to halving its Scope 3 emissions by 2026. The goal is for the team to hit net zero as soon as 2030 – twenty years ahead of INEOS in its totality.

Belstaff, another iconic INEOS sub-brand, is also doing its bit to be more Earth-friendly. INEOS say it uses a 'sustainable by design' philosophy that basically means the products are made to last. We do, after all, live in an era of fast fashion. According to the Ellen MacArthur Foundation, global clothing sales have doubled from one hundred billion to two hundred billion items a year since the turn of the millennium. At the same time, the average number of times that an item is worn has fallen by 36 per cent. The Belstaff belief is that its clothing – hard-wearing and rugged – should last a lifetime. Who can argue with that? It's also embarked on a three year supply chain sustainability roadmap and is demanding that suppliers sign a vendors' code of conduct, all in a bid to reduce the impact of sourcing its materials.

Most of INEOS's operational greenhouse gas footprint comes from emissions linked to energy. It's no surprise: when you're producing and manufacturing on a massive scale as INEOS does, you need lots of energy. Enormous, mind-boggling amounts. Shrinking that energy footprint will be key, but while still managing to keep the lights on. INEOS's energy footprint globally in 2019 was 351.2 PJ, or petajoules. A petajoule is a quadrillion joules, or a thousand trillion. That's an enormous number that's hard to imagine. A sixty watt lightbulb uses sixty joules of energy per second when it's on. We're talking trillions of lightbulbs. But INEOS isn't just powering lightbulbs: it's cooling, compressing, heating and so much more. INEOS has managed to shrink its total energy footprint to 345.5 PJ in 2021, but there's still a long way to go.

Unfortunately, the bulk of the footprint is fossil fuels (about three-quarters, with electricity making up 12 per cent and hydrogen a further 6 per cent). That won't always be the case. The footprint will change shape as INEOS can move to using more renewables – so the energy being used is ultimately less damaging. But to shrink the footprint, INEOS will need to make its current operations more efficient. Making better use of each joule of energy spent means you can use fewer joules to get the same outcome. It's a bit like using all three shelves of the oven if you've got it switched on anyway. These optimizations will come naturally as technology improves, but will also require some clever thinking on INEOS's part. INEOS thinks that optimizations can reduce carbon emissions by 10 per cent.

So INEOS has worked out that it has six main routes to hitting net zero. We'll explore these in detail later in the chapter, but the six are:

- fuel-switching, with a focus on hydrogen and electrification
- feedstock switching to more sustainable alternatives
- optimization so that end results require fewer emissions along the way
- the capture and reuse of carbon
- the capture and permanent storage of carbon
- offsetting against the carbon footprint, through compensation or carbon removal

Offsetting is, in many ways, the laziest option – albeit very effective. It means paying to make carbon reductions elsewhere in the world to plug your own gaps. That's why INEOS is rightly focusing on the first five (especially in the lead-up to 2030) and leaving offsetting as a last-ditch effort to reach net zero.

Hydrogen

Hydrogen is a superstar atom. It's the lightest element, and by far the most abundant. In fact, it makes up about 75 per cent of all normal matter in the universe. It's also highly combustible, which makes it an excellent fuel. In fact, the sun that warms us as you read these words is mostly composed of hydrogen. The bulk of our earthly hydrogen exists inside other molecules. Take water, for instance: it's made up of two hydrogen atoms and one oxygen atom, or H_2O.

Hydrogen is also odourless, tasteless and colourless. But if you speak to those in the know at INEOS – or anyone in the energy game – you'll quickly realize that hydrogen comes in a veritable rainbow of hues. You can't 'see' these colours, but they refer to the different types of hydrogen in the energy industry. You've got green, blue, brown, pink, yellow and even turquoise hydrogen. It's a real headscratcher if your school days rightly taught you that hydrogen is invisible.

Green hydrogen is truly the gold standard when it comes to saving the planet, so INEOS is naturally investigating it. This is hydrogen that's produced with absolutely no harmful greenhouse gas emissions. That means you're producing it using clean and green electricity: think renewables like wind or solar power. This electricity can be used to power an electrolyser. That's a giant machine that can be used to split water into its constituent parts: hydrogen and oxygen.

A basic electrolyser will have a cathode (with a negative charge), an anode (with a positive charge), and a membrane. Electricity will be applied to the anode and cathode across the membrane, splitting up the water molecules. Hydrogen is produced at the cathode and can then be used as fuel. Oxygen is produced at the anode and can be released into the atmosphere – or captured and utilized, if it makes economic sense.

If this electrolysis system is powered using green electricity from renewable sources, then the physical process is carbon free. The result is green hydrogen: a clean fuel that produces water when you burn it. That's in contrast to rival fuel methane, which gives off both carbon dioxide and water when burned. Not good.

In an ideal world, you'll have your renewable energy sources coupled directly to the electrolyser. This means you don't have to transport the input energy anywhere. It's also the easiest and fastest system – but it won't always be possible. Another option is to simply hook the electrolyser up to the grid and get your electricity that way.

In any case, the water you use needs to be pure. This will sometimes already be the case at a chemical processing plant, but if not you'll need a desalination plant to take the salt out too. Once you put that water into the electrolyser (and add electricity), you'll end up with ready-to-use hydrogen. You'll also get loads of oxygen that could be captured and reused. Inovyn's hydrogen business says a key customer of this oxygen could be INEOS Oxide, which – as the name suggests – uses lots of oxygen. This capture and utilization makes the entire process more efficient. Hydrogen could also be used on site by producers, if there's some way to use it. Maybe that's heating a building, powering a furnace or getting the wheels turning on a hydrogen fuel cell truck.

If you can't use the hydrogen on site then it needs to be transported. In an ideal case, that would be locally or nationally – generally through pipelines. A good example of this would be if you were creating hydrogen that would then be used to heat homes. Ultimately the problem with green hydrogen is that electrolysis isn't cheap. It'll take years before green hydrogen production is economical on a mega scale.

Hydrogen isn't always 'green' – far from it. Another type is blue hydrogen, which is produced from natural gas using a process known as steam reforming.

Natural gas is a fossil fuel. It's formed over millions (and even hundreds of millions) of years. When plants and animals die, their remains build in layers and are eventually buried. Immense pressure and heat then transform this matter – rich in carbon and hydrogen – into fossil fuels. It ends up as coal, oil or natural gas. Natural gas is made up of multiple compounds, but the bulk of it is methane. That's CH_4: one carbon atom and four hydrogen atoms. Natural gas also typically includes other gases like water vapour, nitrogen, helium and carbon dioxide.

You can use natural gas as a fuel, burning it to generate electricity, or for heating and cooking. It's also commonly used to manufacture plastics and other chemicals. You'll find natural gas in the cracks between (or pores of) rock layers. Once geologists locate a source of natural gas, engineers build exploratory wells. If it's a good site, the natural gas comes up et voilà: fuel.

Humans have been harnessing natural gas – at least in minor ways – for thousands of years. It only became commercialized in the late eighteenth century, when the British began using it for lighting. This idea eventually expanded globally and the uses of natural gas broadened out to include heating homes and for cooking food. Boilers, too, used natural gas to generate electricity. All of this undoubtedly caused significant advancements for human civilization. Some poorer parts of the world are still waiting for their natural gas pipelines to arrive. But it all comes with a cost: natural gas produces carbon dioxide when refined and burned. It's estimated that over the past hundred years, the production and use of natural gas has made up about a fifth of human greenhouse gas emissions.* In 2020, it emitted around 7.8 billion tonnes of CO_2. That's just under half of coal emissions and about two thirds of oil emissions – but it's still no small figure.

So the fact that blue hydrogen relies on natural gas isn't ideal. It's less eco-friendly by virtue of the fact that creating blue hydrogen releases carbon dioxide. If this carbon is allowed to freely enter the atmosphere, blue hydrogen is then known as grey hydrogen. That's far from eco-friendly. The only way to keep it 'blue' is to introduce a carbon capture and storage element. By trapping the carbon, you can make hydrogen production through steam reforming far cleaner. That's the INEOS vision.

So what is steam reforming? For practical purposes, it's an alternative to electrolysis that can be done at a larger scale. It's also significantly cheaper. You take the methane from natural gas and heat it using steam under high pressure with a catalyst (usually nickel), knocking the hydrogen off the carbon molecule. The result is hydrogen and carbon dioxide. The former is a useful fuel, which is great. The latter is environmentally damaging – or rather, it has the potential to be if handled incorrectly.

INEOS has plans to build two steam reformers at its Grangemouth site to produce hydrogen in bulk. This will naturally create a lot of carbon dioxide. The idea would be that this carbon dioxide could be captured in a concentrated form and then pumped along a pipeline into

---

*   https://ourworldindata.org/emissions-by-fuel

Scotland's Acorn project, an enormous carbon storage scheme that aims to permanently lock away millions of tonnes of CO_2. This would keep INEOS's hydrogen blue. It would also allow the UK to have a powerful hydrogen source, while additionally contributing carbon to an enormous storage project that could drastically reduce our national emissions. More on that later.

Back to hydrogen for now. Hydrogen could totally revolutionize how a mega-site like Grangemouth operates and delivers energy to the UK. INEOS owns and operates the Forties Pipeline System, a huge transport network in the North Sea. It carries around 30 per cent of the UK's oil from oceanic fields to shore and is ultimately pumped to be processed at Grangemouth. Transitioning this system to also include hydrogen is in the future, but it's not as simple as just flicking a switch. As Andrew Gardner, CEO of the FPS, explains:

'One of the difficulties we have is that the Forties Pipeline System can't really shut down, right? It has to run: when the Forties Pipeline System shuts down, the North Sea shuts down. So it has to be run like a utility, like a power station. There is the problem of fuel switching from multiple supplies. We have four or five different ways of getting methane to the site. If you lose one of these supplies, you just go to another one – you have redundancy.'

For the first phase of INEOS's hydrogen switching, it will use methane to make hydrogen with carbon capture. That hydrogen will then make steam and power and be used in the furnaces. INEOS has to keep operational 'redundancy', however, so that if its hydrogen production facility was lost, it could immediately flip back to using methane. The idea is that eventually, INEOS won't be relying on a single source of hydrogen at all. 'The aspiration is – and why we're working with partners like National Grid Gas and others – that in time, say the middle of the 2030s, rather than the UK having a National Grid gas network, it'll have a hydrogen network,' Andrew explained:

'So you'll have multiple people putting in and multiple people putting out. When you get to that place, that gives us alternative sources of hydrogen, rather than the ones we're creating ourselves. Once you have that, you can then take your hydrogen switching all the way to 100 per cent – and that de-carbonizes. But you're probably still with five hundred thousand or six hundred thousand tonnes of carbon. And this is where it'll be technology yet to be developed. A lot of people talk about CCUS. That CC is carbon capture, and US is utilization and storage. We talk a lot about CCS – that's what Project Acorn and Greensand are – but the other thing that we're trying to develop, and over the next five years hopefully we will, is a research centre about taking the carbon and actually turning it into something useful. That's the utilization: maybe for animal feed or some other product.'

INEOS seems sure that hydrogen will eventually play a big part in UK energy systems. The plain fact remains: you burn hydrogen and you end up with energy and water. If you can produce it in a carbon neutral way, it's extremely clean. Now simply massively ramping up hydrogen production overnight would not solve the UK's climate woes, because you need to be able to use it. As Andrew said:

'We're starting some experimental work with Scottish gas networks – local gas networks. If you imagine the UK's millions of boilers in all of the houses that all take methane gas. OK, we can change them for heat pumps or solar. Or the next time you get a boiler, you get one that runs gas or hydrogen. The simplest way to decarbonize without creating chaos is, for example, to make the change that any new boiler has to have hydrogen capability and can flip between methane and hydrogen. Then we start to seed hydrogen into the methane system, the national gas system. So you go from 10 per cent methane, to 10 per cent to 20 per cent to 30 per cent to 40 per cent to 50 per cent hydrogen, so you're decarbonizing millions of homes all the time.'

Andrew imagines a future where we replace the National Transmission System for methane with one for hydrogen. Grangemouth is already hosting research (partly courtesy of some funding from energy watchdog Ofgem) to examine whether UK transmission networks can be repurposed for hydrogen gas. The £29 million project will see INEOS and Scottish Gas Networks feed hydrogen into an old gas transmission line to see if it can carry pure hydrogen.

Ultimately, INEOS hopes that it can deliver hydrogen that won't just be used for heating homes, but also for transportation. The UK is currently shifting dramatically towards electric cars, but there are plenty of sceptics who think that a world where 100 per cent of cars are electric is unrealistic. Hydrogen will have to step in. 'My view is, unfortunately, that electrification of the fleet will get to about 50 to 80 per cent and then it will pause,' Andrew explained.

'Not because of charging points, but because we don't have enough electrical cables in the ground or above our heads to take that base load of electricity: it's a phenomenal increase in the amount of electricity used if you're starting to use it for everybody's car. So you get that 50 per cent energy transition here. And then for the big vehicles like the lorries or the buses, you probably start using hydrogen. You can't make an articulated lorry run on batteries – you'd need about eighty tonnes of batteries – so you don't have any payload capacity. That's probably more suited to run on hydrogen. So you have a hydrogen tank, you fill it up and you then use that hydrogen to create electricity and you run on a small battery because you're basically using a liquid fuel.'

A big problem INEOS is trying to solve with hydrogen – and one that often plagues energy producers – is supply and demand. When it comes to heating homes and businesses for instance, demand for energy is higher in winter than summer. For energy producers – who often have fixed overhead costs – it's generally most efficient to keep producing energy, even in periods of low demand. That means you need storage. Where do you store hydrogen in large quantities and (importantly) safely? As Wouter Bleukx, the Inovyn business director for hydrogen, explained:

'Hydrogen is a difficult molecule to store. You need to liquefy or you need to compress – and you need large quantities. What we are also looking at is storage of hydrogen in salt cavities. We have experience with storage of gas in these cavities, and we have now kicked off a project to look at storage of hydrogen in salt cavities in order to balance supply-demand, and also seasonality. This first project kicked off in the UK.'

INEOS is one of eight companies working on a low-carbon energy project in the UK called HyNet. It's a blue hydrogen project; INEOS isn't producing that itself, but will handle the storage part of the process, as Wouter explained.

'You have production of hydrogen, then you have a pipeline infrastructure that will be built to transport the hydrogen in the north-west of England. Then there will be a pipe infrastructure of CO_2 going to oil wells in the Irish Sea. We will, at the same time, play the storage provider role for that full hydrogen network. That same network can also be used to connect to green hydrogen projects, but at the moment it is a blue hydrogen project. It is one of the two projects that the UK government has taken as priority projects for the development of hydrogen. Our hydrogen storage is in Northwich [in Cheshire], where we have enormous amounts of salt mines. Of course, we first need to do the salt mining before we can have the cavity. We use a lot of salt as a chloralkali producer, so everything starts from salt. So you put water in the ground to create a solubilized salt solution, which you take out. That is then the cavity. Once the salt is almost all taken out – which takes roughly one and a half to two years to create one cavity – then you can start building a gas plant on it, and using that cavity for hydrogen storage. At the moment we are working on a project to create eighteen cavities.'

Ultimately the journey to hydrogen going mainstream is a long one, and certainly won't be realized this decade. Nevertheless, everyone I spoke to at INEOS agreed that hydrogen will be hugely important to the company's future – and indeed all of our futures. It all comes down to that simple scientific fact: burning hydrogen doesn't produce carbon.

Carbon capture

Carbon is what keeps climate scientists awake at night.

Above all else, carbon emissions are the chief human driver of global warming. They make up the bulk of greenhouse gases – if you discount water vapour, which only persists for a few days. Carbon dioxide can persist in our atmosphere for centuries. It's far more abundant than heat-trapping stablemates like methane and nitrous oxide. Myriad industries emit carbon dioxide: transportation, electricity production, heating homes, agriculture, poor land use and so much more.

It's all to do with the greenhouse effect. Whatever their point of origin, greenhouse gases – including carbon dioxide – ultimately make their way into the same atmosphere. Then, just like a greenhouse in your garden, this gaseous shell traps heat that would otherwise have escaped into space. As a result, the Earth warms up. That's the crisis we're all facing: a planet too hot to bear.

One obvious solution is to simply cut carbon emissions at the source. This is happening across the world: governments, businesses and individuals are all scrambling to slash their own carbon emissions. It's a target we must all pursue. But it's simply not possible to cut all carbon dioxide emissions to zero globally right now.

A second option is something called carbon offsetting. This is where a company can buy a 'carbon credit' that pays for the removal of carbon from the air somewhere in the world. This is a healthy part of the solution, especially as carbon is a global issue – so it's all helpful on the journey to net zero emissions. Ultimately it's a stopgap, however.

The third tool to stave off carbon's contribution to global climate crisis is simply to prevent it from reaching the atmosphere in the first place. Carbon capture and storage (or CCS) is how you deal with emissions that can't be stopped right now. It involves trapping the carbon dioxide, then transporting to somewhere where it can be stored underground. This could be a fantastic aid to reducing the carbon burden created by the burning of fossil fuels for power, or certain industrial processes like cement and steel production. Scientists – including the Intergovernmental Panel on Climate Change (IPCC) – agree that carbon capture will be an essential part of meeting the 2015 Paris Agreement to limit global temperature increases.

INEOS has been involved in CCS for a while now, and it's got big plans for the future. For the last decade, INEOS has been capturing greenhouse gas emissions at plants in Antwerp and Germany. It's already removed upwards of a million tonnes of carbon dioxide. That's equivalent to the emissions from eighty thousand cars.

More excitingly, INEOS is working on several projects to store carbon at an enormous scale. One such initiative is Project Greensand, which will involve storing carbon dioxide in depleted North Sea oil fields owned by INEOS. If successful, INEOS says it will make the 'largest single contribution' to cutting Denmark's greenhouse gas emissions.

Denmark is aiming to cut its carbon emissions by 70 per cent by 2030. That's around twenty million tonnes of CO_2 per year. Of that, around eight million tonnes are earmarked for CCS. INEOS's Project Greensand could potentially deliver that full eight million tonnes of carbon capture and storage.

The story begins in 2017, when INEOS bought up the entire oil and gas business from Denmark's DONG Energy A/S. It was an enormous acquisition that gave INEOS a major presence in the North Sea. INEOS has managed to cut costs, develop new fields and deliver significantly greater quantities of oil – helping to keep the lights on, so to speak. But it also created an enormous opportunity for carbon capture and storage on a grand scale.

The North Sea has lots of what INEOS would call 'mature infrastructure'. This includes oil fields that are depleted – so they're no longer useful for energy production. The Greensand site has been producing since 1998, but that's expected to end around 2025–2026. That makes it an excellent candidate for carbon capture and storage. INEOS wants to use one non-producing reservoir (Nini West) at the site for a CCS pilot trial.

Phase one is already behind us. It concluded lab tests, examining cores from the reservoir and exposing them to CO_2 and getting an independent audit of the site's safety and capacity to store carbon.

Phase two will be the physical pilot test, which will involve injecting CO_2 directly into the depleted oil fields. Carbon is already being captured by INEOS Oxide in Antwerp for commercial purposes and held in a liquid state. Instead of shipping that carbon to customers, it will instead be placed into containers. Then it will be trucked for about five kilometres to the harbourside, before being loaded onto tankers. A ship will then carry that CO_2 from Belgium, taking it just over five hundred kilometres to the oil platforms in the North Sea.

The CO_2 – made by liquid through heating, compressing and cooling – is then sent down into the sandstone reservoir via carbon dioxide wells, around one thousand eight hundred metres below ground. Above it are layers of impenetrable rock that will keep the CO_2 from leaking back out. This should keep marine ecosystems safe, and also stop stored carbon ending up in the atmosphere.

It might sound slightly shocking: the idea of pumping millions of tonnes of liquefied carbon dioxide into the ground. The good news for INEOS (and ultimately for us all) is that it's a tried and tested technology that has existed for decades. It's also important to remember that certain types of rock formation are fantastic for storage. Think about it: the Greensand site has been storing gas and oil for between ten and twenty million years. These Paleocene sandstone fields are encased in a sturdy cap rock, in an area regarded as extremely geologically stable. That significantly reduces the risk of a major carbon leak.

Norway's DNV GL conducted a major audit of the area and determined that the Nini West field appears to be suitable for safe and extended storage of CO_2 – at around 0.45 million tonnes of CO_2 per year per well for a ten-year period. The hope is that the entire INEOS-operated area can eventually take up to eight million tonnes of CO_2 per year by around 2030. It would be an enormous win for INEOS and Denmark, as well as for our planet.

Project Greensand isn't the only INEOS effort to lock carbon away. INEOS is also helping to develop Acorn Carbon Capture and Storage, an enormous project in North East Scotland. The aspiration is to lock away between five and ten million tonnes of carbon dioxide by 2027. INEOS says it could do twenty million tonnes a year in the future. By 2030, the Acorn project could be comfortably storing more than half of the ten million tonnes per year targeted by the UK government's ten-point plan.

It'll work by tapping into depleted oil and gas fields in the North Sea. These are old Shell fields that are no longer productive, but can provide value in locking away carbon. Acorn is based in North East Scotland at the St Fergus gas terminal. This is where around a third of the UK's natural gas comes onshore. Scotland has its own vision to become a net zero nation by 2045, and the Acorn project will be part of meeting that target. INEOS has teamed up with a number of organizations to capture and store significant quantities of CO_2.

INEOS will use the project to significantly reduce its own emissions. When the Grangemouth manufacturing site was first bought by INEOS in 2005, it was emitting around five million tonnes of CO_2 per year. That's since been reduced to around three million tonnes – and will eventually dip below two million. This will be achieved through Acorn project carbon capture, as well as investment in hydrogen. INEOS already has pipeline systems that go from Grangemouth to the north of

Scotland, and then beyond that into depleted North Sea fields. That means INEOS won't need to rely on shipping, like Greensand will.

Like Greensand, the Acorn project should be an extremely safe operation. Lab tests have already been conducted to make sure that the sandstone pores can host CO_2. This carbon will be stored at depths of two kilometres, where it will eventually turn back into hydrocarbon fuels.

The ability to store carbon like this is a major benefit. Not all nations are as fortunate as oceanic UK and Norway, who have ready access to depleted oil and gas fields where carbon can be locked away. A country like Germany, for example, will need to be much more creative to store carbon. Almost all of Europe's rock formations identified for carbon dioxide are shared between Norway and the UK and of the sites already designated for storage projects, all are in the North Sea. By 2030 the UK wants four major carbon stores, with two already approved. One is at St Fergus, with the other being Drax power station in North Yorkshire. Storing carbon in this way will be an enormous part of reaching UK climate goals.

It's also clearly a very sensible option. Existing gas pipelines can already take CO_2 directly to the storage sites. Existing CO_2 emissions can be captured from the units at the St Fergus gas terminal, slashing carbon loss from day one. INEOS can pipe carbon up to the site, and ships and trucks can carry CO_2 from other parts of Scotland.

In the first phase, around three hundred thousand tonnes per year of existing CO_2 emissions from St Fergus can be captured, dried and compressed. These can then be sent through the Goldeneye pipeline, which reaches out to the northeast of Scotland to the Acorn storage site. At this stage, the carbon would be injected directly into the sandstone rock, several kilometres below the seabed – and around a hundred kilometres offshore.

In phase two the project hopes to expand, allowing for CO_2 importation at Peterhead's deep water port and a repurposed pipeline stretching across Scotland's interior, allowing for storage of central belt emissions.

The project also hopes to deliver an international CO_2 storage hub in the central North Sea. This would open up access for shipping from across the UK and Europe: think Teesside, Humberside, the Thames, South Wales and the Netherlands and Norway.

It's a great reuse of existing infrastructure. The Goldeneye platform was used for gas exporting for seven years, ending in 2011. It was due to be decommissioned in 2019, but will be used for carbon capture and storage instead. The pipeline is a large carbon-steel tube just twenty inches thick, and it will funnel carbon thousands of feet below ground – trapping it indefinitely.

Carbon capture is an essential part of meeting climate goals. Nations can install solar panels, build offshore wind farms and switch out fossil fuel-gobbling vehicles for electric alternatives – but it won't be quick enough or sufficient to meet targets. Heavy industry will inevitably produce CO_2, and carbon capture is an extremely quick and efficient way to mitigate against that. Where we can store carbon, in other words, we should. The sandstone formations in the North Sea subsoil are perfect for long-term CO_2 storage. In fact, it's estimated that Denmark's subsoil could store the next five hundred years of CO_2 emissions from the nation at current emission levels. Carbon capture can give us and our planet significant breathing room – if we let it.

Carbon capture and storage is a clear route to limiting emissions from the energy industry in particular. Without CCS, the demand for global energy would need to significantly shrink to meet climate targets. This is unlikely, especially as new populations climb out of energy poverty – ultimately driving demand up. When you look at the IPCC's ninety-seven different 'mitigation pathways' to keep global warming below 1.5C, you end up with an average of 665 billion tonnes (or 'gigatonnes') of CO_2 captured between now and 2100. The world will need to significantly scale up carbon capture efforts, and find ways of making it cheaper. Project Greensand and the Acorn project will be fantastic contributions to the cause, but global industry and governments must step up and do more to make super-scale CCS a reality.

The good news is that it's certainly possible, at least geologically. The IPCC's 2022 Summary for Policymakers notes that there's more than enough underground storage space globally to meet targets – although not all nations have equal access. 'The technical geological CO_2 storage capacity is estimated to be in the order of a thousand gigatonnes of CO_2, which is more than the CO_2 storage requirements through 2100 to limit global warming to 1.5C, although the regional availability of geological storage could be a limiting factor,' the report reads.

That's why it's important that countries and industries that have the ability to store carbon underground should take total advantage of it. Oil fields have certainly contributed to the climate crisis, but they can also help us tackle it in their depleted state. It will be expensive at first but thanks to economies of scale, costs will come down. Not only that, carbon capture and storage could help keep ex-oil workers employed. Project Greensand's report rightly notes:

'Denmark has been extracting oil and gas from the North Sea since 1972. It has created a wide range of jobs both on land and at sea. But as part of the green transition, a majority in the Danish parliament has decided that Denmark must stop oil extraction from the Danish part of the North Sea in the year 2050. If we instead start storing CO_2 in oil and gas fields in the North Sea, we will not only solve part of the climate challenges. We will also maintain several thousand jobs.'

It makes perfect sense, given that these oil workers already have the skills, the know-how and the desire to work with offshore platforms. Storing CO_2 isn't miles from the job of extracting oil, so bolstering the CCS industry is a great way to ensure that thousands of skilled workers aren't kicked to the kerb.

The problem is that we're behind schedule right now. INEOS might be storming ahead with CCS projects, but the IPCC warns that current global rates of deployment are 'far below those in modelled pathways limiting global warming to 1.5°C or 2°C'. It makes a few recommendations, none of which are particularly surprising. The first is having better policy instruments: governments need to make it more attractive and easy for businesses to start storing carbon. The second is greater public support, and there's no easy fix for that. A lot of public discourse is dominated by methods of cutting emissions at the source, with far fewer people talking about how we have the untapped ability to lock away billions of tonnes of carbon dioxide before it ever reaches the atmosphere. The third recommendation is technological innovation, which won't happen overnight. It will take bold projects like Greensand and Acorn to test the waters (literally and figuratively), and discover where efficiencies can be made. This will take time, but subsidies and public awareness will help.

Ultimately, this will happen. By hook or by crook, CCS must go global – and fast. The race to reduce greenhouse gas emissions will inevitably include burying hundreds of gigatonnes of carbon dioxide below ground. Governments and big players in the energy industry will be watching INEOS closely to see the fruits of its CCS labour. Thankfully it seems a certain thing that carbon can be safely locked away in the North Sea, but only time can tell for sure. Once INEOS has proven its case, it can begin injecting carbon beneath the sea in enormous quantities, doing its bit to steadily stave off climate crisis. Imagine a future where hundreds of depleted oil fields are turned into dumping grounds for the worst of greenhouse gases, helping to mend their contribution to our climate woes. What sweet irony.

Efficiency and Project One

Part of the sustainability drive is making existing systems better. Take plastics. The world can't abandon plastics overnight. Swapping out drinking straws might be easy, but the same can't be said for all of the plastics that go into medical equipment or health and safety gear. Scientists and big brands need to work hard at developing better alternatives to plastics, but it's a big challenge – and there's no one-size-fits-all replacement for every plastics usage. Part of the solution has to be a reduction of the carbon impact of plastic production in the short term.

That's the thinking behind Project One, an INEOS initiative to make the production of plastics more sustainable. Project One aims to deliver a brand new ethane cracker. In fact, it should be the most environmentally friendly steam cracker in Europe, and possibly even the world.

First off, what the heck is an ethane cracker? It's a plant that produces the building blocks of plastics. First, you need some natural gas. That's what scientists call a gas you can burn that has a mix of compounds – mostly methane, but also ethane, butane, propane and pentane – found deep below the Earth's surface. You take this gas and 'crack' it with extreme heat, breaking it down into ethylene. Ethylene is the base chemical that you use to make the plastics, resins and adhesives that you'll find in almost all areas of our world. Without ethylene, modern life looks extremely different. You'll find it extending the shelf life of food packaging, in medical equipment like syringes, in vehicle parts, in insulation for buildings and the coating for wires, and even in the pipes that transport drinking water.

Crackers for ethylene exist in many places around the world, including in the Middle East, the USA and China. Ethylene is a flammable gas, and shipping it globally, safely, isn't easy – which is why there are dozens of ethane crackers in Europe, allowing it to be produced locally. The problem, as INEOS sees it, is that Europe's cracker infrastructure is very old. The continent hasn't built a new cracker in more than twenty years.

In simple terms, think of the technology you were using twenty years ago. You didn't have an iPhone, Tesla was still just the name of a long-dead scientist and not something you sit in to go fast, and a fresh-faced Mark Zuckerberg was only just finishing high school. Sadly, many European crackers are far older than two decades. We've gained so much efficiency in the realms of technology and science, but we're still using ancient systems to make our plastics in Europe. Project One is an INEOS bid to reduce the emissions of plastic production by using far newer technology. The hope is that this will replace some of Europe's oldest infrastructure, and allow necessary plastic production to continue without having to ship chemicals and goods from distant lands.

It's possible to import liquefied ethylene from the USA, but it's expensive. As a result, INEOS is aiming to build a 1.45 million tonne ethane cracker in Antwerp, Belgium. This state-of-the-art facility was announced in 2019, with a view to having the plant commissioned by the end of 2026. It's a mega project that will probably end up costing in the region of four billion euros. John McNally, the CEO of Project One, told me that there are around one hundred and fifty people working on the cracker right now. By the time it's done, that will rise to around two hundred. Probably more:

> 'Part of the drive is to make sure that it's the most environmentally sound cracker that exists on the planet today. When you're comparing, the most modern cracker is over twenty-five years old. Look at what technology has done in that time. It's like comparing a twenty-five-year-old car to a modern one.'

According to INEOS, the CO_2 footprint for Project One will be less than half of the top 10 per cent of crackers in Europe. It will emit less than a third of the CO_2 of an average cracker. 'There isn't a cracker on the planet that will compare in terms of CO_2,' John explained.

That's important, because lots of people think new ethane crackers shouldn't be built at all. After all, they require significant energy sources to heat ethane to a molecular 'cracking point', and ultimately produce large quantities of carbon dioxide. On the flip side, plastic production can't just vanish globally. Ethylene that Europe won't produce likely ends up being made instead in somewhere like China, before being converted into a solid (like plastics) and then moved to Europe anyway. The carbon ends up in the same atmosphere (there is only one, after all), with higher emissions than we'd see from an ultra-efficient INEOS cracker. If a job needs to be done, at least let it be done right, INEOS would argue. Relying on fifty-year-old crackers in Europe is not the answer.

Let's break down exactly how the system will work. First, you need ethane – and INEOS has a source for that already. It's shipped over from gas fields in Texas and Pennsylvania as a liquefied product at -90C. A large tank will be built at Antwerp – like the ones at INEOS sites in Grangemouth, Scotland and Rafnes, Norway – to store the 'cryo-ethane' in large quantities. Massive ships that can carry hundreds of thousands of cubic metres of ethane at a time will fill up this tank. The Project One cracker will then use powerful furnaces to superheat the ethane to crack the molecular bonds, resulting in ethylene, as well as water, butane and propane. INEOS also wants to use the ultracold temperatures of the cryo-ethane for the cooling process – rather than just using energy – to help with the separation and distillation process, splitting out methane. You can then sell the methane or push it back into the cycle.

If there is a villain in this scientific story, it's methane. When you burn methane, you get carbon dioxide. Even if INEOS can push left-over methane from the cracking process into heating systems, you'll still end up with carbon dioxide. In consequence, INEOS is looking at some solutions to lower the carbon footprint of the cracker.

One simple solution is to make sure that the electricity brought onto the site is from renewables. INEOS has already purchased wind farm electricity to edge the process closer to the ultimate net zero goal.

The bigger problem is that natural gas is used to fuel the furnaces. INEOS hopes that one day, it will be possible to replace all of this natural gas in the boilers and furnaces with hydrogen. Not all hydrogen is produced cleanly, but if INEOS can get its hands on enough green hydrogen, the natural gas could be displaced. Unlike with methane, burning hydrogen simply leaves you with water as a byproduct. No nasty carbon dioxide. The Project One cracker system will be capable of running like this, if hydrogen supplies can be sourced. That's not the case for extremely old crackers that were never designed to run on hydrogen.

Sadly, the fact is that for now, it's not possible to get enormous quantities of cheap low carbon hydrogen. That will change in the future.

Another option for INEOS is to use some carbon capture. Site space has already been allocated for carbon capture and storage. This will allow INEOS to sink away excess carbon that would otherwise make its way into the atmosphere. It won't be a huge project, because carbon emissions from this type of modern cracker are already quite low – and storage typically requires heavily concentrated CO_2 streams, like those from a power plant. Ultimately, carbon leaving the cycle is bad for the planet and also bad for business. INEOS is incentivized to make efficiencies and to keep carbon from being wasted. Reuse and capture is essential for the future.

Ethane crackers are a controversial technology, but Project One should help to clean up Europe's cracking industry. It will automatically be compared with all other European steam crackers in the EU Emissions Trading System (EU ETS). This has a benchmark – determined by the 10 per cent best-performing plants – of 0.68 tonnes of CO_2 emissions per tonne of product. Project One will be at 43 per cent of that benchmark, with 0.29 tonnes of CO_2. As soon as the site goes online, in other words, the benchmark will be forced to shift. If fellow European businesses don't make their crackers more sustainable, they'll pay more for their emission rights. It will force the hand of rival crackers: clean up your act, or shut down. This means Project One should result in lower emissions across European crackers, simply by existing.

It's a pure example of how improving an emitting technology can be a great stopgap in the fight against climate change. Stopping the production of cars would probably help the climate, but it would also plunge us into assured chaos. It's the same story for plastics: we'll still need them for a long time, and we need businesses developing more sustainable production. Simply using outdated crackers or relying on distant nations for plastic production doesn't solve the climate crisis. A new and cleaner European cracker should limit reliance on both of those options. Why turn to an ancient cracker or Chinese plastics when we can produce ethylene more cleanly right next to the port of Antwerp, offering transport routes all around Europe?

This is why, perhaps confusingly at face value, the new ethane cracker – with its carbon emissions – is part of INEOS's grand decarbonization strategy. Driving no car might be the best option for the planet, but if everyone still needs to move around right now then we can't just ban cars. It's better to rely on an efficient 2022 motor than an ultra-polluting banger from the eighties. The same can be said for ethane crackers.

And if INEOS can realize its hydrogen dreams, Project One could become a plastic production miracle. This is the largest investment into European crackers in decades, and should deliver a much brighter future for plastics – while we still rely on them so heavily. Recycling and the circular economy will also play a part in helping INEOS get to net zero. The goal is to reduce wastefulness by reusing – or making better use of – the products and systems that we already have. Ultimately, this should mean lower emissions across the entire production ecosystem.

Recycling and the circular economy

One part of that mission is simply to improve the recyclability of INEOS's own products. INEOS makes lots of products with the capacity for recycling: polyethylene, polypropylene, polystyrene and PVC. If they can be recovered and reused, or recycled in the most maximal way, this will reduce the need for landfills, incineration, and ultimately lower the demand for fossil based raw materials. To make that happen, INEOS has made what it's called the 2025 pledge. This is a bid to transition to a circular economy where less is wasted – ultimately inching the business towards its net zero targets.

So what's included in the pledge? For a start, INEOS has vowed to make sure its products that end up in polystyrene packaging in Europe contain at least 30 per cent recycled content on average. It has pledged to incorporate 325 kilotons of recycled material into its products per

SECCO China. In July 2022, INEOS and SINOPEC sign deals worth a combined value of $7 billion, landmark agreements that significantly reshape INEOS's production and technology in China.

INEOS China – Bird's-eye view of Kaimen site at Ningbo, China, March 2023.

INEOS at Chocolate Bayou, Texas, USA. INEOS's largest plant in North America, covering 2,400 acres.

The INEOS site at Cologne. The largest of INEOS's facilities and one of Germany's largest cracker complexes, employing 2,500 people.

The INEOS site at Grangemouth, Scotland. INEOS's largest UK plant and Scotland's only refinery. Processes 40% of UK's oil and gas via the Forties Pipeline System connected to the North Sea.

INEOS Energy enters US oil and gas production for the first time, acquiring a portion of Chesapeake Energy's oil and gas assets in Eagle Ford, South Texas for $1.4 billion, February 2023.

The Unity platform receives crude oil and gas via six incoming pipelines. The streams are combined into the 'FPS Sealine' to the onshore Cruden Bay Terminal, north of Aberdeen.

Monarch of the Glen – Expedition 1.0 media convoy traverses the wild Ardverikie Estate in Scotland's Cairngorms National Park.

Oh buoy! INEOS Automotive becomes the first manufacturer to cross Morecambe Bay.

Grenadier prototypes saw over 1.1 million miles of testing in the harshest conditions.

Schöckl-ready!

Sir Jim Ratcliffe and Sir Lewis Hamilton test drove the Grenadier together.

INEOS announces its partnership with Mercedes-AMG Petronas Formula One Team at the Royal Automobile Club in London, 2020.

Sir Lewis Hamilton celebrates winning the 2021 British GP.

Egan Bernal, in the famous yellow jersey, won the Tour de France in 2019 for Team INEOS, supported by Geraint Thomas.

Tom Pidcock on his way to winning the Alpe d'Huez stage of the 2022 Tour de France.

INEOS has been Performance Partner to the All Blacks and Teams in Black since January 2022.

INEOS owns French Ligue 1 football club OGC Nice, pictured here, and Swiss side FC Lausanne-Sport.

Sir Jim Ratcliffe, Sir Ben Ainslie, Dave Endean, Toto Wolff and James Allison launch INEOS Britannia as Challenger of Record for the 37th America's Cup, supported by Mercedes F1 Team.

INEOS Team UK as British Challenger at the 36th America's Cup.

Sir Jim Ratcliffe and the INEOS team celebrate on board the AC75 Britannia after winning the Prada Cup Round Robin series in 2021.

Sir Jim Ratcliffe, Sir Ben Ainslie and The Royal Yacht Squadron's commodore Jamie Sheldon launch INEOS Team UK in April 2018 to challenge for the 36th America's Cup.

Sir Dave Brailsford, director of sport at INEOS.

The 'Gin & Tonic Moment', in South America, when the 'INEOS 1:59 Challenge' was conceived.

Eliud Kipchoge becomes the first person to run a sub-two-hour marathon at the INEOS 1:59 Challenge in October 2019.

Sir Jim Ratcliffe and Eliud Kipchoge celebrate after making history at the INEOS 1:59 Challenge.

A world first. INEOS-led Project Greensand carbon capture and storage in the Danish North Sea. By 2030 it could store up to 8 million tonnes of CO_2 per year.

Project Greensand was officially opened by His Royal Highness Crown Prince Frederik of Denmark on March 8, 2023.

2021: INEOS announces €2 billion investment, Europe's largest ever investment in electrolysis projects to make green hydrogen to transform production across Europe.

INEOS signs renewable power deal with Eneco. The deal increases INEOS's total Belgian offshore wind generation to over 200MW and reduces CO_2 emissions by nearly 3 million.

Rafnes, Norway: INEOS secures green power supply deal for its Norwegian sites to pursue ambitious plans to reach CO_2 reduction targets and deliver net zero emissions by 2050.

Sammy Miller winning the Scottish Six Days Trial in 1962 wearing Belstaff.

Belstaff CEO, Fran Millar.

Mercedes F1 driver George Russell models Belstaff.

2021: INEOS launched INEOS Hygienics, a commercial business supplying hygiene products to the public.

The Daily Mile was the official school education fitness programme supporter of the World Athletics Championships Oregon '22.

On top of the Brandberg: at 2800m, it is the highest mountain in Namibia, and second largest monolith in the world to Uluru/Ayers Rock.

INEOS graduates are invited to Namibia as part of the company's graduate challenge.

Children from local schools take part in The Daily Mile GO Run for Fun event, London Stadium, UK.

The Forgotten 40 project helps to improve the lives of children growing up in some of the poorest parts of the UK.

A ladder enables salmon to climb and access new sections of the river for spawning.

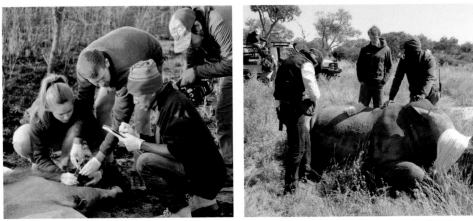

Six Rivers Africa was established by Sir Jim Ratcliffe to protect and develop some of Africa's great wild places.

The INEOS Tour de France Challenge – Each team covers the daily mileage of the Tour de France. In 2022, 2,560 employees cycled a combined distance of 1,283,865 kms to raise £122,000 for charity.

Sir Andrew Likierman and Sir Jim Ratcliffe in front of the London Business School's Ratcliffe Building.

INEOS donates £100 million to create new Oxford University Institute to fight antimicrobial resistance. From left: Professor Chris Schofield, VC Louise Richardson, Professor Tim Walsh, Sir Jim Ratcliffe, David Sweetnam, surgeon and adviser to the INEOS Oxford Institute.

John Reece, Jim Ratcliffe and Andy Currie in 2002.

year. By 2025, INEOS says 100 per cent of its polymer products will be recyclable. And by 2030, INEOS says it will be incorporating at least eight hundred and fifty thousand tonnes of recycled and biosourced polymers into its polymer products.

Reducing waste in general will also be important. In 2021, INEOS recycled or reused 22 per cent of all of the waste it generated. Another 22 per cent was sent for energy recovery. That's when you take waste materials that can't be recycled and turn them into a usable form of energy like heat, electricity or fuel. The overall strategy is common sense: reduce the waste you generate in total and make better use of the waste that you do end up with. This can even be economical: INEOS can sell waste as a recycling byproduct or for reuse as a fuel, or have a business like INEOS Oxide use waste heat to evaporate the liquid ethylene from its storage tanks. Everyone's a winner.

Things are moving in the right direction. The global tally for INEOS waste generation has shrunk over the past few years. In 2019, INEOS generated 0.991 Mt (megatonnes, or a million tonnes) of waste. That was reduced to 0.851 Mt in 2020, and then again to 0.824 Mt in 2021. The more this figure drops – and the proportion that can be reused or recycled grows – then the closer INEOS gets to a truly circular economy.

Not all recycling is the same – that much is clear. Dr Peter Williams, group technology director of INEOS, explains:

'There are two broadly distinct recycling methods. One is mechanical recycling. So you take waste plastic and you reheat it and reform it into something else. The other is what we call advanced recycling, where instead of just reforming the waste plastic – once used or multiple use plastic – you break it down back into the starting materials from which you made it in the first place. The problem with mechanical recycling is it normally downgrades. When you heat these things up and do that again and again, it removes some of the properties.'

One solution that INEOS has used to get around this is to produce part-recycled products using 50 per cent recycled content. This means that you can get a quality product without relying on entirely virgin materials. Mechanical recycling is also tricky because you need a large and clean stream of recycled material. Making sure that your source of plastic is clean is essential, especially if it's going to end up being used in a food or human contact scenario.

So INEOS is also investing heavily in advanced recycling. As far as INEOS is concerned, there are three main types. The first is dissolution: you dissolve a waste polymer in a solvent to remove any additives, colours or impurities. Those are the bad bits that are one of the main problems with mechanical recycling. Being able to remove them means you can have a much more useful end product. Second is depolymerization, which does what it says on the tin. You take polymers and turn them back into the monomers from which they were made. A polymer is a long-repeating chain of monomers – identical molecules that can attach to each other. All plastics are polymers (though not all polymers are plastics). Once you've returned to monomers, you can purify them and then turn them back into polymers, leaving you with a high-purity resin. Great on paper, but difficult to execute.

Giving hope is the INEOS Styrolution business, which has helpfully proven the concept for the depolymerization of polystyrene. It successfully depolymerized waste polymer polystyrene back into its monomer form styrene – before repolymerizing it into a viable product. INEOS has now teamed up with partners to make this process commercially viable.

The third and final method of advanced recycling that INEOS is looking at is called pyrolysis. That's when you take waste made up of mixed plastics and convert it to oil. This is usually done using thermal cracking, which simply means heating it up to extreme temperatures until it effectively 'cracks' apart as a material. You end up with an oil that can be purified and processed, and then ultimately used as a fuel. This could feed INEOS steam crackers that produce the basic building blocks for polymer and chemical production: ethylene, propylene, butadiene, benzene. Thermal cracking is heat-intensive (and therefore energy-intensive) but it can be made better by using more eco-friendly heating systems. And ultimately, the mixed plastics used to produce the oil would be wasted anyway, either ending up in a landfill or being burnt.

One particularly promising project aims to create a circular food-grade polypropylene. It's a type of plastic that is very commonly used for food packaging. It's stiff, sturdy and is translucent but can be dyed to any colour. More importantly, it's got a high melting point, so it's often used for food containers that might end up in a microwave or dish-washer. You've probably bought a yoghurt pot or microwaveable meal dish made from polypropylene. It's everywhere, so getting better at recycling it into a food-contact product again is important. INEOS is part of a UK project called NEXTLOOPP to create a demo plant for the production of recycled food-grade propylene. The plant hopes to produce ten thousand tonnes of the stuff each year. This will be a game-changer for food packaging. 'Polypropylene is one of the most versatile plastics in the world,' says Graham MacLennan, the polymer business manager for INEOS Olefins & Polymers UK.

'It is also missing from our recycling streams in food contact applications. In the UK alone we use over two hundred and ten thousand tonnes of polypropylene in our food packaging every year. It is found in pots, tubs and trays. However, the absence of food-grade recycled polypropylene means that all polypropylene food packaging is currently made from virgin plastics. This isn't unique to the UK but it's a global issue that INEOS and its partners are determined to change.'

One truly sci-fi mechanism to improve plastics recycling is an initiative aptly named HolyGrail 2.0 – of which INEOS O&P Europe is a part. Recycling household waste is very difficult, generally. It's usually a big mix of different types and grades of plastics, making it tough to reuse.

HolyGrail 2.0 will create imperceptible codes that cover the surface of the packaging – like watermarks. They'll be about the size of a postage stamp and invisible to the human eye. They will, however, be visible to special cameras that are connected to high-speed waste sorting systems. This will quickly allow the system to determine the type and grade of a plastic, so they can be efficiently sorted. 'Partnering with HolyGrail 2.0 demonstrates our commitment to taking action across the value chain to create a more sustainable future,' explains Rob Ingram, CEO of INEOS O&P North. 'It fits perfectly with the INEOS goal to increase recycling rates and the use of recycled materials back into everyday products. This is an exciting next step on our path to full packaging circularity.'

Recycling is very fashionable but it is not the only way to make a product more sustainable. You can also introduce biofeedstocks. A feedstock is shorthand for the raw material that supplies or fuels a machine or industrial process. Often this means using a fossil fuel resource, which isn't ideal. This type of feedstock is considered finite (unless you're willing to wait around for millions of years). A biofeedstock is a renewable source of carbon: think plant-based. For instance, normally you would use fossil-based carbons to produce polyolefins and PVC. INEOS is now using something called UPM BioVerno. It's a bio-based feedstock that is made from a renewable residue of wood pulp production. This is significantly better for the planet. The carbon footprint of a bio-material like this can be up to 90 per cent lower than for a conventional product.

INEOS is already offering one such product commercially: the bio-based PVC product BIOVYN, produced by INEOS business Inovyn. You can see where they got the name. INEOS is also able to substitute traditional styrene with a bio-attributed styrene for its Styrolux ECO and Styroflex ECO resins. The end result is greenhouse gas savings, compared to the usage of fossil-derived feedstocks. INEOS Oxide is also making a similar switch. It has completely substituted fossil feedstocks with a renewable biomass for a bio-attributed ethylene oxide. That's a gas used to make other products like antifreeze, detergents, fibres and bottles, as well as for sterilization in healthcare* on items like wound dressings and lateral flow tests. The new product is totally renewable, and it's certified as delivering a greenhouse gas saving of over 100 per cent compared to ethylene oxide produced using normal fossil-based methods. It's part of INEOS Oxide's strategy to be carbon neutral by 2050. More tangibly, it means that many of the products you might interact with on a day-to-day basis have been made in a more eco-friendly way – without relying on harmful fossil feedstocks.

Renewables

It goes without saying that one of the best ways to reduce your net fossil fuel greenhouse gas emissions is to use fewer fossil fuels. Few solutions can ever be as effective. Now it's extremely unlikely that, by 2050, INEOS won't be using any fossils across its business. Science accepts that net zero will be achieved – at least in part – by capturing and then either storing or using carbon. That said, INEOS will absolutely need to replace hydrocarbons at a significant scale. That's where renewables come in.

An energy source is considered renewable (or not) based on simple mathematics. Fossil fuels take an extremely long time to develop underground. When we use them as an energy source, inevitably we use them at a higher rate than they can be replenished. Renewable energy by contrast is from a natural source that replenishes in a much more useful timescale, i.e. not millions of years. If you use wind power, you just have to wait for another strong breeze to have more. You don't have to wait for subsurface chemical processes that take tens of thousands of human lifetimes to create gas or oil.

There are lots of different types of renewable energy. There's wind power, hydropower, geothermal energy and more. Probably best known

---

* https://www.gov.uk/government/publications/ethylene-oxide-properties-and-incident-management/ethylene-oxide-general-information

of the lot is solar energy, which we can harvest using solar panels. Solar panels are used at-scale for industry, but you'll also find them on people's homes – and now even on backpacks for hiking. According to the University of California Davis,[*] roughly 30 per cent of the solar energy that hits Earth is reflected back out into space. The remaining 70 per cent is absorbed, either by the atmosphere (23 per cent) or land and sea (47 per cent). Earth absorbs roughly 3.85 million exajoules (an exajoule is a thousand petajoules) of energy per year. That means that the amount of energy hitting Earth in a single hour could power the world for a year. There's no reasonable way to cover the entire planet in solar panels to capture it all, and nor would we want to. But we can get much better at harnessing the near-infinite energy that the sun chucks at us every day, given how valuable a resource it is.

The problem with solar is that it isn't a catch-all solution. It ultimately depends on sunlight, which varies around the world. If you set up a giant solar array next to the INEOS Grangemouth site just north of Edinburgh, Scotland, you're not going to have much luck. Scotland has many things in abundance (not least mountains and whisky), but it's lacking in sunlight. The same is not true for Texas, USA.

So it's no great surprise that INEOS Olefins & Polymers USA – with operations near Houston – has grand designs on an enormous solar field that could soon power its entire business. To get a better picture of how it works, it helps to understand what the business is actually doing.

The name is the giveaway: it produces olefins, and then polymers from those olefins. You start with a natural gas liquid like propane or ethane, and then heat it up to a very high temperature for a short time. This breaks the bonds down, knocking hydrogen off to create olefins like propylene or ethylene. That's the first process, and it is very energy-intensive. You're having to power furnaces to create extreme heat. This all takes place in very large units around fifty miles south of Houston,

---

[*] https://www.ucdavis.edu/climate/definitions/how-is-solar-power-generated

in an area known as Chocolate Bayou. The second process is to turn these olefins – which are monomers – into polymers, which can eventually be used to make materials that you'd find at the supermarket, or under the hood of your car. The monomers go through a catalytic process to be linked into long chains called polymers i.e. polyethylene and polypropylene. They're sold in the form of little solid pellets – about half the size of a raisin. Creating the pellets is a bit like making pasta. You push the plastic through a die with thousands of holes in it. The polymer-melt goes through the die, with blades on the other side spinning very quickly, constantly cutting as it comes through. The blades are in a bed of water, which instantly cools and solidifies it. Those pellets are ultimately distributed across the US to customers by railcars, and sometimes via trucks. Depending on the type of pellet, it'll end up being turned into the bag for your crisps – or potato chips as INEOS USA would call them – or medical IV devices, or milk bottles, or fuel tanks. They can be anywhere; they're everywhere. INEOS also converts some of the pellets in-house, creating plastic pipe for municipal water systems, mining and also the oil and gas industries.

The bulk of INEOS O&P USA's energy usage is in that very first stage of the journey. 'The olefins process is a very, very, very energy intensive process,' said Mike Nagle, the president of the business:

> '[That's] because it takes a lot of heat to heat up the furnaces to get the temperatures you need. Hydrocarbons like ethane and propane are very stable molecules. They don't want to be broken down, so you need very high temperatures. About 80 to 85 per cent of the greenhouse gas we make are in that olefins process. The polymers process – where you're linking and zipping – tends to be an exothermic process. It gives off heat, as opposed to the endothermic olefins process. So exothermic tends to not use as much energy.'

Building your own solar plant is difficult, even in Texas. You need the right soil conditions, a good environment (hurricanes naturally make matters tricky) and systems to deliver that solar energy to your plant. Sensibly therefore, INEOS has teamed up with an energy giant with lots of experience in solar facilities: NextEra Energy, Inc. 'They were looking to build a pretty large solar project here in Texas,' Mike Nagle explained:

'We told them how much we thought we'd need, and over time we ended up just deciding to partner. They built the solar farm, but it's 100 per cent dedicated to INEOS needs. It will meet all of our purchase Scope 2 needs, but also generate excess power that we can share. It also provides opportunities to electrify pumps and motors that aren't electric today (like steam), or ultimately sell some energy credits to the market.'

The solar plant will mean that the INEOS O&P USA operation in Texas can be significantly cleaner. But it will also have an impact on the local community. 'Even building the solar farm will create lots of jobs,' Mike went on:

'There are almost eight hundred thousand panels that will be part of this solar farm. They all need wiring and cabling and need transformers to turn the direct current from solar to alternating current. The landowners will also benefit from investment. There are certainly going to be changes down the road to train for – and some will have to be retrained. As people are coming through school, they need to learn these new skills. Take automotive: most people take their car to a garage that understands how to fix internal combustion engines. Once we move to electric, we still need mechanics but they need to understand the power, and how to fix and maintain them.'

Once it's live and running, the solar plant will make around four hundred megawatts of direct current power. Once it goes through transformers, you would end up with about three hundred and ten megawatts of alternating current power that can be used. For obvious reasons, solar panels can't work at night – and they're heavily impacted by cloud cover for reasons which are equally obvious. The effective power generation, therefore, is only about 26 to 28 per cent of what could be generated on a twenty-four-hour basis. You end up with about seventy-five to eighty megawatts of around the clock power, in the terms we'd think of when comparing to using gas or coal.

Currently the plan is to have the plant commissioned in December 2025. Around eight hundred thousand panels need to be ordered and put together, with a construction period of about eighteen months to two years. It's spread across an enormous ranch: the property that it will sit on is between two thousand and two thousand four hundred acres. It will generate enough energy to cover the entire business Scope 2's needs – the equivalent of around two hundred and fifty thousand tonnes of CO_2 per year. 'To put this in context, the solar farm is the equivalent of converting about sixty-eight thousand homes to renewable power,' Mike added.

Like all INEOS sites, INEOS O&P USA won't be able to rely on renewables alone to completely clear out its carbon footprint. It will need to have a broad array of solutions to get to where it needs to be by 2050. Hydrogen will almost certainly play a part. After all, the business is one of the largest hydrogen producers within INEOS today. The Chocolate Bayou site is the single largest hydrogen-producing site across the entire group. It's all linked to that initial olefin process – and the molecules involved. The chemical formula for ethane is C_2H_6. That's why it's called a hydrocarbon: it's made from two carbon atoms and six hydrogen atoms. When you turn that into ethylene, you kick off a hydrogen molecule and end up with C_2H_4. And then you have spare hydrogen, as Mike explained.

'All of that hydrogen that gets produced, we collect. Now today, a lot of that hydrogen, we don't use ourselves to burn. We actually sell it to third parties who further purify it then sell it to people who need pure hydrogen. There's no reason that we couldn't use that hydrogen ourselves to decarbonize our fuel system. That's something that we're looking at. But there are some technical things you have to understand and study, as opposed to flipping a switch and closing the valve. Hydrogen has much different burning characteristics than methane, and different metallurgy concerns. So that's what we're in the process of studying, and certainly over the next five, eight, ten years, I envision that we will ultimately recapture that hydrogen we're selling today and consume it ourselves. But then we will also need supplemental hydrogen because we don't make enough to meet all of our energy needs, which is why we're talking with other people about how we or they together can make hydrogen in a blue sense or a green sense to meet our evolving needs to support our business.

'It's an endothermic process, so we need more hydrogen than obviously what we're making from breaking our own bonds. So similar to what we've done here with NextEra on the solar farm, we're talking with people who do this on a large scale today, and are trying to find the right partner or partners to put together a consortium to build large-scale hydrogen production that could have a green or blue (or whatever colour we end up choosing) footprint to meet our needs, and ultimately meet the needs of others in the industry and in society.

'This is an aspect of the Inflation Reduction Act that Congress and the president passed and signed. They are providing not just economic incentives for hydrogen: they're also providing some grants, primarily through the Department of Energy, but there are some others as well. You can apply for project funding. We've formed a group that just three weeks ago filed the initial set of paperwork. This is obviously a multi-year process and there are going to be a lot of people asking for the funding, so there's no guarantee that we will get it. But we will certainly be part of a group of companies and consortia that are trying to see if the government would help to support some of the ideas that we have to make this possible – and demonstrate some of these technologies to help our business, help our CO_2

footprint. But we're even looking at creating hydrogen sites where people in transit, say buses and things like that – and ultimately cars – but mostly buses and trucks to start, can come and use hydrogen as a fuel source, as opposed to gasoline and diesel. All of these things start to intertwine when you think about how an economy as large as the US might migrate to a different set of energy usages over the next thirty years.'

The road to 2050

One of the problems with having a goal like net zero by 2050 is that, well, it's the target year: 2050. It's just shy of thirty years away.

Many of the people at the top of INEOS will no longer be of working age. They probably hope to have retired somewhere lovely, on a planet that we pray has much more sustainable occupants. Ultimately, the torch will be passed. Much of the hard graft will be done by young people in ten or twenty years. Some of those people will only be starting secondary education today. They almost certainly don't know that they'll one day work at INEOS, but they might know that they want to make a difference to the climate.

Thankfully INEOS isn't waiting around. There are already young people making great strides in the energy transition at INEOS today. During my research for this chapter, I had the pleasure and privilege of speaking to two of INEOS's best and brightest – both of whom are in their early thirties, and are relentlessly optimistic about the sustainable future of the business.

Elfie Méchaussie is a carbon and environment specialist working for INEOS Olefins & Polymers Europe in Switzerland. She works to understand and calculate the carbon footprint of the business products. That includes not only the emissions at the plants themselves, but also the impact of the raw materials, energy, importing and transportation. She developed a model that calculates for all of the business's current product. Elfie studied chemical engineering and did a PhD that was actually funded by INEOS – where she ultimately ended up working.

'What attracted me was to be able to make a difference at world-scale plants', Elfie told me. 'Every time you implement a project or a technology step-change, that is automatically linked to a large amount of savings in terms of energy, but also greenhouse gas emissions. It makes sense to work in such a company, and to be part of the change. INEOS has a role to play, and by working on the inside, this is where I could make a difference. That's why I work for a petrochemical company.'

In her current role, Elfie has helped to develop roadmaps for the reduction of greenhouse gas emissions – to ultimately meet the commitment to net zero. This begins with roadmaps for 2030, and Elfie's per-site modelling is essential to making sure that INEOS can reduce its carbon footprint. When I ask her about what she hopes the distant future of INEOS O&P looks like, she's not short of ideas:

'I hope that in 2050, the final applications are much better designed – that we as customers will accept better packaging, neutral packaging designed with recycling and end of life in mind. No more fancy packaging, streamlined: you just want the package and not fancy packaging. That combined with very efficient recycling streams, with integrated recycling plants that can not only deal with mechanical recycling but also advanced recycling. For our plants, I hope we have found a way to have almost no CO_2 emissions coming from the plant, or [that we] find a way to re-use it.'

I also spoke to Alice Dibben, commercial sustainability manager for INEOS Nitriles, who builds the strategy for the business to move to net zero. INEOS Nitriles makes – among other things – acrylonitrile, which is just about everywhere. It's the key ingredient in acrylic fibre that you find in clothing and carpets. It also ends up in ABS (acrylonitrile-butadiene-styrene); that's a thermoplastic that you'll find in cars, phones, computer cases and sports equipment. INEOS products also make their way into nitrile rubber that has many uses, including the manufacturing of fuel pump hoses. UK-based, Alice joined INEOS around eleven years ago on the commercial graduate scheme, but now works purely on sustainability. As she explained:

'In terms of day to day, it started off with developing our strategy in line with what the rest of the INEOS group is trying to do: pulling together our roadmaps, pathway to net zero, and setting up the technical team who are looking at that. I spent a lot of time trying to understand our carbon footprint and what that looks like, where the problem areas are, and we're going through that process now, developing lifecycle analysis models. We have a team working on that which I'm leading. And then it's really trying to find different projects and ways we can reduce our carbon footprint across all of our sites. We have a plant in Cologne, and then two assets in America – one in Texas in Green Lake and then in Lima, Ohio. So within my role there's lots of customer interaction, trying to understand what the market is looking for, how we can help service that and drive it forward. Eventually it needs to be a whole supply chain solution: no one can bear the burden of that as one small element.'

Alice spends a lot of time thinking not only about how to make INEOS more sustainable, but about how to do it in a commercially viable way. She tells me that it's important also to remember that the products INEOS is making have a genuine benefit to society: they end up in wind turbines, hospital equipment and the development of drugs. It's not just about cutting back across the board, but being selective and focused. 'I think some products will quickly be replaced: look at single-use plastic bags. But there are some products that we will continue to need, and then we will make those products in the most efficient and sustainable way,' Alice said.

For her 2050 vision, she imagines a world where INEOS Nitriles hits its emission targets through a mixture of reduction and carbon capture. Even more encouragingly, she thinks the prospects of this grand future actually happening are very realistic. 'I'm optimistic,' Alice explains.

'I feel like already the things we're looking at in the business will make our assets very carbon-efficient. Maybe not 100 per cent, but what we can't stop at source, I think we'll be capturing. I'm sure that the advancements we're going to see in terms of carbon capture technology will make it much more efficient, much more affordable, and will be a global thing. So I think that's one element: the actual carbon we're emitting will be very, very low. The second piece will be around feedstocks procurement. We're already having these discussions with all of our suppliers: what are they doing, and how are they reducing their footprint? Buying blue ammonia where possible; looking at buying green ammonia, but it still needs development in other areas before that's fully viable. But I'm sure that will be well and truly in place in all of our assets by 2050.

'The other thing that we're already looking at right now – and it will be quite interesting to see how it plays out – is alternative routes to producing our products that aren't from fossil fuels. There's one option about bioattribution (partly or fully swapping out fossil fuel feedstocks with renewables or biofeedstocks), but there are complications: there's not really enough product to run into a substantial part of the business yet. But there are other routes to producing our products which actually seem quite viable and interesting. They're in their infancy at the moment, but maybe that will be something that's a second stream alongside. Or – we have two reactors in Cologne for example – one will be purely bio and that will be a segregated stream, and then one perhaps won't be. Eventually that will come down to a cost thing. The dream will be you and I as the end consumers being able to afford to buy these sustainable products. Right? That's the issue at the moment: that the value isn't really there for the end users. It's really hard to make these products when you're not making any money back. But if you can get the feedstocks to an affordable level – which hopefully over time, as more and more people invest, that will happen. That's my vision, and I don't think that's unrealistic. I can see it happening, but I am an optimist.'

The challenge is great, and exceptionally complicated. INEOS is enormous, and growing. A lot of the 'easy' work towards net zero has already been done. It's now going to require immense innovation, brutally tough decisions and significant amounts of capital (from within INEOS and without). There is huge optimism within the business – and for my own part, I do think that INEOS very likely will achieve net zero and remain a commercial success by 2050 – but there are many uncertainties along the way. INEOS can control what it does, but it will always have to contend with governments, technology, society, investment, and so much more. The only thing certain about the future is that nothing is certain. The good news is that INEOS is a company packed to the rafters with truly brilliant minds. There is so much knowledge and expertise within INEOS that it seems almost any task is surmountable.

What's also important to remember when thinking about the future of INEOS is that a net zero target doesn't mean the total abandonment of fossils. I've already explained how carbon capture will have its part to play in the future. But ultimately, some fossil-based systems will be kept on in the business by choice. INEOS makes important products, after all.

'Fossil fuels are used as a fuel, that's an energy source. The energy sources can be replaced. But fossils are also used for highly valuable products – it's value added to a feedstock, and this will not go away,'

explained Greet Van Eetvelde, INEOS global head of climate, energy and innovation.

'It's not possible to replace it all with bio-based; it's not possible to replace it all with renewables. This is not possible, and also it's not meant to be. We're a company that makes so many things, anything. The toothpaste you use in the morning is ours. We are a commodity chemical company, which means that we make the intermediates. You will not see the INEOS name on your toothpaste, but it's in there. This is what we make. The glasses that you wear, whatever you have on your body, on the desk, when you look around you – we're everywhere. You cannot make a car, you cannot drive a train. If someone goes by sailboat to a climate action, by all means let them go. If they glue themselves to the walls, it's our glue. If you want to dissolve the glue, it's our solvent. That's the absurdity of things.

'There are thousands of examples. From the moment you get out of bed, everything you do and everything you touch, one of the INEOS businesses has impacted there. If you have a headache, even aspirin. In COVID times, we were there. It's the plastics in the new cars of the future – if they have to be lightweight. Single-use is a horrible thing; we never make something for single-use except for medical appliances. All the rest: please don't throw it away. Please don't throw away even the tiniest little plastic bag. It's such a valuable thing. We've made it with all of our heart; we've put our technology in there; we've made it as light and as thin as possible. We even help to make it biodegradable now. You wouldn't have solar panels – we make the layer. You wouldn't have wind turbines – we make the alloys, and the oils that help the gear in the wind turbine to not have to be removed or changed as much, so that when they're built in the sea, you don't have to fly there as often. All those lubricants are optimized [. . .] not only for us, but also to make sure that their impact on the environment, and the help that wind turbines give to the people is fabulous. We're just one of the links in the chain, and we are a link in the chain that really takes responsibility.'

When you look at the INEOS strategy for the energy transition, it's all about diversity. This isn't about picking one energy solution and dumping all of the eggs in that basket. There's no one-size-fits-all idea that will help humanity move to cleaner and more sustainable energy systems. The types of energy production that might work for a windy island like the UK can't necessarily be replicated elsewhere. We need myriad ways of producing energy, lowering emissions, capturing carbon and making supply chains more sustainable. It's this sort of relentless adaptation that has allowed human civilization to flourish: the desire to never sit still and to endlessly innovate. The days of global dependency on oil and gas are numbered, and no one thing will take their place.

INEOS is betting on diversity: of its businesses, but also of its solutions for hitting net zero by 2050. Sir Jim's team is pouring money into innovative ways of storing carbon, producing and using hydrogen in new and exciting ways and cleaning up the global chemicals and polymer industries for decades to come. It has a firm deadline, and bold plans to remain commercially viable while vastly minimizing its harm to the planet. That's no small feat for a company specializing in energy and petrochemicals. The good news is that it looks like INEOS can do the job – and that means a better future for all of us. The planet depends upon it.

6

INEOS for All, Consumer

Steph McGovern

NOTHING MUCH SURPRISES ME IN the business world anymore, but INEOS does. It continues to push the boundaries of what a global business with petrochemicals at its core can do. It moves into sectors that you might think it knows nothing about and it confidently challenges perceptions.

Much like one of its huge ethane carriers travelling across the ocean, it's a company that disrupts the waters it passes through. And (unlike an ethane carrier, I suppose) it re-energizes those waters at the same time. It is this that makes the business so fascinating to journalists like me.

I've spent years reporting on INEOS and have seen it go from one of the biggest British companies you've never heard of, to one that is now being regularly talked about in many different circles. Their sponsorship of top-level sport in particular has raised them to the public consciousness, but of course there are other things too. It's become a consumer brand.

Shortly after it was announced that INEOS was going to start building cars, I was at an awards evening in Sheffield. A fellow diner proudly announced that he had ordered a Grenadier 4x4. It sparked a lengthy chat between everyone at the table, firstly about what a Grenadier car was, and more importantly why on earth INEOS was making them.

What did a chemicals company know about cars? I'd asked precisely the same question a few years earlier about INEOS getting into fashion.

In February 2015 I was visiting the INEOS Grangemouth site for *BBC Breakfast*. I was there to talk about what was happening in the oil sector at the time. As was often the case with my visits to company sites, I also used these broadcasts as an excuse to have a good nosey round. Getting to tour a huge production facility and show our viewers the types of jobs you could do there was always a joy. I don't think many people would have known about the variety of jobs that a company like INEOS would have and I loved giving the nation a flavour of the roles I saw in my time at the polymer production site.

As with every visit to a site like Grangemouth, I had to be kitted out in full hi-vis, hard hat, safety goggles, steel-capped boots and ear defenders. The whole health and safety shebang. It's not the most flattering look, nor is it in any way trendy. It's all about keeping you safe and it was pretty clear to me that day that INEOS takes safety very seriously indeed. I had learnt the hard way what happens when you try and walk up the stairs without holding the handrail: you get a bollocking. I get it. When you're a company dealing with products that have the potential to cause incredible harm, safety has to run through the core of the business, no matter how trivial the risk may seem.

Still, as I wandered round admiring the facility in my oversized hi-vis gear, which was hot and uncomfortable, I did wonder why no one had designed safety gear that was functional, comfortable and cool. But hey – it's a chemicals company. Why would they care about fashion?

At no point during that visit did I think that INEOS was a company with fashion in its sights. Yet just two years later, they took over Belstaff, the British clothing brand, specializing in classic outerwear.

I also didn't hear any talk in those days about INEOS making hand hygiene products, although of course we couldn't know at that point what would be waiting for the world around the corner.

It's this move into consumer goods that I want to focus on in this chapter. There's the automotive side with the building of the Grenadier, the fashion venture, with the purchase of Belstaff, and then there is the most recent move into the fast-moving consumer goods arena in the form of Hygienics.

They are three very different sectors. When you scratch the surface of each business, though, you see the commonality between all of them. The linking thread is Sir Jim Ratcliffe's vision, along with that of his co-founders Andy Currie and John Reece, which is woven into the fabric of all INEOS businesses and into every decision that is made. Through understanding the core values that the world's most successful industrial entrepreneurs have built into the ethos of INEOS, you soon realize that it makes total sense for this huge chemicals business to be making the consumer products that it's chosen to make.

Although the structure of the business is a federated one – meaning that each business is fully responsible for all of its functions – there is consistency across the group, supported by these core values. In fact, they're values that each new starter gets a presentation on, to welcome them into the INEOS way of life. I'll come back to that later.

This story that I am about to tell now has emerged from my chats with the key players in the consumer businesses as well as from my various visits to different INEOS sites.

The move to widgets

The branching out into 'consumer' starts with automotive. I won't dwell too much on the story of the Grenadier car here because that is the focus of the Automotive chapter. However, it's important to mention it briefly because it also helps to explain why it was that INEOS went into fashion.

In short, Sir Jim wanted to challenge a market that he saw as having become stagnant. As a big fan of off-road driving, he regularly asked why it was that there wasn't much choice. He was also, of course, a big fan of the old Land Rover Defender, which he learned was to end production. With these things being true, Sir Jim decided that he would try to create a new 4x4 which would disrupt the market.

As INEOS communications director Tom Crotty explained to me, the INEOS team knew that they were good at manufacturing chemicals but they wanted to see whether the skills that they had developed in process technology could be transferred into making widgets, mechanical things, and components. This is what then led to the start of the automotive dream that is now being realized, with the Grenadier about to roll off the production line in significant numbers for the first time.

This also got the management team thinking about other prestigious British brands that had lost their way, that they might be able to take over. It was because of that that Belstaff came onto the INEOS radar. Just like the Land Rover Defender, here was another iconic British brand that INEOS thought needed rescuing. Jim doesn't dream idly about such things. They actually happen.

In October 2017, INEOS bought Belstaff. As Jim said to the media at the time: 'We have a lot in common. We are British, we are entrepreneurial, straightforward, adventurous and most importantly we are successful.'

So how did they get to that point?

The history of Belstaff

I need to take you back a century, to the end of the First World War. A Latvian Jewish immigrant called Eli Belovitch, who was living in Stoke-on-Trent, had spent the war supplying waterproof fabric to the British Army.

With the war over and motorcycle racing becoming a thing, Eli and his son-in-law Harry Grosberg saw an opportunity to set up a business that produced protective motorcycle clothing. So, in 1924, they founded Belstaff – the name coming from a combination of the surname Belovitch and the place the company was born: Staffordshire. The two opened an army, navy and general store where they sold waterproof clothing, and eventually trademarked the Belstaff logo in 1927.

It's a brand that's been synonymous with adventure and innovation from day one. Belstaff was the first company to use waxed cotton in the manufacturing of waterproof apparel for motorcycling: a cost-effective alternative to leather.

The Belstaff clad customer list reads like a who's who of twentieth century history. They included the British Army officer T.E. Lawrence – known of course as Lawrence of Arabia – whose tunic of choice was a Belstaff 'colonial coat'. In the world of aviation there was Amelia Earhart, the first female aviator to fly solo across the Atlantic Ocean, who was also a fan. As was Amy Johnson, who wore a Belstaff jacket when she became the first woman to fly solo from England to Australia in 1930. Mountaineer Chris Bonington was wearing Belstaff gear when he made the first ascent of 'The Ogre': a steep, craggy and (as its name rather implies) exceptionally challenging 23,901-foot peak in Pakistan's Karakoram range.

During the Second World War Belstaff was one of the largest suppliers to the military, providing parachutes and aviator suits. Over the past century it has kitted out some of the most daring people that the world has ever seen. Another big name to throw into the mix is Communist revolutionary Che Guevara, who was a fan of the Trialmaster jacket.

The Trialmaster was launched in 1948, designed to weather the harsh riding conditions of the Scottish Six Days Trial: an historic, internationally recognized, off-road motorcycle competition – the oldest in the world – which takes the riders through hundreds of miles of the Scottish Highlands. The Trialmaster jacket was designed to allow for ease of movement on a bike, and was made from water and wind-repellent wax. Details of the jacket include a four-pocket silhouette with a slanted map pocket, curved-arm construction for mobility, and adjustable throat-latch collar and waist belt.

It was first put to the test by eighteen-year-old Sammy Miller, who went on to compete in over a thousand races wearing Belstaff. There is even, as a result, a line of jackets named in his honour.

However, it is the actor Steve McQueen who is credited with really widening Belstaff's appeal. He it was who took the clothes to the silver screen, wearing a Belstaff jacket in the classic 1963 wartime film, *The Great Escape*. It was this which took the brand to cult status.

It made another notable silver-screen appearance as part of Will Smith's ensemble in *I Am Legend*. To demonstrate its now-iconic status, the Belstaff clobber has popped up in lots of Hollywood films, including *Mission Impossible*, *The Curious Case of Benjamin Button*, *Harry Potter and the Half-Blood Prince*, *Eastern Promises* and *Sherlock Holmes*.

Along with the Hollywood films come the megastars wearing them in real life too: Ewan McGregor, Brad Pitt, Hilary Swank, Angelina Jolie and even Kate Middleton, the Princess of Wales, to name only a few. Or supermodel Kate Moss, who hit the headlines for signing a deal with Belstaff worth over a million pounds in 2006. Or Hollywood actress Liv Tyler – another star to be paid megabucks when she put her name to a twelve-piece collection in 2016–17.

To the outside world, it was all looking good. An array of stars was wearing Belstaff clothes, and glossy flagship stores stocked them in all the important fashion cities across the globe. In March 2017 lads' mag *Maxim* gave the brand a glowing review:

'At its core Belstaff always made what the *Independent* refers to as "old-fashioned British motorbike clobber", designed to keep riders warm, dry, and comfortable, even in the worst conditions. It just happens to be superstylish as well. And while the lion's share of its customers these days may not be avid motorcyclists by any means, a Belstaff jacket can certainly make you look like you just climbed off a smoking, chrome-plated Triumph Bonneville. And that's proved extremely profitable.'

Although it turns out that, despite appearances, it wasn't actually 'extremely profitable' at that time. Anything but.

The Italian owners, JAB Luxury GmbH, which also owned the high-end fashion labels Jimmy Choo and Bally, had decided a few years earlier to take the brand from luxury to uber-luxury. They wanted Belstaff to be up there with the likes of Chanel, Gucci and Louis Vuitton, to name only a few luxury brands.

The price of the clothes shot up. And so too did the money that they spent on PR. One notable campaign which caught the eye of the mainstream media in 2013 was David Beckham riding a motorbike down Bond Street, while kitted out in Belstaff clothes. This marked the opening of their flagship London store, on one of the most sought-after bits of real estate. The photos at the time of the opening show various pop stars and celebs draping themselves over the bike outside the store. The pictures were all over the papers in the days that followed.

From then on the Italian owners of Belstaff continued to spend a fortune on rents, on materials, on PR. But it didn't work. This was when INEOS started hovering around, thinking that here was a classic British brand which should be more than it was.

Chris Tane has worked with INEOS for almost twenty years. He was the CEO of Inovyn and chairman of the automotive side of the company when he was asked to go to a meeting with Sir Jim to talk about moving into the consumer arena. Over a lengthy lunch the team was asked to come up with some ideas for brands that they could buy. Chris explained to me that this request seemed 'pretty weird' – 'a substantial departure' from what he and the INEOS team were used to, but they started brainstorming nevertheless.

'For the next two hours we racked our brains trying to guess what sort of new opportunity it might be . . . we didn't come anywhere close!' They decided to go away and do some research on the types of brands on which INEOS could work their magic: brands that had what Sir Jim was looking for. The net was cast far and wide with one key requirement.

'Jim said the only requirement [for choosing a consumer brand to acquire] is that it must be a cool brand. The only problem was that we could never agree on what constituted "cool".'

I had to laugh when Chris said this to me. What does that even mean? Cool to whom? What's cool to me is unlikely to be cool to Chris and I can't be the only person who is cringing at the thought of how this 'cool' conversation between the INEOS bosses went.

Given that there are no criteria for 'cool', it was simply a case of waiting to see what felt right. As it happened, they didn't have to wait long. Belstaff was in a bit of a mess, and the existing owners had no idea how they were going to turn it around. After nearly drowning in the heady waters of the uber-luxury brand world, the Italian owners then went on a cost-cutting exercise. That didn't work either.

Meanwhile Barbour – a business with a very similar backstory to Belstaff – was seeing its products fly off the shelves. Here's an interesting stat that Chris told me about sales at that time: Barbour jackets cost three times less than Belstaff ones, while they were selling ten thousand times more of them. You don't have to be a mathematician or have much of a business brain to see that things looked an awful lot healthier at Barbour.

In many respects, Belstaff was on its last legs, and so was put up for sale. And given the precarious position that it was in, it had a cheap price tag (unlike the clothes that they had been trying to flog). It did also meet the important criteria for which the INEOS team was looking, as Chris explained:

'Whatever else we thought about it as a business proposition, we all agreed it was definitely cool.'

For INEOS this acquisition was seen as a way to gain insight, with very little financial risk. Plus given Sir Jim's interest in finding a cool brand, this would give INEOS, and perhaps him, some elevated street cred. Belstaff also seemed a relatively low-risk opportunity to learn about managing consumer brands. What they learned would then prove invaluable for other businesses: for Automotive and for Hygienics.

So the mergers and acquisitions team at INEOS, which had been snapping up businesses for years, was brought in to get the deal done.

Even though INEOS had very little to offer in terms of fashion experience, they were confident that they could turn things around. Chris pointed out that:

> 'INEOS has a very strong, and pretty unique, management process which we apply in all our businesses. We were confident that would help us improve Belstaff's performance. But would that be enough?'

It was a challenge that INEOS was up for. Of course they were. Challenge is in INEOS's DNA. That said, surely Chris, with his wealth of experience and success in the chemical sector with INEOS, must have thought that the move into fashion was a bit mad? Some sweaty palms? Some nightmares? Here's what he said when I asked him:

> 'One thing my twenty years with INEOS at that point had taught me was that Jim, Andy and John might sometimes have ideas which sounded pretty crazy, but turned out to be inspired – so who could say this wasn't one of them?'

Trust: they had earned it. Also, although Belstaff itself might have been at stake, such was the success of INEOS's core business that that was not jeopardized. This was not a gamble like the ones Jim had taken in INEOS's early days.

In October 2017, INEOS bought Belstaff from JAB Luxury GmbH for next to nothing. In fact, the company was in so much trouble that Chris says they practically paid INEOS to take it off their hands. This purchase by INEOS was not just significant because Belstaff was a 'cool' brand that had clearly lost its way, but it also brought the prestigious British brand back into British ownership.

Synonymous with enduring style and function, and with a strong racing pedigree, the brand has proven a natural fit with INEOS's sporting elite. Belstaff created the onshore collection for Sir Ben Ainslie and INEOS Britannia as they challenged for the 36th America's Cup (the oldest international trophy in world sport). It's also the official outfitter for the world-class cycling team, the INEOS Grenadiers. In spite of this, and the incredible brand history, though, the acquisition of Belstaff has not been without its challenges.

As Chris explained, his team had managed to get them out of the long and expensive lease agreements which were sitting heavy on the balance sheets. But although this, along with some other changes, did certainly save money and improve things a little, it did not do so by much.

Crunch point

In the summer of 2020, things came to a head. Belstaff was losing money – a lot of money: around £25 million a year. So two options were put on the table. They could get rid of the business, or they could have one last roll of the dice, with some key deliverables put in place, and a new person at the helm. With option one feeling like accepting defeat, you might not be surprised to learn that it was option two which was chosen.

Fran Millar started on 1 October 2020. Now here is an interesting fact. Fran doesn't have any background in fashion. While most bosses in the fashion world were probably trying to get a seat next to Anna Wintour on the London Fashion Week FROW (what fashion types call the front row), Fran was busy managing a cycling team.

Not just any cycling team, of course: one of the most successful professional road cycling teams in the world, the INEOS Grenadiers. Fran was with the team from the beginning, in its early life as Team Sky (which began in 2009), before it was snapped up by INEOS in May 2019. As CEO Fran led on the development of the team's operational and governance systems, alongside all of its business and engagement strategies.

So what made one of the world's top cycling bosses want to make the move from the high-energy world of competitive sport to what some would see as a much slower pace of life in fashion? Especially given the fashion brand that you're about to take over is failing. Well, I'm sure you've already guessed it: Fran wanted the challenge.

In general, INEOS's management thrives on taking on seemingly impossible challenges. It's also this on which, as they repeatedly tell you, their success was built: 'challenge and seeking new opportunities'. So, with that in mind, it is obvious why Fran would want to make this move. Fran is competitive, daring and sporty. You might wonder why I mention being sporty. It's because I actually think that that's a key attribute to fitting in at INEOS.

You only need look at the huge gym in the Knightsbridge office, the Tour de France team cycling challenges that lots of people take part in across the business and the incentives for new graduates. This is a company that's obsessed with fitness, and with competition.

I am used to seeing companies offer things like discounted canteens and a chance for flexible working. INEOS incentives are next level, with fitness and competition at their health-focused heart. Take their graduate scheme, for example. You can read more about it in the Next Generation chapter, but, briefly, every year graduates at INEOS can choose to participate in a great African adventure. Now when I first read this I was thinking, 'Oh, that sounds nice, a safari holiday'. This is what I continued to think until I reached this bit on the company website:

'For six days you'll be challenged to go beyond your personal limits and test your mental and physical fitness. You'll discover what you're truly capable of as you complete a 320km run, cycle and hike through the Namibian desert. Don't worry, we have developed a comprehensive nine-month training programme to prepare you for this unique opportunity of a lifetime.'

Don't get me wrong, I like a challenge and have done the Great North Run a couple of times. But 320km through a desert? Are you having a laugh? That's definitely not an incentive for me.

Nor does it stop at the young graduates. This love of competition and fitness runs right through the business, whatever your age. Chris Tane defended it when I questioned him about it:

'The fitness side of INEOS is all about helping people to set challenges that are appropriate for them. For some (not me!) that's running double marathons; for others it's more about maintaining a healthy level of exercise.'

It's great, of course, that INEOS is proactive in wanting their employees to be healthy. And I imagine that there will be people for whom this is a huge incentive, driving them to work for the company. I have to be honest: personally I found this approach quite intimidating – and I do imagine that this would put off some people who otherwise would thrive in the business.

This incentive for staff does, though, explain a lot about the mentality of the people who work for INEOS, and especially about those who reach the top echelons, as Fran has. Fran's love of triathlons (and having a brother who is professional road racing cyclist David Millar), along with having proven herself as CEO of INEOS Grenadiers, makes her perfectly aligned with the INEOS ethos and of course one of Sir Jim's people.

The challenge

So back to Belstaff. Fran was tasked with 'making it more INEOS'. Which she described to me as being a lean, efficient, future-proofed business:

'Basically, I was given five deliverables but told, beyond that, to do it however I felt was the right way to do it. I needed to reduce marketing and overhead spend by 50 per cent, to get it to operationally break even within two years, to retain the existing brand equity and not damage that, to grow ecommerce and to retain the existing retail footprint. So I then spent the remainder of 2020 and the first quarter of 2021 coming up with a strategy that would enable us to achieve those goals. And that's what I've been delivering.'

Within a year the Belstaff team managed to increase revenue to £64 million. This year (2022–23) it's set to hit between £74 and £75 million, whilst also very nearly breaking even operationally. As Fran explained:

'So year one, we managed to improve the EBITDA (Earnings Before Interest, Taxes, Depreciation and Amortization) position by about £19 million. A huge improvement in the first year, predominantly from stripping the cost base out, changing the operating model, changing the channel strategy, evolving the product, going after a younger customer, and also just evolving the brand to be a little bit more relevant and current.'

In other words, Fran has completely overhauled the business. As you'll have worked out from the brief history lesson that I gave earlier, the brand has a really remarkable backstory – clothing and making tents for the British military, or being worn by every megastar going during the twentieth and twenty-first centuries.

A backstory is a backstory though: it isn't relevant right now, apart from as a rich source of imagery and iconography on which the brand today can build. No image rights to pay for! And as the clear rationale for Belstaff constituting a rebellious brand – an icon of independent spirit. All of which needed to be utilized in order to attract a new audience, preferably while not losing the fanbase that they had built up in the past. It isn't easy to do that quickly in fashion:

'You know, one of the things that's hard to grasp when you're not in it is that fashion takes a long time to change. The product that's hitting the stores now and since August 2022 is really the first product of mine. And that's the real reset. The new sites have gone live, the stores have been refreshed, the product is very different. And we're seeing great traction.'

I saw that reset for myself when I went into the Regent Street store in London in November. It was a busy Saturday. A flagship store, in the heart of the capital, in the run-up to Christmas.

I'll be honest, my image of Belstaff was that it was a brand for what I would call 'hairy blokes'. The rough and ready fellas of the world. The kind of men who might be adventurous with their hobbies but are certainly not with their clothes! Is that a bit harsh? You know what I mean, though. However, I have to say that I was very surprised by how trendy the store was. The staff all looked effortlessly cool. And the whole vibe was one of 'this is a luxury place to shop'. This feeling was confirmed, I have to say, when I picked up a bobble hat that I rather liked the look of and was told that it would cost £95.

Still, everything about the store felt classy and sassy. I like my clothes and I'm partial to a label or two, but I had never considered buying Belstaff before. And yet here I was in the womenswear section, which I'd forgotten that they even had! And I found myself mentally adding various items to the Christmas list that I'll likely be handing to my partner at some point.

So how did they make that transition to be more relevant? Fran told me that they really had to think hard about what the brand was, and why Jim loved it, and why it was that he had bought it in the first place.

'It is quite a rebellious brand. It's got that rebel spirit. People who choose to wear a Belstaff over a Barbour, it says something about you, right? It's a style piece. It's much more elevated, it's a higher price point, it's a more luxury item. So we wanted to really reposition the brand first and foremost. I think the key to that is to not alienate the existing customer, because whilst we hadn't broken the £50 million revenue barrier, prior to coming on board, it was still £50 million and we still had customers who were very passionate and loyal to us. So making sure we retain our wax cotton and leather proposition and making sure that we still do that in a really credible and authentic way, but adding to the portfolio product that speaks more to our broader heritage.'

It's no easy task to try and get new customers, whilst not putting off the people who have been spending their hard-earned cash with you for years. Loyalty to a brand can easily be lost if the customer feels that they don't know what they're going to get from you anymore. So how did Fran and her team marry the two together?

One decision was to bring Gore-Tex back into the range. Another significant decision involved the use of colour. Historically, Belstaff has been a brand which is navy, brown or black. No bright colours. But Fran tells me that all customers, but particularly men, have brightened up a lot in terms of their palette choices. Menswear, she tells me, is a much brighter, much lighter proposition than it used to be. Once any shop could have relied upon it that a men's lavender-coloured shirt would not sell well. But now, on the contrary, it has been one of Belstaff's best sellers.

Now what Fran says about colour is interesting because, prior to entering the Regent Street store, I certainly didn't think that Belstaff was a brand that loved colour. There was a subtle scattering of it with some bright orange pieces, some neon green tops and a few bits of light blue.

When I say 'scattering', they were of course anything but scattered. These elements of colour were immaculately placed, with not a sleeve or a collar out of place. I couldn't help thinking that the military precision of INEOS's decisions was reflected in the folding of the clothes just as much as in their huge factories pumping out chemicals.

These, though, were subtle pops of colour in what otherwise was a sea of dark neutral shades. Now, as Fran had explained to me, there was this juxtaposition of their history with their new-found edge: colour, more lightweight products, more interesting printing techniques and garment dyeing. Not just leather and waxed cotton then.

Importantly, the plan seems to be working, Fran was excited to tell me:

'We already had seen great traction in wholesale and we're seeing great traction in our stores and online. So the aim is to close out this year at £74 to £75 million, which obviously is a huge improvement. It's the biggest sales revenue number that Belstaff has ever achieved in its hundred year history. And our EBITDA will be so close to breakeven. So it will be an improvement of about £23 million loss to about £2 million loss.'

The numbers speak for themselves. Belstaff is on the right trajectory again and it's doing it whilst also living by the INEOS values.

So you might think that the next move would be to ramp up sales and move the brand into new markets, but for Fran's team at Belstaff it's about sustainable growth:

'I think next year is very much about getting everything stable. There's a temptation to go to Asia or to go and do something really bold. I'm not quite sure we're ready for that yet. So for the next year, it's going to be about consolidating on the new brand position, consolidating the offering to the new customer and making sure that we continue to appeal to, and speak to, our existing core customer as well. Then it's actually our centenary year in 2024. And that's the point for the brand where we would hope to be really starting to look at aggressive global growth.'

Here's another twist to the turnaround story. Alongside repositioning the brand, the Belstaff team has also fundamentally changed the infrastructure of the business – and in turn has made it even more British.

In recent years, Belstaff was a business with its headquarters in Italy.

All of the product development and production was done there, alongside a lot of the logistics and the finance team. Those operations in Italy have now been closed down and all functionality has been moved to London.

It's now back to being a brand that isn't just paying lip service to the label 'British'. So what next? Fran says that the concept has been proven so now it's about consolidating. That buzzword that keeps popping up when I talk to Fran.

'I think that kind of structural and organizational change takes a while to bed in. So I'd quite like a year of really consolidating the business, getting all the processes in great shape, baking efficiency into how we operate and what we do, getting really good discipline and rigour into how we're doing range planning and focus as a business. And then from that platform we'll be a profitable business with a very clear strategy with a clear, consolidated customer view. Then in 2024 we'll go for big global growth.'

What does that look like in the longer term? Well, for Fran the sky is the limit. She tells me that she is convinced that Belstaff can be a global superbrand – up there with the likes of Stone Island, or Moncler, or Canada Goose. That's her ambition, she says. And if that wasn't enough, such is her success in making a consumer brand sing the way that INEOS wants it to that she's now also been put in charge of another consumer brand: Hygienics.

INEOS Hygienics – the need for speed

The INEOS Hygienics business was born in the pandemic and at lightning speed.

In March 2020 the world as we knew it suddenly ground to a halt and businesses all over the world had to work out how to survive. Some of the more generous ones also wanted to know how they could help.

As Tom Crotty explained to me, INEOS had lots of discussions with politicians about what they could do:

'The government asked us all sorts of questions, like "Can you supply the oxygen?" Which we couldn't. Then we talked about what we could do given we make all of the industrial alcohols that people need to make hand sanitizer. So we thought, why don't we actually take it a step further and make the sanitizer ourselves? So we took the challenge on.'

It all came down to chemistry. INEOS is the biggest producer of ethanol in the world, and ethanol is the main ingredient of hand sanitizer. When you buy hand sanitizer, it normally quotes about 75 per cent ethanol in the bottle. So the majority of those bottles we were carrying round for months will have had a product in them that INEOS will probably have made.

Despite INEOS having never produced hand sanitizer, or any type of cleaning product, Sir Jim wanted to make it quickly, and to give it to the NHS for free. George Ratcliffe was running the INEOS compounds business at the time, where the first Hygienics plant was built.

'Jim was the one who said, "I saw China build a hospital in ten days. We should be able to build a hand sanitizer factory in ten days". We actually did it in seven days but gave ourselves a three-day buffer for testing.'

This first sanitizer plant was built where I grew up. I remember reading the headline on 24 March 2020, and being so pleased that they'd chosen somewhere in the North East, where investment is often lacking. Teesside has provided a great home to the chemicals sector over the years but it is often overlooked for new investment so deprivation is a big problem.

The Newton Aycliffe site was the perfect choice for the first sanitizer plant for lots of reasons. It was a site where they made compounds. They had an empty shed there. (Not a shed like you might keep your lawn mower in.) They had people. So they thought that that was the place – and not only was it perfect but this would give Newton Aycliffe a 'shot in the arm', a new lease of life.

This was all a bit of a shock to the people who worked there. Wayne Dixon was brought in from the compounds side of the business (the bit that makes PVC pellets) to help put the plan into action. As he explained to me, no one at INEOS had any experience of making hand sanitizer, but that wasn't going to stop them:

> 'We were told we were going to start making hand sanitizer. And we were like, "that's a really good idea – way to go, INEOS." And then our general manager said, "Let me rephrase that: *we* are going to start making hand sanitizer." We were like – "What are you talking about?" He said, "We've been told there's a press release going out this afternoon that says we will be producing in ten days." So we just sat around in disbelief waiting for somebody to pop out and say "candid camera" or something like that. Then we were like, "Right, OK – we'll have to figure something out, then."'

After emptying the hundred-metre-square warehouse – or 'shed' – and borrowing some tents from the INEOS sailing events team in which to keep the bits from the warehouse, they then had to suss out how actually to make hand sanitizer. You might think at this point that there would be a sophisticated process, in a futuristic-looking lab with some elaborate formula. The truth is that they watched some fella in his kitchen on a YouTube video who was showing the world how to make it. Such were the times we were in!

> 'We had absolutely no idea what we were doing. We found a formula from the World Health Organization, the one that everyone was using to make sanitizer with. So we watched the online video and

thought that will do for now because we don't know how else to make it. Our boffins downstairs in the lab coats went through it and they worked out that to make it in a certain quantity you'd need x amount of ethanol, x amount of demineralized water and x amount of peroxide.'

So they worked out the quantities they needed and the recipe to put the ingredients together, but they still didn't know how they were going to do it, especially on a mass scale. Basically, Wayne tells me, a couple of their engineers drove around the North East with a bag of cash, trying to work out what people had which might be useful, and then buying it from them.

Inevitably they ended up paying over the odds for some things that they didn't use. That didn't matter. The important thing was that they had managed to cobble together a makeshift production line, with various manual stations and a bar pump being used to put the sanitizer into bottles, which would then be passed on to someone to put the lids on. Wayne described it to me as looking like Steptoe's yard: *Steptoe and Son* was a British sitcom from the sixties about the rag and bone business. For the same company that was using a fabulous ex-Mercedes factory in Germany in order to build its Grenadier 4x4, this definitely wasn't a compliment! Not only was it a very manual process, it was an expensive one too.

'At the time it was probably the most expensive production line that INEOS has ever done because our general manager was doing it, I was doing it, our operations manager was doing it. The hourly rate for workers on that line would have been through the roof. And don't forget we had the compound business to run at the same time.'

The trial and error nature of this whole experiment also meant that – inevitably – they hit some sticky situations: like the ethanol that they were using eating into the pipework and the welds. Meaning that all had to be scrapped.

Let's not forget that this experiment was all happening over hours and days, not weeks and months, such was the speed at which this production line needed to be built. There was also an interesting rivalry going on between the different INEOS sites across the world, who were also all trying to make sanitizer. In France, Germany and the United States, teams similar to Wayne's were all using the WHO formula, and all working at speed in order to get a sanitizer production line up and running. All the same, in the end Newton Aycliffe *was* the very first to get a useable hand sanitizer off the line. And it was no accident, as Wayne recalls:

> 'I got a phone call from George one evening and he said that he had just been told they were going to start producing in Germany tomorrow so can you get somebody on site to go in and at least pour some so we can be first. At which point I told him "no", because I didn't trust anybody else to do it, so I said, "Hang on a minute" and then I shouted to my wife to tell her she was going to have to put the boys to bed because I have to go back in to work. So we came back in and poured it.'

Wayne poured the first five-litre bottle of hand sanitizer that was going out to the hospitals where it was desperately needed. It was a moment in history for the INEOS team – and Wayne was keen to show me all the photos. He is a Northerner, so there was no bragging. But his pride at what they had achieved was written all over his face. He promises me that he really did think, in his heart of hearts, that they would be able to do it – although he admits that there certainly was a lot of pressure, with people working at weekends or late into the night.

The simple fact was, he says, that having publicly taken up the challenge, 'we had to do it'. It was another reminder that nothing is impossible at INEOS. There is never a view that something to which they put their mind can't be done. It means that they work in a high-pressured and stressful environment. 'High adrenaline' might be a more neutral way of putting it. But, in spite of the time pressures, and the pressures that people saw on the news every night, they clearly did enjoy it. It made for 'a really good atmosphere', Wayne tells me: 'everybody was in it and they were invested in it'.

This notion that 'everybody was in it' is an important one. INEOS may function as a business with very separate entities, which definitely causes a bit of friction when it comes to who owns which sites and how the leasing of those sites works, and it might also be a place where rivalry between departments is encouraged, but Wayne said that there was a team spirit during the pandemic which really made a huge difference:

'Lots of businesses that I didn't even know we had gave us stuff. The INEOS cycling team let us use their vans and the sailing team gave us things too. Everyone came together to get the job done.'

George Ratcliffe explained that everyone in INEOS was given the mandate to help and to prioritize pandemic support: 'We just looked around the whole of INEOS. And everyone kind of chipped in and got it going.'

Including the INEOS director of sport, Sir Dave Brailsford. Dave, as I'm sure you'll know, is one of the most successful cycling coaches in the world and was even knighted for it. There is much more about him and his work in the sports chapter, as well as in others. His team was crucial to getting the sanitizer out to hospitals, as George explained:

'Getting the hand sanitizer out to the hospitals where it was needed in the UK, Europe and the US was quite difficult. So for example, in the UK the London hospitals were getting loads of PPE, but the hospitals further away from London were struggling. Dave and his team are experts on logistics because they spend their life travelling to more than two hundred different cycling events with all the catering trucks, cyclists, bikes and mechanics. It's amazing what they do. So he did the logistics, which was impressive.'

The Mercedes Formula One team also donated loads of vans and the America's Cup gang made all the labels and signage. Also in France, the OGC Nice football club did a lot of the French deliveries themselves, where things were really tough.

At Newton Aycliffe, the team was also supported by new employees who were brought in to help. At a time when other businesses were having to lay people off, INEOS Hygienics *took on* forty new employees at the Newton Aycliffe site. Many of them came from the other businesses which were based on the same industrial estate, whose production lines had been stripped right back because of COVID. I am sure that it was a huge relief for them to secure a new job at a time when very few companies were employing, although I imagine at that point no one really knew how long that work would last, or even what exactly the job would involve. As Wayne explained, they were in a really unusual position:

'We weren't an established business from a hygienics point of view but we were in terms of INEOS. We were training them, as we were learning ourselves.'

When I picture those early days setting up the Hygienics business it makes me think of the famous opening line to the Charles Dickens novel *A Tale of Two Cities*:

'It was the best of times, it was the worst of times, it was the age of wisdom, it was the age of foolishness . . .'

On the one hand, you have these super-slick factories making PVC pellets and resin, with an experienced and highly qualified team, and then next door was a makeshift production line, run by a load of people who didn't know what they were doing! Obviously this is a simplistic view of events – and I should also point out that there was nothing reckless happening. Wayne was keen to make sure I understood that safety was a priority. Further evidence, not that I needed it, that INEOS was prepared to take lots of risks but never at the expense of safety. That aside, it is fascinating to imagine this juxtaposition of these two very different INEOS worlds.

Its very formulation as a business was everything that INEOS stands for: innovation, challenge and the notion that the business can solve problems. That shed became one of four plants in Europe which were built quickly to produce millions of bottles of hand sanitizer every month, to supply hospitals free of charge at a time when medical professionals desperately needed it. As George explained, this was an opportunity for INEOS to give back in a worthwhile way and on a large scale:

'We do have a global responsibility, a corporate responsibility, to give back and I think in the pandemic Hygienics was something we thought we could do on a meaningful scale. It's not just little bits here and there, like helping one hospital in the North East of the UK and maybe another hospital close to one of our companies in the US, for example. This had a global impact.'

It was an award-winning move by INEOS, and in October 2020 it was announced that INEOS Hygienics had been recognized at the 2020 European Responsible Care® Awards for its ambitious response to the COVID-19 pandemic.

The European Responsible Care® Awards are a recognition of the chemical industry's work to enhance safe chemicals management and to achieve performance excellence. In 2020 the awards had a particular focus on 'Caring in COVID-19 times', specifically highlighting the commitment of Europe's chemical industry to keep critical supply chains functioning, to protect workers and to support local communities in these unprecedented times.

The three-person judging panel for the awards particularly commended INEOS for supplying critical sanitizer products to frontline medical staff in the UK's NHS and in hospitals across Europe, all completely free of charge. Commenting on the award win at the time, George Ratcliffe admitted that it had been a challenging period:

'From our first internal conversations, our objective was crystal clear; to get the supplies [that] hospitals needed to them as fast as possible. The herculean efforts of our workforce and partners ensured we were able to commission three facilities in just ten days, and our first deliveries reached UK hospitals within two weeks – something that was a real highlight for everyone involved.'

But as generous as INEOS was at the start of the pandemic, they decided that they couldn't keep giving it out for free. Plus, as medical demands eased, the company's executives realized that people's long-term attitudes towards hand hygiene were likely to change. So they turned their focus towards consumers themselves.

The same product that they were giving free to hospitals was what they now wanted to get into people's houses, handbags and pockets. INEOS thought that they had found a gap in the market: no one else was providing hospital-grade-quality sanitizer for consumers. Plus not only had they managed to build factories which were able to produce the hand sanitizer, but they could also do it cheaper than some of the established players in the market for the simple reason that they already made important raw materials. And given that they make plastics, there was a longer-term plan to start making their own bottles too.

However, the demand for hand sanitizers was not in reality what they had originally thought it was going to be. Fran said there needed to be an evolution of the business:

'As the pandemic has changed the world, I think so has people's need for, and requirement of, hand sanitizer. What we all thought the world would look like post-pandemic, and what it actually looks like, are quite different. So rather than just deciding, well, we'll just bin the business, we know we've got loads of great talent in there and we've got a really great brand proposition.'

The master brand

A bit like the crunch point for Belstaff in 2020, the Hygienics business was having one of its own. It was time to ditch the entire business, or to evolve. It doesn't surprise me that they chose the latter.

They'd come this far. Why wouldn't they have a go at disrupting another market in which they didn't have much experience? Also, this was a market that hadn't seen much change, as Fran explained:

'The industry of fast-moving consumer goods, especially in the hand wash and hand sanitizer space is actually quite stale. And there are no brands really challenging and disrupting the status quo. So we thought, well, we're here now: we may as well at least give it a try.'

This, Fran observed, was just about the only product which actually had the INEOS logo on it. Chemicals didn't – not that you'd put them in your house anyway.

This was such an important point. The hand sanitizer was branded: INEOS. This was now an opportunity to get the name into people's homes. There are other INEOS consumer brands, the clothes and the cars, but it's different with them. Belstaff is owned by INEOS, but it is not branded INEOS, and very few people would have a clue that it is owned by a huge chemicals business. The Grenadier car is branded INEOS but it's such an expensive product that there simply isn't the same global access to it that there can be with hygienics products, which are at a much lower price point. With the Hygienics brand, there was an opportunity to move into the 'fast-moving consumer goods' – FMCG – market: products that are sold quickly and at a relatively low cost. An 'interesting proposition' was how Fran described it:

> 'Then we could get the INEOS brand into people's hands and into their homes at a price point that was pretty universally accessible. The hand sanitizer and soaps are in the one to two pounds category. And I just think that level of visibility, that level of access, is an interesting one. And I also think having that spectrum of a one-pound product right up to a £65,000 product in the consumer space means that people can see the scale and breadth of what INEOS does. And, similarly, FMCG marketing is the kind of marketing where you can do really great challenger disruptive stuff that speaks not just to the hand sanitizer and hand wash business, but to INEOS as a master brand.'

Now *marketing* is the key here. The FMCG market is huge, worth trillions of pounds to the global economy. Within it are some of the world's biggest companies, including Procter & Gamble (P&G), Unilever, and Reckitt Benckiser to name only a few. Within these businesses are huge global brands, brands with which INEOS was now going head-to-head.

People knew that it was a serious undertaking to take them on. Getting a new FMCG brand up and running from scratch – it's extremely costly, and it takes time. Competitors – like Carex, or Dettol: they are hundred-year-old brands which people trust. The INEOS consumer brand, by contrast, was only two years old. The only solution was a bucketload of money pumped into marketing. But was that where INEOS wanted to go purely for soap and sanitizer?

What INEOS also needed were people who did work for those brands to jump ship and to give them the inside steer. Rory Tait, who joined INEOS as its new chief operating officer of Hygienics in March 2022, was one of those people.

Rory had worked for years at Reckitt Benckiser, which makes most of the things that you have in your home, like cleaning products, or some food and healthcare products: the list goes on. Rory's role there was running their biggest brand, Dettol (or Lysol, depending on where you live in the world). Fortunately for INEOS, Rory had been looking at what Hygienics was doing in the FMCG space. And he wanted to be a part of it. He loved the idea of taking capabilities and experience in one area and trying to transfer them to another one completely, and he offered to help. It was, he thought, a 'bit of an experiment'.

Rory thinks Dettol, which is primarily a home hygiene brand, has many commonalities with what they're trying to do with INEOS, and that this shows just how successful it could be. Dettol too was playing across many different categories: surface cleaning, disinfection, personal care (deodorant, shower gel and body wash). Similar to what INEOS was trying to do, in terms of being a master brand which operated across different categories.

What INEOS has over brands like Dettol, though, is something that is quite unique – the ability to produce, to manufacture and to supply sanitizing products themselves. No need for third parties to package or to create a variety of their products. And this is a very important difference. 'We have access to the raw ingredients that make our products, which also has a variety of environmental benefits because we are extracting multiple steps out of the production supply chain,' as Rory says. Obviously there are economic benefits as well.

The point about the environment and sustainability is an interesting one. So too is the fact that INEOS has the chance to challenge the orthodoxy of the FMCG market, which up to now has consisted of very large brands in very large categories. As Rory explains, these brands don't want to take risks. They are happy with 1–2 per cent growth, year on year. Stability – that's the goal. Not challenging orthodoxies. They have taken decades to build a secure, solid position. Obviously today you might create a brand differently, based perhaps upon an environmental slant.

It means that INEOS, because they are starting from scratch, don't have to reverse engineer sustainability into their supply chain, or have to try to extract the wasteful elements of a cleaning product. As Rory says:

> 'You can create highly efficacious products, which deliver on their intended purpose, without the bells and whistles. I think the big brands have over-engineered multiple categories to eke out a few margin points year on year. I think we can take a fresh approach and actually create products which are fit for purpose at a fair price off the back of a brand which is built on purpose. And for me, that's a fascinating idea. Because you're turning on its head a hundred years of FMCG orthodoxy and starting again, creating a brand fit for today's world. That's maybe me romanticizing a bit too much what I think I'm doing, but that's why I'm here.'

It all sounds very positive and you might think that INEOS have all the things needed to smash this business. But Rory is extremely aware of the challenges that INEOS has to overcome, and mainly the fact that it has predominantly been a business to business (B2B) company for so long. As a result, the mindset internally needs a bit of a reset. Previously the starting point was not the consumer. It was: 'How can we utilize this byproduct in order to make some money?' But now it needs to be. INEOS has become, in these areas, a consumer-facing business.

The other big challenge is the one that George Ratcliffe mentioned earlier: the marketing. Marketing is key to doing well in this sector. And once again INEOS needed another big brand insider who knew how to get consumers on their side.

Caroline Reynolds had been head of category at PZ Cussons for twelve years when she was approached by INEOS to join the team. Under her watch was Carex – the global leader in hand wash. Carex was the first brand to introduce into the UK market liquid antibacterial hand wash (in 1993) and hand gel sanitizer (in 2008). Caroline had a big part to play in the brand's success, including designing the pebble bottle for which Carex was renowned.

Caroline told me that it was a huge leap for her to move to this unknown brand. Like lots of other people, she admitted, she hadn't actually heard of INEOS, but was reassured that when she spoke to George Ratcliffe, he was asking the right questions. INEOS, she could tell, was going to do this properly. A consumer market in which all the brands have been around for a very long time also seemed ripe for new and interesting brands to emerge.

I dare say that there was some big money put on the table too, and in July 2021 Caroline joined INEOS Hygienics as its head of marketing and innovation. Essentially Caroline left the comfort of a steady ship that she knew well, to get into an INEOS tanker that hasn't yet begun its voyage, with a crew that have never done the route before, and with a map that hasn't been properly drawn.

But that didn't matter, because what lay ahead in the FMCG waters was an exciting challenge – and if I've learnt anything by now, it is that the glue that unites all of the INEOS employees is their love of a challenge.

Breaking habits

Trying to break consumer habits and brand loyalty has to be one of the biggest challenges you can set yourself in the FMCG market.

According to the Customer Loyalty Index 2022 UK (source: Emarsys), 73 per cent of UK consumers consider themselves 'loyal' to certain retailers, certain brands and certain stores. Add this to the fact that only a third of people said they have switched from a brand that they were loyal to due to a bad experience, and it makes it nearly impossible to penetrate into a market where there are incredibly successful brands that have been around for years.

This, Caroline knew, was her biggest challenge. People liked brands that had been around for a long time – it was a short cut to knowing that they were of good quality. So initially it was hard – 'because you're trying to break down that relationship someone has with a brand and then get them to try you instead'. Getting them to try you in the first place – that is half the battle. At least half.

So what I'm struggling to get my head round at the moment is how they're going to do that. There can't be that much you can do with hand wash, can there? Caroline says it's all about trying to do everything differently. For each product in the category, they pick the key things that people are looking for. With hand wash, for instance, it's about two things: moisturizer and fragrance. Those are the two things that INEOS really looked to improve, in order to give people a better product.

This is still a big ask, because as far as I can see, the other brands do stuff with moisturizing and fragrance too. However, what the other brands don't have is unbridled access, through sporting teams, to the world's best performance scientists and doctors, all of whom can give insights into how they can develop their products so that they make a real difference to consumers' daily lives. Rory Tait sees this as their superpower:

'Access to the insights from our performance scientists and athletes is what's helping us design our portfolio. When we think about some of our product launches, we've just launched a hand soap where we have an ingredient strategy within it that uses fragrance as a way to promote mental stimulation. So we're taking elements from performance science and weaving it into our propositions.'

Performance scientists were also able to help them improve the hand sanitizers. They found that one of the biggest barriers to effective hand hygiene is the fact that traditionally, sanitizer dries people's hands out. It causes the skin to dry and crack, which was particularly bad for nurses and doctors who use it fifteen to twenty-five times a day. This would stop consumers from using it as often as they should. If you engineer hand sanitizer which is moisturizing and better for your hands, people use it more often. So usage of hand hygiene products goes up enormously – and unintended germ transmission goes down.

And of course, what that also means is selling more products. Now, the thing that gets me here is: surely the other big brands have scientists too? So what makes the INEOS scientists so special?

It is true, of course, that the rival hygiene firms *do* have scientists, but the INEOS ones have an important advantage: they also come with athletes who use the products. As Rory explained, when he was at Reckitt Benckiser he would have given his right arm to be able to develop hand sanitizer products with seven-time Formula One world champion Lewis Hamilton – who of course is on the INEOS books through their part-ownership of the Mercedes F1 team. This sort of access – 'wow', Rory exclaims. Not only is he an absolutely massive name but he really believes in the importance of hand hygiene, because he doesn't want to miss more training days than he has to through sickness.

Having people like Lewis on the books already – that means that they don't have to pay the millions of pounds that other companies would have to pay to use them either for product development or for marketing. Inevitably, for retailers, when they're deciding whether to stock INEOS products, Lewis Hamilton's backing makes it a much more attractive proposition – as it does for consumers as well, of course. This, as George Ratcliffe says, gives them an important edge:

'Most of our competitors say how much they spend on marketing every year, because when you go and talk to Boots or Tesco or whoever, they ask "Why do we want to put you on our shelves?" We'd respond and say, "Because we're going to spend x million on marketing a year". We quantify it, roughly. And if you can say "Oh, we've got Lewis Hamilton too," then you can sell it. For any other brand, that would have cost them two and a half million, for example. So for us, it kind of boosts our numbers, and it makes it a more attractive product when you're showing it on the shelves in front of the customers. So the retailers like that, that value add.'

This marketing extends beyond what happens at a retail level. Stars like Lewis, or like the All Blacks, can work with psychologists to create a programme of educational support which can be used in schools or in homes anywhere, in order to help people to learn about the importance of wellness, physical exercise and of course good hand hygiene. Not just physical wellness, of course, but mental wellness too. This easy access to major stars, Rory remarks, is 'absolutely one of our USPs'.

Thinking about schools is also a shrewd move: get to your future customers early doors and build brand awareness from a young age. They're all going to grow into potential consumers of hygiene products. And then they'll know all about INEOS. Although Rory is quick to point out that it's about more than that – it's about generating awareness of the brand but it's also about demonstrating the important role that INEOS has to play in people's lives.

This consumer crossover between the INEOS businesses also means that they have cost-effective and innovative ways to market stuff across all of their consumer brands. One of my favourite examples of this is the INEOS Belstaff floating billboard. The world's largest ethane carrier was given the name *Pacific INEOS Belstaff*. INEOS is already known in the maritime world for bold mottos emblazoned upon its vessels' hulls. In the case of Belstaff, though, the vessel serves as a floating billboard for a separate business – bearing the name and logo of another INEOS brand in letters which are roughly three metres high.

I love this idea of a huge ship with the Belstaff logo on it, but I did also wonder: what really was the point? Not many people are going to see this in the middle of the sea and surely you're not going to find many people at container ports who would be your target audience either. Nevertheless, it was a proud moment for Belstaff CEO Fran Millar, who regarded herself as 'godmother' to this new member of the INEOS fleet, and who publicly enthused about the Belstaff logo being introduced to all sorts of places around the world.

When I talked to Fran about this, she herself was quick to point out that this wasn't about advertising jackets but spoke simply to the scale and size of the business:

'INEOS has these huge boats that are crossing the ocean and they need to call them something. So let's call them things from the INEOS portfolio. There's a Grenadier one. There's a Belstaff one. And that's just cool. It's the biggest ethane carrier in the world and it's called the *Pacific INEOS Belstaff*. I'm totally into that. It speaks to the scale and size of the business. This business has everything from however many trillions of tonne ethane carriers to a one pound bottle of hand sanitizer to a thousand pound leather jacket to a professional cycling team. So Lewis Hamilton and Mercedes F1, and all these other things in between. And it's phenomenal, the ambition, the challenge, the "why not" element of it. I find it absolutely inspiring to be a part of a business like that.'

Also, when you think about it, INEOS has lots of moving billboards all over the world with the cycling teams, the racing cars, the footballers and so on, all adorned in whatever INEOS wants us to see. They use opportunities and there are lots of them – the sides of ships or the sides of cars: opportunities with no additional costs because these are part of the INEOS family anyway. It's a big family and their approach to everything is about the small changes that together can make a big difference.

Marginal gains

I'm sure you'll read a lot in this book about marginal gains. That's the theory made famous by Sir Dave Brailsford that runs right through the very core of the business – the idea that accumulated small changes can make a very big difference. And this idea is one which can be applied to health and wellness.

From a hygiene perspective, there are three primary vectors of germ transmission: hands, surface and air. As we know, INEOS Hygienics started with hand sanitization, but although that's important for good health it's a small category to compete in with a handful of major play-ers. The market for hand soap is bigger. After that, the next primary factor of germ transmission, where INEOS can make a material impact on the health of consumers, is their surfaces. So there is an ambition to launch into surface sanitization quickly, through wipes and sprays. That's around double the size of the hand soap category. Then there is fabric. So the laundry category will be one that they plan to conquer in the not too distant future as well. It's an ambition that I got to see when I visited the Hygienics plant.

Visit to Newton Aycliffe

In November 2022, I visited the Newton Aycliffe site where the first hand sanitizer plant was built. As previously mentioned, I do love a chance to have a nosey round a production facility and this one was particularly appealing to me because I used to live and work just up the road. I was an apprentice engineer at the nearby Black + Decker factory, not long after INEOS had also made a home for itself here. Funnily enough – perhaps not surprisingly – some of the staff I met at INEOS that day had also previously worked at B+D.

The site has an interesting history. In the middle of the Second World War, it was home to a munitions plant. The Royal Ordnance factory operated twenty-four hours a day, with workers filling shells and bullets and assembling detonators and fuses for the war effort. The majority of the seventeen thousand workers were women from the surrounding towns and villages, who became known as the 'Aycliffe Angels'. The site was even visited by Winston Churchill during the war.

When I arrived, it was a very foggy day, making it impossible to get any sense of the scale of the fifty-five acres that INEOS occupies here. Of course, this sort of weather is not uncommon in the region. In fact, legend has it that one of the main reasons why the site was chosen for munitions was precisely because of the fog. The hope was that this would stop the Luftwaffe being able to see the buildings in order to bomb the site. Is this true? I have no idea, to be honest. But when I arrived, staff were certainly quick to tell me the old story.

After the war, the site was taken over by a chemicals business, and then eventually it was bought by INEOS in 2008, as part of its acquisition of Hydro Polymers. I did wonder whether this fog might also help INEOS hide away from prying eyes – it would keep industrial espionage at bay! Not that business competitors are likely to be armed with bombs.

It did certainly feel like outsiders were kept at arm's length. This was not a company that anyone could walk into, which is not a surprise given the nature of the business. Although having to show my passport did feel a bit much, there was no budging the security guard on that one. No ID, no entry. But perhaps this is just a regional thing: I got very much the same response as a teenager trying to get into local nightclubs!

Once through, I was straight into PPE. The hi-vis that I know and love was back on. This time it was a neon orange tabard, a matching reinforced baseball cap and some safety glasses. I'd come prepared in my own steel-capped boots because I have learned the hard way that they are invariably ill-fitting and uncomfortable. I can't deny that I am disappointed that INEOS hasn't upped their game on the safety gear front, given that they now own a fashion brand! I can only hope that one day, safety gear will be a bit more stylish. Or even, dare one hope, just a bit more comfortable – and a bit better-fitting for women in particular.

I was walked around the site by Mike Wainwright, the head of operations at INEOS Hygienics. The whole site is fifty-five acres, as I say, and there are three INEOS businesses here. The project to build the sanitizer factory started six months before he joined. 'I remember walking down this path nearly two years ago', he told me, 'when I came for my interview, and this was a warehouse just like that empty one' – not much to get excited or inspired about. But the broader story of Jim's vision, his overarching business, and the philanthropic side of things, along with the fact that this was INEOS's first business to consumer (B2C) operation meant that there was in fact rather a lot by which to be inspired.

I was whisked through the doors of the warehouse and into the labs where the quality control and research and development magic happened. The place was so clinical-looking. The flooring and walls didn't have a single blemish and the air was a heady mix of fresh paint and sanitizer.

Mike was keen to explain how the air in the factory was changed every eight hours and the doors were air locked to make it as sterile as possible. It was at this point that the safety gear was stepped up a notch. After washing my hands I had to put on a lab coat underneath the hi-vis tabard, a hairnet on underneath the baseball cap, and some shoe covers over my steel-capped boots. If I'd had a beard, which to be honest has been known, I'd have had to cover that with a hairnet too.

The factory is split into three main areas. The first is dedicated to wipe production and then in the middle we have the bottling lines, each of various levels of automation. The least automated line does around one thousand bottles an hour and then the new fully automated line which they were keen to show off will do ten thousand bottles per hour when it gets going in 2023.

It was explained to me that the manual lines gave them the flexibility to test out innovations that they fancy trying with the products. Then – the next stage – they would move to the semi-automated line. And then eventually to the fully automated one.

Now forgive me while I indulge in a bit of geekery because I love learning about how these production lines work. And manufacturing manager Marc Coates was keen to tell me. Marc joined INEOS Hygienics in May 2021, having worked at Warburtons for over a decade. He explained how the sanitizer wipe line worked. Today they were making the travel size ones, each pile of fifteen, wrapped in plastic, sealed and cut, weighed and metal-detected, before being loaded into boxes ready to be put out (by people) on the pallets.

From the wipes I move on to the bottling machine. Here the bottles go in at one end, get sorted and stacked onto a conveyor belt. From there they go through a high-speed labelling machine, before being tipped and given a little blast of air to ensure that there is no dust or debris in them. Only then will they be filled, and, depending on whether they are to have caps or pumps, will be fed through in one of two directions to complete the process.

At the moment there isn't an awful lot happening in the plant, and only one production line is running at a time, but the hope is that soon this will be a busy hive of bustling bottle, soaps, wipes and detergent manufacturing.

I had an interesting chat with Caroline Reynolds about the product packaging. She explained that when the brand first launched, it had 'INEOS Hygienics' on everything. But they did some research and found that people tended not to understand really what hygienics actually meant. Also, it felt a little too connected to the pandemic – which is something that, understandably, everyone wants to move on from now.

So, one of the things they've been working on is making sure that the consumer-facing brand represents everything for which INEOS stands. So, for example, on the pack of wipes I'm currently holding, that have just come straight off the production line, it has the words 'science + performance' written underneath the INEOS logo. Which of course links back to the science on which INEOS is built, and their dedication to performance, whether that be in the business world or in the athletics one. I am sure that all of this is reassuring to the consumer, and certainly Caroline and her team have thought long and hard about it. 'The whole idea behind the product range', she tells me, 'is that, essentially, it's a marginal gain – so keeping healthy, keeping clean, helps you to live a better life: you get more out of life.' Although this branding is relatively new, she says, it's 'on everything we have now'.

Nor is it just the wording that they've changed. The cross in the middle of the O of 'INEOS' is being removed, because it's seen as being too clinical. One other tiny detail I ask about is why the O of INEOS is maroon whereas the usual INEOS logo is blue. It turns out that the maroon was a random choice but has gone down well with consumers, and is now viewed as being a distinctive part of the branding. I noticed that the factory doors are in the same maroon. These are hasty choices, though, so it's really just about being recognizable in a shop. This is what really matters.

I do wonder, though, whether the branding is still a bit too industrial. The pack of wipes I'm holding look like ones I'd be handed in the office rather than something I would choose to go in my handbag or on my bathroom shelf. But maybe that's also something that makes them distinct from their rivals.

Standing out on the shelf is one thing; being trusted by the consumer is another. Why should anyone *trust* INEOS as a hygiene brand? It is something, Caroline tells me, that takes time, and you do have to work much harder as an unknown brand – which is why everything that INEOS does has to be really high quality.

Also, for INEOS, things always have to have the company's core values at their heart. INEOS is currently running a campaign with Hygienics, Fran tells me, which uses the slogan, 'You can handle anything,' and that is something based absolutely upon INEOS's core values. 'Anyone who comes into INEOS and works here', she tells me, 'knows that one of the mantras is, "you can handle more than you think you can and you will be given more than you think you can handle but ultimately, you'll be able to handle it"'.

Aligned with this is Hygienics' overarching slogan which is 'Go Humans': the idea that you can unlock human potential if you just give people the right backing, and the right encouragement. That, says Fran, is a very 'INEOS' approach to things:

'This is the INEOS philosophy, this idea of asking big questions, getting remarkable people and giving them the backing and the support. Ensuring they've got grit, rigour and humour within them. You will achieve incredible things, you'll get extraordinary outcomes from that. And I think what the hygienic business enables us to do is to tell all those stories and to land all that brand proposition in a way that we've not historically been able to do, and in a way that we wouldn't be able to do if we didn't have an FMCG brand. It's almost a Trojan horse for the master brand as well. As well as being a fantastic product that's outperforming Carex in consumer research.'

Award-winning

INEOS's venture into the hygiene market got a ringing endorsement in February 2022, when their hand sanitizer won the title Product of the Year in the Personal Hygiene category of the data and insights company Kantar's sponsored awards.

Product of the Year is the world's largest, annual, consumer-voted award for product innovation, with ten thousand UK shoppers picking their winners, and providing valuable insight into emerging, post-pandemic FMCG trends. The winning products represent key consumer wants and habits, serving as a barometer of buying patterns and behaviour in the UK. The citation given about the win observed that hygiene has been – as one might expect – a growth industry during the past few years. Loads of products had flooded the market – some with excellent credentials, some purely opportunistically. Winning in a crowded space demands brand excellence. This INEOS example, the citation declared, displayed the age-old principles of brand-building:

'A product that delivers and supports its promise with relevant and tangible reasons to believe (hospital grade and data- and science-led). A brand that builds emotional trust and credibility through its umbrella narrative (parent brand with world-leading expertise and scale to respond to consumer needs at a time of challenge).'

It was impressive, the citation remarked, that INEOS had been able to do what it had done at speed. 'Simple', was the conclusion, 'but excellent.'

So, it's winning awards. But my question remains: are people really noticing the brand? I'll be honest: I've yet to spot it when I'm out and about in the shops where I buy my hygiene products. In terms of aware-ness of a brand, there are different ways in which to measure it.

Let's start with 'prompted awareness', which is a measure of how many people have heard of a brand when it's told to them, or they are shown a prompt such as a logo or advert. This is an interesting one for INEOS because it's a master brand for so many different things. So if you're asking consumers: have you heard of INEOS hand sanitizer? then they might say yes, on the basis that they've heard of the cycling team or one of the other businesses. So, you do have to take the num-bers with a pinch of salt, in terms of what they mean for hygiene recognition. Nevertheless, prompted awareness of INEOS hand hygiene is up 250 per cent, year on year.

The more interesting research involves what is known as 'spontan-eous awareness' – a measure of how many people, when asked, can quote a brand without any assistance. So when asked: 'what brands do you think of in hand hygiene?' INEOS comes out the same as Dove and Sanex, with 6 per cent spontaneous awareness. This is a huge achieve-ment, not least because INEOS has only been making hand hygiene products for two years. Fran thinks that this is about the positioning of the brand:

'The way that we've positioned the brand is we want it to be innova-tive. We want it to be a challenger. We want it to be disruptive. We want it to be empowering. All of the things that we believe the INEOS business is and we want to be using hygiene as a tool to tell that story.'

So it's growing, and there is greater awareness. But it's also still early days as far as George Ratcliffe is concerned:

'I think we're still very much in the learning phase, despite being two and a half years in. It's a pivot because a year ago, we were a hand sanitizer company. And today, we're moving into the household cleaning range, which is a different category altogether. So you're almost starting from scratch again, talking to different buyers, which is challenging and another cost.'

It's debatable as to whether it's worth it because, as George went on to say, it's taking up a lot of time and money. Positive growth results might still actually involve small numbers – not comparable to what INEOS is selling in the rest of its portfolio. Because it's a brand-new business, Hygienics gets a disproportionate amount of management time. There is an understandable desire to look after it, and to look after the INEOS name. There is a desire not to get it wrong. 'I think we've got another couple of years to see how it goes,' George Ratcliffe concludes. 'It needs to be a business that makes enough money to justify all of the people and management time that goes into it.'

And in the meantime, while they decide what to do with Hygienics, are they planning any more moves in the consumer arena? Tom Crotty thinks not, for now: 'We probably feel we've got indigestion and need to settle down a bit,' he says:

'We have the Grenadier as project one of the automotive series and then project two, which is smaller scale, will be an electric version of the car, in 2025. And we'll go on from there. I don't envision us being a one trick pony. On the fashion side, if we're successful with Belstaff, I could see us looking to maybe add some acquisitions there and grow that business.'

So – never say never.

The INEOS DNA

INEOS is used to being top dog, or at least in the top three players, when it comes to the chemicals markets in which it operates. So this step into the consumer world through fashion, cars and hygiene is a very big change. Suddenly, they are the new kid on the block.

Without doubt these new directions have given them a huge lift in terms of brand awareness, increasing from near zero to over a fifth of the UK population now being aware of INEOS. It's also given them the ability to talk directly to the public about who they are and what they care about. INEOS can now get their message out in a meaningful way, rather than the press telling everyone what INEOS is, and what it does. You could also say that it's brought a certain level of that 'cool' that Sir Jim and his team were looking for.

What blows my mind in all of this is that there doesn't seem to be an overall game plan as far as I can tell. It's just whatever takes their fancy at the time. Not something you would get from a publicly owned business, or even many privately owned ones for that matter.

When I first spoke to George Ratcliffe about why INEOS had ventured into the different consumer brands, he said that there wasn't one big strategy, that there isn't a golden thread, and that all businesses have been treated separately. As I mentioned earlier, it's only recently that Belstaff and Hygienics have come under the same roof, with Fran Millar in charge to make sure that the same message is being heard by all INEOS customers whether they're buying a jacket, hand wipes or a car. Fran essentially is the gatekeeper of the brand. But what is the brand? Is it INEOS or is it a house of brands? I guess this is something that they're still trying to figure out.

But while the businesses might operate in silos, there is without doubt a shared DNA. There is a mindset which sees that INEOS has business ambitions beyond what is conventional in the sectors in which it operates.

There is a grit, rigour and humour with which they are intent on bringing change. It's something I've seen in everyone I've met in the company, from the first interview I did for the BBC with INEOS communications director Tom Crotty back in 2013, right up to the team I met at the Newton Aycliffe site nearly a decade later.

It's a company that is good to people, especially if you're competitive and sporty. However, life is anything but safe and cosy. You might think you've got a job for life as a manager in the chemical sector and then suddenly be brought into a meeting to be part of the group tasked with buying a fashion brand. Or you might think you're going into work one day to make PVC pellets and then find yourself putting a formula together to make hand sanitizer. They challenge their staff and very rarely take the easy route. Scary on some levels. Not suited to everyone. But for those who thrive on this, it does make it an exciting environment in which to work.

The way I see it, INEOS does more pivoting, and causes more disruption to the status quo, than a *Strictly* contestant does on their route to the final. What's at its heart is innovation and what makes this successful is the stability of the leadership. The three captains of industry, Jim, Andy Currie and John Reece, have been steering this tanker together from day one.

Given the size of the business, you might think that it would struggle to be agile. In fact it's quite the opposite. Its decisions are made quickly, and what's really impressive is that these are not just based on profits but on what its leaders think is the right thing to do. It's a business that takes risks and which invests in projects that others might dismiss as impossible. In fact, I reckon that the word 'impossible' is very rarely said in the corridors of power at INEOS.

What is impossible though, is to predict what INEOS will do next in the consumer world – or in any world, for that matter. And that is nothing if not exciting.

7

Next Generation, Youth Development

Lord Sebastian Coe CH, KBE

ADULTS TODAY OF ALL AGES have strong memories – positive or extremely negative ones – of running at school.

Cross country. Laps of the football pitch. Jogging in the mud and the rain. Smears across the face or on the knees. Shouts – encouraging or irate – from the PE teacher. For most of us, this was part of the ritual of growing up. Some (like me) had an appetite for it but of course I know that plenty didn't, that plenty *hated* it, and usually it *was* competitive.

It is no coincidence that, as Elaine Wyllie tells me now, The Daily Mile – the revolutionary and quite astonishingly successful initiative that she founded – was given its very first spark by an elderly volunteer. He, she remembers now, had recently begun to help at the school of which she was the head teacher in Stirling, Scotland.

After watching the children's PE lesson, he turned to Elaine, who was standing next to him, also watching, on the touchline. He asked her to look at the class carefully. You do know, he said, the children really aren't fit. Her initial reaction, she recalls, was outrage. Hers was considered a sporty school after all – with a reputation as such among other local schools. Her pride, inevitably, was more than a little wounded by his suggestion.

Still, it made her think. And in time she came to accept that this reputation for sportiness was based upon a small minority of the most athletic children in the school. For the majority, when they went for a short run, the experience was very different indeed: 'they were exhausted by halfway, they had a stitch and they were fed up. It was awful', she admits. So gradually her outrage dissipated. 'Actually', she admitted to herself, 'he has a point.'

This, she now recalls – and for the millions of children across the world who have benefitted from the simple routine she instituted – was the moment that changed everything. This was the gift from an older generation to a much younger, new one.

A healthy mind in a healthy body

I was going to begin this section with a quotation in Latin. Then I thought: Jim at least won't care for that. I should give him his full name and title: Sir Jim Ratcliffe, although I'm aware that this might get the same response!

And to be honest, I agree. I grew up in Sheffield, he pretty close by, in Manchester. With regard to the quotation, you can't have a book part-entitled 'grit' and then go throwing Latin quotations around. The phrase is well-known in English anyway – no need for any dead languages. A healthy mind in a healthy body. The ideal.

What about the late Stephen Hawking, you might say? A brilliant physicist trapped in a paralysed and little-functioning body, traversing the wonders of the universe from his motorized wheelchair. Well, I can only respond that very few humans could exist entirely in their brains in the way that he did. I know that I'm not one of them. What INEOS is trying to do is to think about the vast majority of people who are like me in this respect.

I was an athlete, though, so I know that in *that* respect at least I am not typical. The Daily Mile programme is emphatically not one that caters for any sort of elite. It is entirely non-competitive. It is about the benefit of exercise for everyone. When I talk about health and fitness here, I certainly don't mean running a four-minute mile, let alone a sub-two-hour marathon (which only one man has ever done).

Most people are content to operate at a much lower level. Exercise for many might mean a regular half-hour walk, hour of busy gardening or a few flights of stairs taken at a moderately brisk stride in preference to the lift. No competition need be involved at all. Some like it and find it a helpful motivation; others do not. Either way the point is the same: physical activity promotes good health, both physical and mental. To be beneficial to one's health, the exercise need only actually be quite gentle.

Nor are the positive effects of physical activity seen only in the young. Here of course I *am* a case in point. The athletic performances for which I am most noted took place decades ago. The times and results might remain in the record books, as do those of almost all athletes, whatever the era in which they competed (Jesse Owens and Fanny Blankers-Koen along with thousands of others), but I am well aware that racing against me now is scarcely going to worry a latter-day Olympic athlete. No one, least of all me, thinks that I am likely to threaten any current world records. Time ticks for all of us. I had my day – my time on the track – and now it is in the past. Yet the physical activity of my youth continues to benefit me today as I approach my seventh decade.

On a personal level, I still enjoy and feel the benefit from doing exercise. Mountains of scientific evidence attest to the health advantages of being physically fit, even relatively late in life. Among this evidence, furthermore, is research which stresses the beneficial impact of physical activity upon mental performance. This doesn't have to be 'aerobic' exercise – exercise which leaves the person performing it out of breath. Taking the dog for a walk, or doing some gardening, is enough. The beneficial effect on one's mood is also pronounced.

There are a variety of wise quotations on the subject. Take one from that recurrent coiner of wise quotations (as well as being a general brainbox), Albert Einstein: 'intellectual growth should commence at birth and cease only at death'. This is another way of saying that learning is lifelong. It is common now to emphasize that our brains, even in later life, are plastic and malleable.

'Neuroplasticity' is the buzzword. We should not assume that once we have reached adulthood, all development stops just because our physical growth stops. We might not go to school anymore. Our limbs might not be getting longer. But pushing ourselves to learn new skills, or to memorize new information, retains its benefit. 'Anyone who stops learning is old, whether at twenty or eighty,' said Henry Ford; 'anyone who keeps learning stays young.'

Or take this example from the famous sixteenth century Frenchman, Michel de Montaigne: 'There is nothing more notable in Socrates than that he found time, when he was an old man, to learn music and dancing, and thought it time well spent.' It is increasingly understood that our bodies are constantly refreshing themselves. Some muscle cells might live for decades but the majority of those in our bodies are replaced in a matter of months.

In early human history, people had to hunt to survive, and hunting required physical activity – we had to run, often for a long time. In settled, agricultural communities too, even once it wasn't necessary for most of us to hunt to survive, physical hard work was an inevitability, not a choice, whether in fields of crops or in maintaining a home without any of the labour-saving devices to which we have now become accustomed. As a species we have evolved to possess the capacity to do this, and to have the physical expectation that existence will involve a lot of effort.

Today we live in an era where inactivity has become the norm. But it certainly was not the norm in the past, indeed for almost all of previously recorded history. The modern era is one in which it is no longer necessary for most of those in the developed world to work in any physical way, rather we tend to work sitting at desks in an office environment. And at the same time food is plentiful. Calories are too easy to come by. Manufacturers of processed food, soft drinks and ready-meals pack them with cheap sugars and sugar-substitutes which promote addiction and addictive behaviour. Supermarkets even deliver them now: the days of wandering around with a trolley – of walking at least to stock up on BOGOFs – are largely in the past.

The predictable result has been a massive spike in obesity, accompanied by a precipitous decline in physical fitness. For most of our history, in Britain and across much of the world, it was considered a mark of wealth and high status to be overweight. Only the rich and the richly honoured could possibly afford to eat too much, and to exercise too little. In remote indigenous communities today, one still sees this correlation between weight and status, but certainly not in the US, the UK or in similar countries.

Indeed, in the developed world, in a remarkably short space of time, a complete reversal has taken place. There is a clear correlation these days between being overweight and being of *low* rather than high status: eating too much cheap, high calorie, processed food, making use of cheap labour-saving devices and exercising little. Readily affordable amusement activities are often static in nature: playing computer games, watching television, or reading social media feeds (yes, even these utilize the vocabulary of consumption) are all pastimes which do not require getting off the sofa.

Unlike activity that is more physical, none of these pastimes discourage the almost-unconscious habit of eating while performing them. In fact they are more likely to do the reverse. The habit of munching popcorn or a calorific snack while watching films or television is ingrained. Not for nothing do cinemas have a large array of crisps, sweets, chocolates and soft drinks – served of course in vast receptacles – prominently on offer as people enter the screening room.

· People considered, or who consider themselves, of higher social status do not labour, of course. As a rule, they certainly do not till fields or clean offices or deliver mail. But they are much more likely to go to the gym, or to have a personal trainer, and to eat in a health-conscious fashion.

The Daily Mile

What those like Elaine who were closely involved in establishing a charity like The Daily Mile have recognized, and have attempted to shift, is the habitual inactivity which far too often affects our current crop of young children.

This is an inactivity which, much as the word 'habitual' implies, accustoms them to an inactive lifestyle. It is one which inevitably they then take with them into later life. The more ingrained such behaviour becomes, the harder it is to change, and the more likely it is to be emulated by their children and grandchildren.

INEOS's founder, chair and CEO Sir Jim Ratcliffe is himself a keen runner and adventurer. The Olympics came to London in 2012 meaning that everyone had seen plenty of elite runners. They, in general, didn't need promotion or encouragement. But Jim wanted to promote running in particular to those kids who might not otherwise acquire the habit. Not to this generation, but to the next one.

For him, physical challenges significantly improve our mental and psychological capacity: physical fitness and mental fitness go together. And so for him this enterprise was one in which he passionately believed and continues to support. It is one whose potential benefit for society both in the short and in the longer term is enormous. It is one which I, too, am proud to be associated with and help in any way I can.

As mentioned at the outset, Elaine Wyllie was the head teacher of a primary school when she founded The Daily Mile. I use the past tense only because she has retired from that role now. She ran (no pun intended) a school called St Ninian's in Stirling, central Scotland, the city which is described as being the 'gateway' to the Highlands.

As head, prompted initially by that elderly volunteer who commented on the fitness of her pupils, Elaine became increasingly aware of their relative inactivity and the lack of physical fitness. School was for everyone – sporty or not. It was pointless, she realized, having a reputation as a sporty school if that reputation depended upon little more than a tenth of a year group. The absence of children's physical conditioning was little known to previous generations when then, a large percentage might have walked or cycled to school. Now, few did. They sat on the bus or a train or in a car. These days the tendency for bicycles to be electric only increases this trend: the one activity which used to require physical exertion no longer does, or markedly less of it at any rate.

Nor was this a class issue. It is true that, say a century ago, the differences between classes were more conspicuous than they are today, still pronounced as they undoubtedly remain. I recall them being much more apparent when I was a child than they are now. Then, the very affluent, the titled and entitled, might have had servants, chauffeurs and so on, but it was nevertheless true that children were much less insulated than they are today. In general, the gulf of separation between the adult world and that of children was much larger than it is now across the population.

Their parents would tell them – with physical activity implicit in the very instruction – to 'run along'. Fun would consist of sports, or outdoor games. Walking and running were a part of life. And inevitably, therefore, exercise was too – for upper and lower classes alike. Concerns about health and safety have certainly diminished risk in many environments – but in helping to reduce activity they have unknowingly and *decidedly* increased risk as well.

Nobody, of course, doubts or denies the huge gains that washing machines and cars and all manner of labour-saving devices have brought for average households, and perhaps most particularly for some parts of humanity – women most obviously – in a world still massively divided according to gender. Men have always been, and still are, spared a lot of manual labour which is often pure drudgery and which brings very real health risks, far outweighing benefits to health. Washing clothes by hand, or using a Victorian mangle, were physically demanding activities but did not improve the wellbeing of those expected to perform them.

Elaine saw, however, that the loss of lifestyles in which regular exercise was part of the world that children knew was damaging not only for the children's educational attainment, but also for their broader chances in life. And she thought about what she might be able to do in order to help her pupils to improve their prospects.

At the time, her thoughts were directed at the relatively small number of children who attended the school of which she was the head teacher. To have had any larger vision at that stage would have seemed hopelessly unrealistic. So early in 2012, Elaine's first move was to institute a routine in her own school whereby all the pupils would run, jog or, if necessary, walk or wheel themselves around the playground for a quarter of an hour every single day, regardless of the weather. There must have been days when, peering at rain thumping down onto the grass or the playground tarmac, the prospect did not appeal. But as every runner knows, rain isn't really that bad. It's only water! Even cold rain. With exercise the body warms up and the rain becomes cooling, and positively welcome.

I have always thought that there is a sort of spirituality to running in really inclement weather. The world is a much quieter place, populated only by committed dog walkers or runners. And it is somehow more tranquil. External noise is quashed by the rain – dampened down, quite literally – and the noises that one hears are by and large only rhythmic, repetitive ones: the noise of one's breathing, the metronomic contact of one's shoes pacing the ground, the rain drumming on the tarmac, along perhaps with the less rhythmic shouts of anyone who is watching. Being alone with one's thoughts under these conditions is almost transcendental.

I accept that much of this might not be the case when we're talking about a gaggle of wet, excited and bedraggled schoolchildren. That is certainly somewhat different to a runner going for a solitary run in the rain. But regardless, rain is without question vastly preferable for any runner to great heat – not that the latter is often a problem in Scotland or indeed anywhere in Britain.

Jim came from Manchester and, as everybody knows, it rains a lot there as weather systems blow in from the Atlantic, clouds form over the land and over the hills and dump their contents on the north-west. There's not much that you would accomplish in life if you were put off every time there was a shower.

I must admit that when Elaine initiated what would later become the much broader Daily Mile initiative, I barely noticed. It was then just a few months before the Olympics and a great many rather good, experienced and established runners among other athletes, were coming to London. The general noise surrounding the build-up was increasing, as I can well attest. It was certainly in the media. And for me at least, and I suspect for others too, this rather drowned out Elaine's important but – at the time – localized venture.

Anyone who has tried running and stuck with it can vouch for the human body's remarkable capacity to improve at performing a repeated and accustomed activity, whatever that activity might be: running, juggling, playing a racquet sport or a musical instrument. Our brains and our bodies are constantly learning and adapting: they are, to use that current buzzword, 'malleable'.

Muscles become larger and fitter, regions of our brains become more packed with neurons and with the connections which make particular skills possible. 'Practice makes perfect', people used to say. Nowadays they have dispensed with the final adjective – we aren't aiming for perfection. Perfection, people rightly object, is hardly a realistic goal. 'Practice makes permanent' is what teachers say now. And this encapsulates the sense of the value of repetition. As we repeat, so our bodies and our brains adapt and are moulded.

It is true, of course, that some people have more natural talent for a given activity than do others. I could play tennis all day every day for years on end, even in my youth, and I would still never have become as good, or indeed anything like as good, as Roger Federer. I just don't have his – as the expression goes – gifts. Very few do, of course. The same goes for being as good a footballer as Lionel Messi. And, unfortunately, for being a jazz musician – a skill for which I would happily exchange any talent that I have for athletics, but which I have reluctantly come to accept that I don't and will never have. The name 'Sebastian Coe' is unlikely ever to be uttered in the same breath as 'Thelonius Monk' or 'Nina Simone' or 'Oscar Peterson'.

I was lucky enough, though, that I did have natural ability when it came to running, and this fact allowed me to achieve much more in athletics than other athletes who might have worked just as hard. Not that I didn't work very hard. Talent doesn't get you *that* far, and my father made very sure that I focused. From deep inside, an unquenchable determination certainly did drive me – but it does seem possible that it drove others too. Both determination and ability do need to be present: certainly in my case, I would have found it very difficult to access that determination had I not also had the natural ability which allowed me to perform well.

This being said, there is no doubt that practice – whether for the oft-mentioned ten thousand hours said to bring mastery of a skill, or for rather fewer – certainly does make a substantial difference. The first time it is attempted, a run is hard. No one is good at running without training: not Haile Gebrselassie or Eliud Kipchoge. Not even a sprinter like Usain Bolt, who, it is true, was probably no slouch before he honed his fitness or technique.

Think of all those runners that one sees on New Year's Day, who look precisely like what they doubtless are: people desperately fulfilling a resolution, paying a price for too much seasonal indulgence and attempting to turn over a new leaf. They don't in the least look like they jog habitually or are remotely enjoying the activity! And in the majority of cases, they probably won't be jogging at the beginning of February and almost certainly not at the beginning of March.

People might object to my observation on the basis that I have run all my life, so what would I know about starting out on the process? Well, the objection is fair enough, I suppose. But putting me on a rowing machine or an exercise bike or making me swim as fast as I can for ten lengths does give me some idea of what it is like to acquire familiarity in a new discipline, even if I am well-used to the similar process of exertion, breathlessness and recovery which accompanies it.

In any case, we are not talking here about getting to an elite level, or even necessarily to a competitive one. This is emphatically not what The Daily Mile is about. We are talking only about acquiring the *habit*. About taking pleasure in performing an energetic activity and in doing so with regularity. About making this activity, and the satisfaction one derives from it, a part of one's life. This is something that everyone can do, something that everyone can derive pleasure from doing and feel the benefit from doing. It is a deeply ingrained, very natural activity.

At first, anyone who tries a new sporting activity finds it hard. This is one of the reasons that Elaine recommends what she remembers being referred to as 'scout's pace': running for a bit, walking for a bit to allow recovery, and then repeating until the walk becomes shorter along with the recovery too.

One of the things that drove her initially was the realization of just how unfit, just how physically unused to exercise, most of her pupils were. Astonishingly quickly, though, it became much less of a hardship for them. And any sense of discomfort from being out of breath also diminished. Rapidly. As we know, exercise promotes the release of endorphins – the body's natural drugs, as the uncontracted form of endorphin, 'endogenous morphine', clearly suggests. These chemicals greatly reduce pain and can create a marked uplift in mood. Just like other drugs. And just like other drugs, they are addictive. They encourage one to seek another hit – secure in the knowledge that, in this case, they are associated with long-term benefits and not with any risk of overdose or harm. Or with the career-threatening consequences in athletics of the detection of unnatural and illegal substances. Unless that harm be to one's relationships, while training for some long-distance endurance event and disappearing from family life for hours on end! This addictive quality explains why it was that Elaine remembers finding both pupils (and even their parents) *wanting* to run more, out of hours, so addictive and so rewarding did they find this previously almost unexperienced activity.

Elaine's idea – as good ideas tend to – very quickly caught on. By later that year the entire school was taking part and the impact that the activity was having on her charges was being talked about much more widely. It was having a hugely positive impact on the general levels of physical fitness at the school. It was also having a positive impact – noticed by many teachers – in terms of the willingness and ability of pupils to apply themselves to *mental* exertion. And it was having a very positive impact psychologically, on the general mood of the children. As my fellow athlete, long-term INEOS employee and keen supporter of The Daily Mile, John Mayock, remarked to me: 'Running makes you happy.' It really is that simple. Very soon this new form of regular group exercise was proving a fantastically good thing in the kids' lives in every way.

At the end of that year the school's nurse carried out a medical checkup on all of the school's pupils. As anyone who has ever taken part in a medical check-up will know, you do not need to be much over the ideal to be classified as 'overweight'. Well, Vitality estimates that four in ten children leaving primary school are overweight. Research sponsored by Public Health England at around the same time, meanwhile, showed that more than half of primary school children in England were not getting enough exercise. It estimated that 30 per cent of two to fifteen year olds – almost a third, and a pretty similar proportion – should be classified as overweight or obese. What a burden, psychological as well as physical, to carry into later life, for an unacceptably high number of this country's children!

It is hard to imagine that the situation is much better in Scotland. But in spite of this, when they were measured not a single one – not one – of the fifty-seven primary school children at St Ninian's was deemed overweight, let alone obese. It was a remarkable result. And mightily impressive testimony to the value of the routine which Elaine had instituted.

The school years are also immensely formative ones for young people – a time, more than any other time in life, when enduring habits are set. I recall Tao Geoghegan Hart, the INEOS Grenadiers cyclist who became an ambassador for The Daily Mile, talking about precisely this, and it struck a chord. 'When you're [school] age', he said, 'sport can inspire you and take hold of you and transform you more than at any other age. Yes, we all go on journeys with sport – but when you trace those journeys back, [they go] to your childhood'.

Not long afterwards, in 2015, Elaine retired from her role as head teacher. But since then, along with her husband, John Wyllie, she has dedicated herself full time to promoting The Daily Mile much more widely. Its huge take-up and equal popularity suggested an urgent need. And so from Stirling it has rolled out across the UK and well beyond that. It has become an international phenomenon, touching the lives of a vast number of children – much greater than the pupils at her own school about whom she was originally thinking, all of them wanting what John Mayock memorably refers to as 'that piece of magic that's happening in Scotland'.

Quite rightly, Elaine has been honoured for her extraordinary efforts. Who could possibly object to seeing her name among the party donors and career civil servants on the country's honours list? Her achievements and contribution to the wellbeing of young people are a great deal more obvious than many of theirs. One article in the press in the spring of 2014 noted that ten thousand children had taken part in events since the previous August while many more – more than a hundred thousand – were expected to take part in around 250 events planned for the following three years. When I asked John Mayock about it recently, towards the close of 2022, he reported that there were almost four million children involved, from some fifteen thousand schools across the world. Participation has since passed the four million children and sixteen thousand schools milestones.

The sheer scale of it takes one's breath away. Without any question, Elaine sits more than comfortably on any honours list. I have met and spoken with her many times before but at our most recent meeting I was keen in particular to ask her about the genesis of her creation. I spoke to her in her Stirling home, using our post-pandemic technology skills.

Elaine logged on alongside her husband John. Both were decked in Scottish knitwear to protect against the winter elements – not surprisingly, since an influx of northern air had plunged us into a cold snap that is noticeable right across Europe. They were sitting close together already but I urged them to get closer still so that I could see them both clearly on my screen. John's shoulder is lovely – don't get me wrong – but I did hope to see more of him.

They must have told the story of the germination of The Daily Mile many, many times before. But they did so again with the same infectious enthusiasm as ever, Elaine recalling how it was an elderly volunteer – accustomed to the norms of childhood in a previous age – who first drew her attention to the fact that the children now did not seem fully fit.

Anyone who has tried running – almost everyone – knows that it's no fun at all if you're not fit. It was then, she remembered, that she first suggested taking the children out for just fifteen minutes every day, in order to get them to build up their fitness. To begin with, she fell back upon an old technique that she remembered from her own youth and which I have already mentioned: 'scout's pace'. I can vouch for the fact that the basic concept goes up to the highest level, where 'interval training' is its more professional-sounding name. Athletes run fast for short distances, then allow themselves to recover before doing it again. As a young athlete in training I did this on hilly roads near my home, with my father timing me in his car. Some might use a running track, but there is absolutely no need. Lamp posts will do. 'We have cherry trees as markers', Elaine observed. The general idea of 'scout's pace' is, she enthused, 'a brilliant thing: I love it!'

She recalled, however, not initially being optimistic that the strategy would work. In fact, the beneficial effects were remarkably quick in appearing. The children 'started to come in shining, and, you know, just in a good mood. They really wanted to keep going. It was unbelievable', she remembered. And their progress was astonishingly rapid. While initially many had struggled, soon most could run for the whole fifteen minutes without stopping.

There was also another, largely unexpected benefit. They didn't only enjoy it at the time. They were in a noticeably better mood throughout the day. And all day they were much more focused. Really, she recalled, it was quite amazing. Initially the experiment had only been with one class, but very quickly, inevitably, word got around. 'Other classes, teachers, parents, children, were saying, "can we not do that?" And so it wasn't long before the entire school, even the nursery children, were joining in. We all loved it.'

As Elaine said, nobody in a school would ever recommend something which hadn't been embedded for at least a year. Too many ideas have seemed good ones at first but then failed to stay the course. So in the short term, the idea wasn't pushed onto other schools. But other schools did hear about it and didn't, for obvious reasons, want to wait a year. Before long, some had taken it up. Then it spread like wildfire and Elaine was rather bewildered about what she had started.

While initially there was no particular name for the scheme, somebody at Elaine's school dug out a measuring wheel and worked out that the children were covering 99.99 per cent of a mile each time they ran. It was too good to be true. Thus the activity became a children's running charity and was christened with the obvious name of The Daily Mile, a label which has stuck ever since.

As John, who has also been closely involved since the outset, observed, 'the beauty of it is that it taps into something that is natural in children. You know, when you see children going outside together in a playground to run, they *want* to do it. It's not something that's forced upon them. It's not punishment. They really enjoy it. All we're really doing', he went on, characteristically understating the galvanizing and organizational role that he and others have of course played, 'is opening a door for them into something they already want to do'.

Help and support

It goes without saying that an operation as large as this one has become has major running costs, requires substantial organizational effort, and desperately needs a significant corporate backer – a corporate backer like INEOS. In 2016, INEOS committed to being the principal, 'title' sponsor of The Daily Mile initiative. They helped Elaine to establish The Daily Mile Foundation. Its employees were provided with office space at the company's London HQ, so that they had no need to look for or to pay for alternative office space.

As Elaine happily acknowledged, INEOS already had a children's running charity – and a good one at that – called 'GO Run For Fun'. Which only goes to show what a massive impact her concept had upon Jim Ratcliffe, whose style is certainly decisive but who wouldn't have taken on another such charity without very good reason and careful consideration. What was the appeal? Large companies like to be associated with philanthropic ventures, of course. It helps their public image. But for Jim, it was much more than this. It was something deeply personal.

He knew from his own experience both the psychological and the physical benefits of regular exercise. He was brought up in a Manchester council house where the spoons were definitely not made of silver. 'Council house billionaire' has been the label that the press has loved to apply to Jim. And he credited running when young with instilling a healthy, lifelong passion for exercise, as well as what he calls a bit of 'northern grit'. He believes passionately in the value of what Elaine has been trying to inculcate in young children.

What appealed to Jim was precisely the inclusive, non-competitive nature of the project. He, along with so many others, had seen and been inspired by the elite, high-level runners who came to London during the Olympics. But he wanted to do something very different: something aimed at children, at all children, especially those without access to expensive facilities or expensive coaching. Exactly what Elaine's scheme was doing, in other words. Because The Daily Mile is emphatically not about levels of performance, rather it is simply about the benefit of exercise – something that is as true for those who are less gifted by nature as it is for those who are.

It is in general true that while developments in technology have made it possible for people in large parts of the world to lead lives which are much less physically active than those led by their forebears, the bodies we all inhabit owe their skeletal structure to hundreds of generations of evolution and are largely (though not entirely of course) shared by other members of the animal kingdom. These bodies evolved to cope with demands very different from those we face now. They are shaped by natural selection. And while we no longer have to operate in an environment where only the fittest can be sure to survive, they still benefit from exercise – something that's no longer a given in the routines and rhythms of everyday life in the industrialized world. Not much energy is required to secure a meal these days: a protein fix requires only a car trip to the nearest fast-food outlet.

So we must ensure that exercise forms a normal part of life, in a manner which is voluntary rather than mandated. Fortunately, this does provide its own rewards: it feels good in the short term, and in the longer term too. And this feel-good factor offers a powerful incentive for exercise, even in a world in which it is no longer essential.

This is what Elaine was focusing upon – and why The Daily Mile has proved so sensationally successful. It has that magic, just like so many success stories: that 'of course' factor, which makes everybody who tries it, or who touches it in any way, wonder why they didn't think of it first.

Forgotten 40

When it comes to the next generation, I also want to focus on another of INEOS's major philanthropic projects. A philanthropic project? You may well conclude that this would more appropriately be featured in the Philanthropy chapter.

Well, yes, I'll admit that it certainly could be. But its strong emphasis on children, and on the future, means that it also sits comfortably here. We are, after all, talking about the next generation. As such, its focus upon the distant future marks it out – the length of time that it takes a glint in the eye, or a baby, or a young child to grow into an adult. The adult carries none of the biological cells of the baby that it used to be, but still has that baby's memories and personality traits deeply embedded within it.

In the political world, as I know all too well from personal experience, our short-term thinking is often driven by a focus on the need to get re-elected. This gives politicians very little incentive to invest in the long term or to train resources on things that will only bear fruit many years down the track, the benefits of which may not always be easy to quantify. They probably won't be in office then. Their party might not be in office. And even if they were, would they be given any credit for a policy which they had initiated that long ago? I think we know the answer, and so do most politicians.

This opens a space for the crucial role that is played by philanthropic initiatives and private support. Unlike political parties, business is not driven by the electoral cycle. It does not need to be widely credited for the good that it has done. On the contrary: it is quite enough for the individuals concerned to know – and the same holds true for those who work in a business like INEOS, and for Elaine and John Wyllie.

The benefits of The Daily Mile became evident, as we have seen, in the very short term – shorter than even Elaine had anticipated – as well as being enduring. But the similarity in terms of the priorities and the ambitions of another of INEOS's major programmes, such as Forgotten 40, is clear. It is certainly no coincidence that both Elaine and John have also been asked to sit upon the board for this venture. Their experience, and Elaine's public profile, are great assets.

As one might expect, this is also something about which they both feel passionate. The motivations which drive Forgotten 40 chime with much of what Elaine herself witnessed while working as a head teacher.

From the moment that it was described to them, their belief in it, and their enthusiasm for it, were infectious.

That remained true when I spoke to them. I got the impression that when something stays with them, it *really* does stay with them. It was January 2020, John recalled, when they first read something about what, at the end of the previous year, had been the *Sunday Times'* Christmas appeal. The bit that made the biggest impression on them was about children in the country's most deprived communities not even getting a Christmas present. It was – as of course it was intended to be – a heart-rending illustration of lives lived in real poverty and deprivation, without even the small but very important comforts and excitements of the festive season.

'We received an email', John remembered, 'asking us if we had any ideas.' What, he says, they settled upon was basically 'this notion that if head teachers were given money to spend on the community that they knew best, then they could sort out some of the problems for these children – that was the essence of it'. Elaine enthusiastically concurred. Head teachers, she observed, were people you could really trust – and she wasn't simply saying that because she was one. 'Out of a hundred head teachers you could probably trust a hundred to do their best . . . They know their community, they know their children.'

The road to being a head teacher is often a very long one when you take into account the years of experience gained along the way, all of them under the watchful and critical eyes of colleagues. And this was a message which was ideally tuned to Jim's ears. There was, John said, 'no middleman, you know, just quite like The Daily Mile in many ways. Completely simple'.

I found it very easy to talk to Elaine and John – not just because they were so obviously likeable and enthused but because we were entirely on the same page. We shared a feeling that both The Daily Mile and Forgotten 40 address deep-seated problems that have proved resistant to orthodox political solutions.

I'm known primarily for running, for athletics, as well as for organizing large scale events *involving* a lot of running, even if they are not only about that – like the 2012 Olympics. Or, at the time of writing, I'm also known for heading World Athletics, the body responsible for administering the sport of athletics globally. So what, you might ask, am I doing talking about a philanthropic venture which is really not about running at all?

Obviously my involvement with The Daily Mile derives fundamentally from my being a well-known name in athletics. But this chapter is entitled 'Next Generation'. It is about the future, and about trying to ensure fairness in the future. Athletics just happens to be a part of that fairer, fuller world in which Elaine and I both believe.

The Daily Mile is not, at its root, *about* athletics – and it is certainly not about the element of competition – something integral, of course, to the sport. (Even if one of its virtuous byproducts could be the unearthing of a future track star.) Elaine and John's passion for Forgotten 40 – for remembering and helping them and trying to ensure that they are not forgotten any longer – is one I share.

The concept that sits behind the name Forgotten 40 is simple. The number of children in the UK who are living in poverty is estimated to approach 40 per cent, even before the recent pandemic affected everyone – some much more severely than others. That figure made me sit up. The definition of poverty is a little complex and varied. One could get bogged down, and I don't want to get bogged down here. I am no academic, and this is not an academic treatise. Suffice to say that often a household living in poverty is defined by Trust for London as one with an income beneath 60 per cent of the median household income in that year. And as Elaine observes, relative deprivation was made much worse during and after COVID-19. This global crisis (ignoring the significant health issues for a moment) made the gulf between the haves and the have-nots very much larger than it was.

A deprived start in life is so often an enduring disadvantage and barrier to attainment. The educational achievements and health outcomes of those from such backgrounds are markedly worse than those of the other 60 per cent, and their subsequent achievement in adult life is lower too.

Few of this 40 per cent have an effective voice in adulthood, adding to the sense of being 'forgotten' – of their being unable to escape the circumstances of destitution and hardship. The problems are perpetuated. A lost generation follows on from a lost generation. It is a cycle which should sit uneasily with politicians of all persuasions, and which needs to be broken.

In order to understand more about the Forgotten 40 programme, I spoke to another husband and wife pair which has been very closely involved with it from the outset: Brian Padgett and Sheila Loughlin. Both have worked for very many years in the school system, and both have been Ofsted inspectors.

They were articulate – as you might well expect – and their sense of frustration was palpable: 'really', Brian said, 'it is quite an angry feeling'. That much was obvious. It was a quiet, measured outrage expressed in words which, when I spoke to them, were powerfully reflective.

Interestingly what most moved them – as they told me directly – was the same story referred to by Elaine and John, printed in the *Sunday Times* in January 2020 about children in disadvantaged circumstances simply not being treated to the small things that bring so much pleasure to almost all children (surely all children in the UK at least?) at the close of the year. 'This is wrong, you know, these kids haven't got Christmas dinner', Brian splutters. 'They're not having Christmas presents, in Britain in the twenty-first century? This *can't be true* – we must do something.'

As he said, this is certainly not a new problem – not something that we can blame on the pandemic, even if that indubitably made things worse. 'Seventy years, we've been trying to tackle this issue. Why is it that kids from poor backgrounds simply don't do as well as kids from rich backgrounds? And it's never got better'. We are the fifth wealthiest country in the world, he said, despairingly. It needn't be this way: this is a *political* decision.

We have ample resources to resolve this issue should we so wish. This sort of extreme poverty could be eradicated, but 'we choose not to do so'. Children from poor backgrounds are made to feel as if their under-achievement is *entirely up to them*: that 'it's their fault'. It is of course not their fault. The only question – and where Brian and I might differ – is over the solution. But in terms of the efficacy of what INEOS is doing, we agree entirely.

Sheila did not talk as much as Brian, but she very clearly feels pre-cisely the same way, and no less passionately. She talked about how much worse the gap in the experience of children in different social groups became during the pandemic. Suddenly children who had spent 85 per cent of their time at home – a large percentage already of course – were spending 100 per cent of it there, and schools were quite unable to do what they had formerly been able to do, in terms of equal-izing the unavoidable and very stark differences in domestic experiences.

What they found then, not surprisingly, was 'a huge gap' – a gap that was even wider than before – 'between the experience of [more privileged children] and those children who were in disadvantaged areas'. For the disadvantaged children, she lamented, 'life just stopped – absolutely'.

I am writing towards the end of 2022, a year – very unusually – of three prime ministers. Soaring inflation and a dire economic forecast, certainly not helped by the political chaos which has been affecting the UK look set to affect deprived households very particularly. For the Forgotten 40, meanwhile, matters seem certain only to get worse. And, in spite of their very great need right now, they are in danger of becom-ing less visible – more forgotten – than ever.

It is impossible even for those who are not on what is commonly known as the 'breadline' to be unaware of food prices rocketing upwards. For the affluent, or at least the comfortable, this might mean fewer trips to restaurants, where the prices on menus tell their own story. For the poor it is much more important, and more depressing, being simply about scraping by. All of this only makes the help INEOS is able to offer them that much more important. As Sheila said, for pretty much the first time in any of our lives, she is aware of a sense that things are not getting better. She was not talking about short-term economic downturns, which of course have always taken place. But in general in the past there was a sense that, for our children's generation, things would be better than they are for ours:

'There was always that sense that things were getting better. It was getting better for us, and maybe it will be better for the next generation. And that's – that's gone.'

What has replaced it, she lamented, is 'a sense of helplessness'. Brian entirely agreed. (I was going to say that he agreed 'enthusiastically' but of course he couldn't be less enthusiastic about it.) And it's very personal: 'I mean, I'm a miner's son from South Yorkshire, I had free education in primary school, I didn't have to pay when I went to university.' Now, he sighs, when you look at certain pockets of the country – particularly in the north of England – they've had the industrial heart ripped out of them. 'These are devastated communities.'

There are obviously issues at play which are long term. To return briefly, though, to the very damaging impact of the recent pandemic, there is no escaping the fact that its consequences fell in a manner which was markedly uneven and very unfair. It was uneven in terms of class, uneven in terms of ethnicity and uneven in terms of age.

Just as certain older age groups in society, as well as certain ethnic groups, were most at risk health-wise, so certain younger age groups suffered a much greater impact in terms of the measures which were taken to combat the virus. Some of the least affected in terms of the health risks of COVID-19 were the most affected in terms of the impact which the measures to combat the pandemic had upon their lives. Most of them had older relatives, or knew others who were gravely affected, so they could have understood the reasons for the tight restrictions. But it could have all seemed very unfair nevertheless.

Even if everyone was in some way affected, it was also true that the severity of the impact depended enormously upon personal circumstances. The closure of schools and of other educational institutions, for instance, affected some children, some teenagers and some young adults much more than it did others. For those at university, or doing public examinations at school, the impact was very severe. Attempts were certainly made to keep life going. And it was possible to interact more using modern technology than it would have been, under similar conditions, even a decade ago. But it is impossible not to be conscious that much of university life, and much of school life, is social as well as purely educational.

Zoom, and the internet generally, helped to reduce isolation substantially. But we cannot pretend that these could entirely compensate for what was lost. Drinks parties or discos worked poorly over Zoom. That kind of communication works much better as a way to preserve existing relationships than it does as a means to form new ones.

Furthermore, large sections of the community – disproportionately those who are impoverished and disadvantaged – were unable to capitalize even upon the advantages which the internet could provide because of a lack of the necessary equipment, skills or social support.

Home life came to represent 100 per cent of a youngster's experience. It was a massive change. Suddenly the quality of a school was no longer able to serve as a counterbalance, was no longer able to act, as it can in normal life, to equalize differences. It goes without saying that the nature of that home life varied to a vast degree. And simple fortune played a significant and undeniable part in that variation. What INEOS has tried to do is not to offset entirely the importance of fortune – that, sadly, would be an impossible undertaking – but at least to mitigate it.

I have mentioned the critical role played by schools, which was highlighted all too obviously during the pandemic. It is no coincidence that this Forgotten 40 initiative has sought to work with and through primary schools, as by far the best way of reaching all children from a young age in the environment which (in normal times anyway) they were in almost every day.

At first the approach was purely consultative. What INEOS wanted to discover was simply the best means of directing resources in order to provide meaningful assistance. Much of the objection, after all, to high levels of taxation, focuses upon the high level of waste – money that is gathered but not then spent in a good cause. So the means of minimizing this waste, and of effectively targeting the philanthropy, was all-important.

What INEOS decided to do, therefore, was to select a number of primary schools, in some of the most disadvantaged postcodes in the UK, and then consult head teachers at those schools about the best way of making a meaningful difference to the childhood of their pupils. What it also sought to do was to improve communication between these schools such that experiences, and ideas, could be shared. To this end a newsletter, a website, and regular conferences were organized, to allow all schools to pool their ideas, to share what they found had worked well or not so well, and their thoughts about what might be done differently in future years. It is probably no surprise that Elaine in particular enthusiastically backed the general approach of consulting head teachers. After all, for much of her career, she was one! But I have to say that it makes considerable sense to me.

Head teachers after all are deeply embedded in their local communities. The quantity of additional administration for them or for their schools to be involved in the Forgotten 40 projects would be minimal. The cross-section of society that they see would vary enormously from school to school, but in general the head teacher of a local state primary school sees a broad slice of local life. Better almost than anyone, therefore, they understand the lives and the needs of their students and are in a pretty unique position both to identify these needs and to suggest ways of addressing them. They can identify barriers to learning – be they social, emotional, family issues or issues of mental health – and they can best work to resolve them.

As you might expect, or hope, a huge amount of feedback was received, although Brian talked amusingly about the unsurprising difficulty that they encountered in getting schools to believe in their intention simply to give them large sums of money with no strings attached. OK, he was frequently asked, what's the catch, what are you selling? The female voice, he told me, was found to be somehow more persuasive in this context than the male one – and often Elaine or Sheila were tasked for this reason with the duty of making the initial contact with schools.

What became all too clear in the course of the Forgotten 40 trial phase was simply the quite enormous differences which affected different communities. No useful 'one size fits all' approach towards improving childhoods was discovered. And it turned out that this was because there really wasn't one. This was itself a useful thing to know. It prevented the scheme from doing what central government has too often done in the past: wasting time looking for something which did not exist, or wasting huge sums of money on the assumption that it did. What was needed, on the contrary, was the freedom for local communities to come up with their own creative solutions, suited to the needs of their particular environment.

So, in September 2020, a pilot for Forgotten 40 kicked off. A group of head teachers, drawn from twenty primary schools serving some of the most disadvantaged communities in the UK, were each granted a £20,000 donation for the academic year. In each case, they could use the donation with considerable freedom, putting the money towards whichever initiatives seemed likely to them to make the largest difference in terms of transforming the childhoods of their pupils. While the money could not be spent on additional teaching staff, very few other limits were placed upon its use.

Plenty of very creative concepts were tested, and the money was spent upon a wide range of 'enrichment' activities: organizing a student breakfast club, buying reading books and setting up a two day reading festival, a food bank or Christmas hampers and presents for children in need (inspired, clearly, by that influential newspaper article), cultural residential visits for years five and six, Google Chromebooks with paid internet connections for those without computer access, musical instruments and tuition for all children.

It has always been absolutely key to the Forgotten 40 programme that impact did not need to be short term or indeed measured in any way. Short-term, measurable things are what the government does. Here the interventions could be long term and non-specific. Sheila talks about the astonishing impact of all sorts of things which were outside these children's normal experience, like going to the seaside, seeing cliffs, seeing the horizon and learning the language around these things. Somewhere which might physically be quite close but which, for many children, was an entirely new world:

> 'These children have such limited opportunities for broadening horizons and enrichment in their lives. And that's a real block. When you talk about, say, sheep and cows – they haven't seen them. If you talk about the railway – they haven't been on a train.'

You could *see* the distinct difference that this kind of experience made, she insisted, even if you couldn't measure it. Brian nodded his head vigorously in agreement:

> 'You take this child to Chester Zoo, and somewhere down the line, they pick up on animal welfare, and make a career. You don't know that's going to happen. It may not happen for everybody. And it may not happen for a while. But this is what education does for you.'

These sorts of things were only some of the ideas which were put to the test. There really was no 'normal'. One head teacher mentioned by Sheila and Brian had spent the money on the construction of an outdoor swimming pool, under a marquee, so that children at his school could learn to swim much more easily – something that had, he reported, proved an absolutely fabulous improvement for the school.

One thing that was fundamental to the programme was that the money was provided *directly* to the schools. There was no middle layer of bureaucracy, with all the waste that would involve. The concepts tested were designed by teachers, and, throughout, the tests were carried out in consultation with teachers. At all points the idea was to utilize the long-acquired expertise with children of those who work with them day in, day out.

In general, the pilot was a huge success. All twenty head teachers remarked upon the positive difference that the additional funding had made in the lives of their pupils. What they were talking about, and what INEOS had always intended, was that the benefit would be seen not simply in the raising of attainment. The effects of poverty are much more diverse and the aim was to target them all. And since INEOS's intention had always been to increase their understanding of 'scalable interventions' which could then be applied more broadly, the team involved made the decision – not, fortunately, a difficult one – to continue and to expand the programme, building a network of a hundred head teachers in primary schools that served the most deprived areas in the country.

Through this enlarged programme, concentrating on the same enrichment activities, the hope is to ensure meaningful change in the lives of many thousands of children. The hope is to expand horizons: gang violence, to cite only one example of the effects of deprivation, makes much less sense once one realizes that the estate, or the local area, is not the world. The hope is to inspire. And to motivate. To make dreams, and aspirations, possible. To ensure that no children feel trapped: that escape from a deprived environment feels conceivable, and possible.

The hope is to make those who grow up feeling like they are forgotten, feel that there are people who remember them. The signs are that it has been working, in what has been a peculiarly difficult period, and that it will continue to work.

The INEOS graduate scheme

Thus far the initiatives about which we have talked have been ones targeting children. They are ones in which the hope, obviously, is that the changes to many of the children's lives, and to their habits, will prove lifelong. They are the ones for whom, as a rule, the largest percentage of their lives lies in front of them – for whom major, life-changing decisions have not yet been taken, and for whom any changes, in that sense, will make the biggest difference.

When we are talking about the 'next generation', though, we must also include those who, although they are adults already, are definitely young and at the outset of their professional careers. Their entire working lives lie in front of them. Not just *work,* mind you. Most of their *lives* lie in front of them.

The world when they retire will look very different to the world in which we live today. I'm not a professional historian. But history has always been a real love of mine, and indeed I studied it at university. From the reading I've done, it seems fair to say that at no point in the past has it been more true than it feels right now that a few decades will mean a very fundamental change in the world.

For most of human history, the planet that people left when they died was pretty much the same one that they came into when they were born, however far and in whatever direction they ran when they were alive. These days, though, technological change feels like it is on fast-forward. Even the world of my childhood – no home computers, no internet, few electronic gadgets at home of any kind – feels very alien to the one in which children live now.

INEOS may not be able to change the world to the extent that these innovations have changed the way we live now. It is an ambitious company, and likes taking on large projects – but that might just be too large even for them. It can, though, try to help, and perhaps in a small way to shape, its environment and its employees in a constructive and a positive way.

It is fair to say that habits acquired now can have a decisive and formative role in shaping the futures of these young employees. They might be in their twenties. They might even, God forbid, be in their thirties! But that is not too late. This is about *potential*. No less than it is for a baby or a small child. We might be done with formal education by adulthood. We might be done with school and higher institutions. But we are still learning. Learning a lot I should say about learning being lifelong!

This, for INEOS, is the focus. It's a cliché but it's true: all that anyone can hope to do is to maximize their potential. All they can hope to do is to make the most of the skills which nature has granted them. Be the best that they can be. Nobody could ask more than that – and the fact that INEOS has employed them of course indicates that the company must have seen considerable potential in them and that they have a good reason for confidence.

The thought of arriving in later life bearing an all-consuming sense of regret, a sense of never having pushed in order to learn where our limits lie, seems tragic to me. Of course, for most people the limit is rather less clear-cut than it is with the world record for running a certain distance. Most people are content simply to be good at things rather than to be the best ever in the history of humanity. I know – in almost every area of my life, that has always been true for me too.

The principle is the same regardless. I was once told a quotation attributed to the poet T. S. Eliot which struck a chord. 'Only those who will risk going too far', he is supposed to have said, 'can possibly find out how far one can go.'

This, I have always thought, is true in athletics and it is true in life. At the right time, one needs to throw caution to the winds. One does need to pick the right time, of course. We want to risk going too far – to risk 'blowing up' – at a time when it wouldn't matter much if we did. At the wrong time, the consequences can be very severe.

One thinks of those cyclists in the Tour de France race who expend too much energy riding up a mountain, and who lose as a result a catastrophic (catastrophic in sporting terms of course) amount of time, in the process ruining their race – and ruining many months of training. But they do need to do it in training. Because often this might mean the discovery that one can travel much further or much faster than one realized one could.

Imagine the confidence that is given to a cyclist – to continue the analogy – by the knowledge, regularly tried and tested, of one's maximum output. One can push with so much more confidence – just as one could if driving a car that one knew capable, if necessary, of travelling faster whenever required, at only the touch of a pedal.

Almost everyone will be familiar with driving on the edge. At maximum speed, or, more likely, with an empty fuel tank – the fuel light resolutely on. It isn't a relaxing experience. It instils the opposite of confidence. And, of course, there is so much else that we want people – whether in sport, or business, or just in life – to focus upon.

A chance to test your limits

That's why INEOS offers the Nambia challenge, known as the 'In Nam' project, to its fourth year graduates, those who are in their fourth year of employment at INEOS in the Core Graduate Programme. For six days they are offered the opportunity to complete a 320 kilometre run, cycle and hike through the Namibian desert. A nine-month training programme prepares them for this unique challenge. For recent graduates, setting out on their careers, what better time to discover their limits in a safe environment? This, it seems to me, is what the challenge in Namibia is all about. It is an extraordinary adventure in itself. It is the sort of thing most people are very unlikely to do in the course of their day-to-day life. It is a place to which they have probably not been. It is the sort of thing that they will remember, and which will make an impression. It is about so much more than a memorable holiday.

The Namibia challenge is an opportunity for those who are involved to learn about themselves, to go to places mentally that they have not been, and to make changes which will be important throughout their working lives – throughout their lives. Knowing where their limits are breeds confidence – a lasting confidence which will make a genuine difference throughout the years and the decades ahead.

From a rainy, wintry Europe I spoke to safari guide Phill Steffny, who is in South Africa, many hundreds of miles to the south. For many years now Phill has run the 'In Nam' – a project which he knows is renowned among competing organizations, since he has run safaris for leaders at other large companies who have spoken about it in inquisitive, almost reverential tones. Once graduates have signed up (and, as he is quick to emphasize, it is by no means compulsory that they do), he takes charge of leading them through the many months of training. Building towards, and culminating in, what must to most if not all seem a completely unimaginable endeavour: more than three hundred kilometres of hiking, running and cycling through the Namibian wilderness.

A voice call is technically simpler than a video one, so I made do with mental images. He was jovial, and an excellent talker who's confessed to being much happier in speech than in writing. You can tell what good company he would make on a safari, which is what he has been doing since his late teens. It was his summer when we spoke, which is – counterintuitively for northern Europeans like me – the off-season for him in terms of leading safaris.

It isn't only this that is counterintuitive. The world in which he lives, and the life he leads, are so unrecognizably different from those of most Europeans that I felt as excited to talk to him as I had talking to Elaine – despite the hundreds of miles of distance between them. Indeed, there was much which struck me as quite similar about their general attitude – to other people and to what we can all achieve. And I was often reminded of something that Elaine had said or done while I was talking to Phill. They both back the *underdog*. And this is also why they are both so closely aligned with Jim, and why he found kindred spirits in them.

They all love that person who is willing to put themselves out there – that person who is willing to give something a go, despite not feeling that an activity plays to any core strength. 'That is Jim's philosophy in life, you know', Phill told me. 'Go for it; open that door, get your backside in there, because you're not going to die – you'll only benefit.'

Since this is the off-season for him, Phill uses the time primarily to train. Which meant that on the morning that I spoke to him, a weekday morning, he had spent a couple of hours surfing. And then he had gone for a long run – fifteen kilometres – in the mountains above Cape Town. In the afternoon, he thought that he might play a round of golf. For most people all of this (or some of this) might sound like the activities for a day out of the office. For Phill, it is essential preparation for his professional life. Even if, as he did admit, it is 'not everyone's idea of work, I guess!'

During the 'In Nam' expedition, the graduates scale the Brandberg mountain, the local Namibian landmark which seems to 'burn' in the setting sun. It is something that fewer than one hundred people do every year, more than half of them from INEOS. There, in the deep darkness of the African night, they sleep out under an astonishing canopy of stars. By day they might see rare desert black rhino, or even lions, in their natural habitat.

An important part of his job, Phill told me, is to make sure that those taking part appreciate what they are seeing: 'because', he emphasized, 'it's special'. It is so far outside what might constitute the normal run of things. The whole experience might well, as he said, be the single most memorable achievement of many participants' lives. They will tell their kids about it, he assured me. It stays with them, and they pass it on.

He recalled how the experience of meeting and talking with Jim Ratcliffe was, for him, one that was utterly life changing. Hard as it is now to believe, he used to be, he told me, significantly overweight. He might have led safaris, but he was a big drinker and a big eater. For both activities, he said with a wry laugh, he played for the first team. He had never so much as owned a pair of sports shoes. If you were to look at a photograph of him then, he admitted, and compare it with him now, you would hardly recognize him as the same person.

Then one day Jim and a group of runners who were in training for an ultramarathon persuaded him to join them, refusing to take no for an answer. '"Get off your fat arse, you'll like it", they insisted', he laughed, '"even if you only run one kilometre." And that', Phill told me, 'is the kind of ethos, in terms of the whole programme.'

Jim's attitude, he recalled, was relentlessly positive. You can do this. What have you got to lose? 'He never looked at me', Phill chuckles, 'and said, "geez, you'd better sit down, you're going to have a heart attack"'. It was always, for him, the other way around and that, Phill told me, is really the pitch now to each year group of INEOS graduates. 'Anyone can do this. You don't have to, but here's an opportunity. I'm telling you, you're going to love it!'

Phill also told me about the extraordinary experience of one INEOS graduate which remains etched in his mind. A man who, much like his own younger self of course (and no doubt this in part was why it made such an impression) was massively overweight – perhaps six hundred pounds, extremely unfit, and the very last person one could imagine completing a challenge like this one:

'Big, big fella, but he signed himself up, and he turned out to be the most incredible team player . . . He was just so joyful, so appreciative of what he'd actually managed to get himself to do. You know, he had tears summiting the Brandberg. Tears of achievement. I don't think that he thought that he could manage it. He never stopped, he never complained. His result in my mind was one of the most incredible results – I do think it's one of the best achievements of his life.'

This long expedition in the wilderness of Namibia all sounds utterly remote and utterly idyllic and utterly unattainable. But Phill would say that stories like this one show that it is *not*. Not unattainable. For anyone.

And when these graduates return to business life, wherever in the world they are, they will have acquired resources which they can reuse in a very different environment, because there is much which is transferable:

'The concept of being patient, being rigorous in your preparation, having the grit to drill through the hard times, having the sense of humour to manage the difficulties, but also being aware of what's going on around you and taking it all into account. The idea really in Jim's mind is if you can get yourself through a marathon, you will have learned your mind and the ability to push through way more than somebody that hasn't. That then relates to a tough negotiation, for example, where you're being pushed hard by your competitors. It's a similar mindset. You can't rush into it. You can't make rash decisions.'

These are benefits for taking part for the long term – benefits to their careers at INEOS, benefits for the company, but first and foremost benefits to the participants' lives. No wonder it is an experience that participants recall with such fondness.

Conclusion

So what is it that unites these three quite different projects? Well, I would say that they are all about laying the basis for a future that is better. All of them have at their heart a fundamental belief that the future *can* be better than the present, and that it is worth making assumptions on that basis.

I would say that they are all *optimistic* projects. Of course, like all charitable endeavours, they recognize shortfalls in the present which they attempt to improve. Spectacles are not rose-tinted. But they also focus upon a future which can be brighter. Let's walk towards the sun, they seem to say, towards that mountain which is reflecting – which seems almost to burn – in the warm evening light, because it is brighter there.

I remember something John Mayock said to me in this regard. He was talking about what it was that the three owners of INEOS all had in common. He mentioned innovation, creativity, taking risks, taking ownership and so on, but he also mentioned *forward thinking* – thinking about the future, not about a past that one can't alter or change in any way. This, it struck me, is really what these projects all have in common.

The benefits of doing daily exercise at school, or of enjoying the many different provisions which the Forgotten 40 programme allows access to, or of undertaking a unique adventure in the Namibian wilderness as a young adult, are all ones that can be felt immediately. But they are also, more importantly perhaps, ones that can change somebody's life fundamentally, for the better, and for the long term.

Many of us, perhaps, have been sufficiently fortunate to have been on nice holidays, or had nice periods in our lives which haven't left any lasting impression. That adjective 'nice' rather says it all. We might have sat in the sun by a swimming pool, or on a beach, or somewhere similar. It was lovely *at the time*. It might very well have felt restorative and important if we had been tired or stressed or both. I am certainly not downplaying this: batteries need to be recharged. But it probably did not leave an impact that was in any way lasting.

All of the projects discussed here are meant to be very much more than that. If you learn to swim, or to love books, or animals, or hills, or the countryside; if you learn to appreciate the joys of physical fitness and activity and get to appreciate that your limits – physical and mental – are further in the distance than you ever realized; if you learn to work better as a team and to appreciate for the first time how much more you can achieve that way: all of these are things which will remain with you not just in the short term, but for life.

It is this eye to the long term, I think, which has attracted INEOS to all of these projects. And it is this which private philanthropy can do much better, actually, than government can – because governments really can't think about the distant future. They are far too bound up with measurable improvement in the relatively short term. They can't say: well, maybe one day you will come to see that this experience was life changing. We think that it's worth the bet, and worth the investment, but in truth we just don't know.

INEOS can do this, though. It is making bets which it believes will prove to be good and valuable ones. It doesn't *know* that. It knows that not all of these bets will pay off. But it believes that some of them will – and it has good grounds for believing it.

This is the sort of belief in the value of its input, and of its investment, which has shaped all of INEOS's success in different areas of business life. There is no reason now not to believe that it will be true too of the next generation. What, after all, underpins the human desire to reproduce? Yes, of course, there are sexual instincts which we humans share with much of the animal world. But contraception has made reproduction – at least where it is available – a deliberate choice. And you cannot have children without also believing that the world for them, for the next generation, can be better than the world in which we live now. We want to make it so, and INEOS wants to do what it can to help in that journey.

8

A Helping Hand, Philanthropy

Sir Andrew Likierman

IN THE EARLY YEARS OF INEOS, philanthropy was not a big part of the story. But involvement by the company and by its founders has risen dramatically over the last few years.

It's not difficult to understand why. In the early years, the founders were completely focused upon growing the business. Indeed, at times they were battling to make sure that it survived at all. It goes without saying that there would not be any room for philanthropy if the core business was not proving successful.

As the business has matured, however – and indeed has become extremely successful – the founders have had both the time and the interest to look at what they can do for the communities in which they operate. To think, too, about making their contribution to some of the big issues which are facing the planet. The nature of the work that INEOS does means that it can play a leading role in efforts to protect the environment more broadly, in addition to the work that they do to reduce the impact of their own manufacturing processes on the natural world.

As with everything at INEOS, philanthropy is a fast-moving story. It goes without saying that the position set out in this chapter is true for 2023 – the company's twenty-fifth year.

What's covered in this chapter

Not all of INEOS's philanthropic activities fit neatly into this chapter alone. I don't think that a way of separating chapter themes perfectly exists. For this chapter, therefore, and for others, there are overlaps.

A car, for instance, is a consumer good. But it's a big deal, making a car, when you have no history in the carmaking industry, and in consequence INEOS Automotive gets a chapter in its own right, distinct from the Consumer chapter. Likewise, major philanthropic ventures – like the Forgotten 40 initiative, or The Daily Mile – are dealt with in the Next Generation chapter rather than here: because their main focus is upon the future, and upon a generation which is currently very young. Hopefully this makes sense, and needless repetition is avoided.

In some cases, of course, the rationale is clear cut. The Oxford INEOS Institute, for instance – the substantial research institution which concentrates upon antimicrobial resistance, a major concern for all of humanity – is one such example. Conservation projects in Iceland and in Africa are clearly and purely philanthropic, and therefore are covered in this chapter alone. There is no cause for doubt about which chapter to look for these in.

Some philanthropy, however, is linked to other aspects of the company's philosophy or operations. One example is the initiative to support the Royal Zoological Society's giant panda research. As part of this work, two giant pandas are now housed in Edinburgh Zoo – the only animals of their kind in the UK and one of only three pairs in Europe. This support not only combines conservation with education but is also based upon a community initiative, since it is the result of the decision by INEOS's Grangemouth plant to provide local support. But this initiative was, nevertheless, clearly linked to what the company was doing: in this case, a refining joint venture with PetroChina.

I have mentioned philanthropic initiatives like The Daily Mile which are dealt with elsewhere. The hand sanitizer initiative is another, of course. The decision to produce this as fast as possible at the beginning of the COVID pandemic was a way of helping the NHS at a time of great stress – clearly a philanthropic venture. It was only when COVID abated that it became, subsequently, a commercial operation. Nevertheless, because it has clearly now become a part of INEOS Hygienics – a commercial venture – it is dealt with in the Consumer chapter rather than here.

It is worth mentioning another possible area of confusion. In the case of some philanthropic activities, the founders might be involved in a personal capacity rather than with their INEOS hat on, so to speak. Some of these ventures are covered but not all, largely depending upon their personal preference.

Four principal themes

The philanthropic initiatives taken over the past few years are grouped together loosely by the company into four main categories – health, community, education and conservation. The largest number of initiatives are in health, with seven, while community has four initiatives and the other two have three each. The financial amounts involved, though, vary enormously, from a few pounds for many local community gifts, such as kit for a women's football team, to £100 million for the INEOS Oxford Institute – a donation which would fund a fair few football strips. The local community initiatives undertaken by individual INEOS sites come under the community umbrella, though in practice the giving from individual sites covers a wide variety of charitable activities.

As noted, INEOS does often and inevitably combine areas of philanthropic interest, so that these four categories are far from being discrete. GO Run for Fun and The Daily Mile, for instance, combine health and education with community. The health of schoolchildren is something that is important for society as a whole so it is concerned with more than

the wellbeing of individual children. The programme is also about providing help for the schools which constitute such an important influence
in the children's lives. Similarly, the Forgotten 40 initiative, also dealt
with at length in the Next Generation chapter, seeks to deal with issues
of deprivation in certain areas of the UK by letting schools judge what
will give them the best chance of addressing the problems that they face.

Let us take a look at the specific philanthropic initiatives which fall
under each of the four main categories – including, under community,
one example of philanthropy undertaken by an individual INEOS site.

HEALTH

INEOS Oxford Institute

The scale of this initiative, involving a donation of £100 million over
five years, dwarfs all of the others in the health category – which is
scarcely surprising in view of the huge scale of the donation involved.
Resistance to antibiotics (or Antimicrobial Resistance – AMR) is one of
the world's greatest global health challenges. According to *The Lancet* it
already causes an estimated 1.27 million excess deaths per year globally,
and this figure is expected to rise to ten million per year by 2050.

The nature of the challenge is set out in the description of the project:

'The alarming – and escalating – development of bacterial resistance
to antibiotics will be the primary focus of the institute. Without effective antibiotics, the world will no longer be able to fight many
common bacterial infections, making taken for granted procedures
like caesareans, organ transplants, joint replacements and many cancer treatments unviable. In a post-antibiotic world, even a simple cut
may have dire consequences.'

Obviously these include the immediate health implications. But quite
apart from the mortality and these health implications, there are also

the economic effects of lost output to consider – and these are likely to affect low- and middle-income countries in particular. So why is this happening? Well, the institute has identified two main causes. One is global overuse of antibiotics, in humans but also – particularly – in animals and agriculture. The second is simply that too little work has been done in this field for decades.

The institute sees its first task as being to understand and to address the global scale of the antibiotic resistance problem. It has said that it will be working on developing animal-specific antibiotics for use in agriculture: these then might be used instead of the 80 per cent of anti-biotics currently used in agriculture which are estimated to be human drugs. This very widespread usage in agriculture is, not surprisingly perhaps, significantly increasing resistance to those antibiotic drugs which are available for human treatments.

The institute will perform part of the more general research effort which is looking to identify novel human antibiotics. And finally, there is a goal in terms of communication and action: both to increase public awareness of the problem of AMR, and then to influence public policy in the field of effective antibiotic stewardship – in the direction of mak-ing it harder, hopefully, for resistance to develop.

It is not an accident that Oxford is the focus of the AMR initiative. The university has a long history of research in the field, going right back to the 1940s and the discovery of penicillin, which scientists at Oxford first developed into a viable human medicine. The driving force now behind the AMR initiative is the orthopaedic surgeon, David Sweetnam. It was his passion, as well as the vast importance of the issue, which first attracted the attention of INEOS.

In part, no doubt, because of the size of the donation and of the global importance of the research, the project is different to other phil-anthropic initiatives – in the way that it involves senior INEOS management, and the way that regular meetings take place between INEOS and leaders of the AMR Institute. The objective is to ensure that academics are able to maximize their impact. As the announcement about the setting up of the institute put it, the company:

'... can add more value than simply funding. Famous for delivering complex, large scale, ambitious manufacturing and sporting projects, INEOS will lend its management expertise to the Institute while safeguarding the total academic freedom of its research scientists. We believe this close association to be a promising, powerful alliance.'

It is in the interests of all of humanity that the partnership does indeed prove, over the coming years, to be as fruitful and productive as all its participants hope that it will be.

Defence Medical Rehabilitation Centre

In 2019, INEOS donated more than £25 million to the UK's new Defence Medical Rehabilitation Centre (DMRC) for wounded British soldiers. The bequest was for the sum that was needed in order to complete the fundraising campaign for this facility, which was being built in order to replace the former Ministry of Defence (MOD) rehabilitation centre at Headley Court in Surrey. Specifically, the money was earmarked to fund the facility's new prosthetics wing, intended to enable those who have lost limbs to get the very best treatment and support.

The establishment of the new facility on the Stanford Hall estate in Nottinghamshire builds upon the work of the late Duke of Westminster. It was he who first conceived the idea of a rehabilitation centre for injured servicemen and women, which had the potential also to help NHS patients.

The DMRC is one of the world's most advanced clinical rehabilitation centres, providing expert care and facilities for members of the British Armed Forces since 2019. The new prosthetics wing opening in late 2024 will serve wounded servicemen and women who are in rehabilitation following traumatic injuries sustained in action. It can also help civilians, thanks to the first ever specialist NHS rehabilitation facility which is constructed on the same site. At the same time, it functions as a training facility for specialists across the UK.

Former corporal Andy Reid – who lost limbs when stepping on a bomb while on a routine foot patrol in Afghanistan in 2009 – talked about how the new INEOS Prosthetics Wing will be able to make a massive difference to wounded servicemen and women. 'I know from my own experience how important it is to have the right facilities as well as the correct expertise to help people through their rehabilitation,' he said, 'because the journey back from major injury is tough.' INEOS's help does not stop the journey being tough, but it does make it manageable.

Walking With The Wounded
Another initiative that seeks to help wounded veterans is Walking With The Wounded. This is a charity working to help injured former servicemen and women in the British Armed Forces move across from the military to civilian life. It includes the provision to vulnerable veterans of security and independence through employment.

Part of the shift to peacetime life involves the surmounting of significant challenges – and with these of course INEOS is perfectly geared to assist, given the company's love of and regular use of expeditions. It holds them, for instance, for its own young graduate employees: a long trek through the Namibian wilderness mentioned in the Next Generation chapter. Walking With The Wounded has organized for teams of injured veterans to take on similarly major trials, including the dragging of sleds to the South Pole or the climbing of Mount Everest. These expeditions serve both to raise awareness of the cause and also to raise impressive sums of money for the charity's work.

One recent example of the way that INEOS gets involved with the charities that it supports was seen, for instance, at the time of Walking With The Wounded's tenth birthday. Following a very significant donation of £150,000, INEOS (including the INEOS Grenadier team) was at the time of writing supporting a team of veterans in their attempt to make a four-hundred-kilometre journey on foot through the harsh Empty Quarter desert of Oman.

The Daily Mile and GO Run for Fun

I will mention these initiatives here because they are clearly philanthropic in their aim – in this case to make running a regular feature of children's lives, all over the world. As has been mentioned, Sir Jim Ratcliffe is himself a keen runner who believes very strongly in the value of exercise, so it is scarcely surprising that their ambitions were ones that coincided with his own.

The Daily Mile initiative is featured in the Next Generation chapter so I will not explore it at length here. Suffice to say that INEOS's support of The Daily Mile Foundation started in 2016, after the Scottish Grangemouth site heard that schools near the site were involved. Since then, the company has gone further and supported research at Imperial College London into the impact and efficacy of The Daily Mile programme.

At the time of writing, the programme has involved sixteen thousand schools and over four million children around the world. It is very major indeed. And there are further, extraordinarily ambitious plans to help make this a truly global initiative by involving *all primary schools globally*.

GO Run for Fun was one of the very first INEOS philanthropic initiatives. A foundation was originally set up with the help of Newcastle's Great Run Company, founded by the athlete Brendan Foster and designed to encourage primary school children to exercise with their friends. It is now supported by a team of international sporting ambassadors, one of the most prominent being Eliud Kipchoge, whose association with INEOS has of course been close since the company helped to fund and to organize his successful attempt upon the two hour marathon barrier.

Other prominent ambassadors include Sir Andy Murray, Sir Mo Farah, Lady Tanni Grey-Thompson and Paula Radcliffe. By 2022, more than three hundred and fifty thousand children in eleven countries had taken part. The events are usually held near INEOS sites, and the company supports the events with volunteers, many drawn from the local INEOS plants. To date over ten thousand INEOS employees have joined in. One GO Run for Fun event in France in the autumn of 2022 was reported upon as follows:

'Lavéra, Marseille, played host to two and a half thousand children from eighteen schools. Some unusually mild weather saw temperatures reaching twenty-one degrees. One of the hallmark events of the year, the day saw children take part in a two kilometre run as well as fun workshops on vortex throwing, long jump and health and wellbeing. During the lunch break a special guest, Monseigneur Christian Delarbre, gave a brief address to the children and staff before the start of the afternoon session. The local athletics club (Athletic Club Miramas) provided some brilliant demonstrations of hurdles and long jump for the children with the local athletes showing off their skills.'

GO Run for Fun also has a Global Buddying Programme which pairs up schools internationally so that they can complete activities together. Furthermore, it runs a pupil-led educational programme which provides resources to enhance children's health and wellbeing. As with The Daily Mile, there are ambitious plans to expand these activities: it is planned that schools in more countries will join the eleven which are already involved, while the pupil-led programme is being developed into a broader activity series in partnership with The Daily Mile Foundation.

Southampton Children's Hospital

INEOS was founded near Southampton and has always had either its headquarters or an administrative office in the area. Reflecting the continuing interest in the local community that INEOS has maintained, the company donated the last £500,000 to the £2 million campaign to fund a children's emergency and trauma department at Southampton Hospital.

Until the department was opened it had been necessary to treat children in the adult Accident and Emergency department. The campaign to raise the necessary funding for a distinct unit was spearheaded by the Southampton Hospitals Charity and by the Murray Parish Trust. The latter was founded by Sarah Parish and James Murray, two members of the acting profession who lost their daughter, Ella-Jayne, to a congenital heart defect.

The new unit includes a children's emergency X-ray department and a short stay unit. More than that, it aims to address directly the profoundly unsettling experience of a child being in hospital. So there is a specialist sedation room, an area for observed play, a child-adapted X-ray department, distraction equipment to help prepare children for tests and an eight bed short stay area for children requiring longer observation or treatment. In every conceivable way the environment is designed to ease anxiety and to provide distraction during procedures and tests, giving children, young people, and their families privacy and dignity at a time when they are likely to be frightened, in pain or both.

Jeneen Thomson of the Southampton Hospitals Charity commented on how the local community had rallied to the cause:

'We couldn't do what we do without the support of our local businesses and community. They have literally changed care for thousands of our young patients.'

The thing which most struck Sarah Parish and James Murray – as well, of course, as the positive decision to advance significant financial help – was the extraordinary pace of decision-making at INEOS, by comparison with their experience of many philanthropic organizations:

'What's unique about dealing with the kind people at INEOS is the speed with which they decide if a campaign is a worthy cause or not. Where so often bureaucracy hampers progress in the charity sector, INEOS recognizes the importance of a swift decision.'

COVID-19 pandemic

Reaction within INEOS at the time of the outbreak of the COVID-19 pandemic in the early months of 2020 was to ask themselves in what way they could help.

The company was aware that the large volumes of ethanol and iso-propyl alcohol (IPA) that it produced in Europe could potentially help to stop the spread of the coronavirus, since these were ingredients of disinfectant hand gel. It therefore diverted resources and the necessary chemicals from non-essential work at a number of sites in the United States, mainland Europe and the UK in order to provide the means of doing so, as well as helping to protect those making medical materials and equipment.

In response to the British government's call for support in fighting the pandemic, the company decided to build new production lines for medical grade hand sanitizer, and to give the product away free to hospitals. They reacted with astonishing speed, taking only ten days to create new production lines in four countries – the UK, Germany, France and the US. You can read more about this extraordinary response at an extraordinary time – and about its long-term ramifications for INEOS, with the growth of INEOS Hygienics as a commercial operation – in the Consumer chapter. It should be said here, though, that further significant donations were made after the pandemic to Ukraine in 2022.

EDUCATION

The Forgotten 40

This again is a major philanthropic venture which I am only not exploring in depth here because I know that it has already been covered in the Next Generation chapter which obviously focuses in particular upon the future. The Forgotten 40 have not been forgotten for a second time. Far from it: the project to ensure that they are not forgotten is one of the most important that INEOS runs. But I would recommend reading about it at length there.

The 1851 Trust

The 1851 Trust is the charitable foundation that is linked to the UK sailing team which aims to win the America's Cup. So, what makes the year 1851 so special?

It is special because this is when the first America's Cup sailing race was held, initially known as the Hundred Guinea Cup. It was won in its first year by the yacht *America*, after which (not after the country or the continent) the trophy derived its lasting label. The charitable foundation was launched by Sir Ben Ainslie and Sir Keith Mills during their British challenge for the thirty-fifth America's Cup.

The trust uses the Cup – which has been called the 'Formula One of sailing' – to bring STEM subjects (science, technology, engineering and mathematics) to life. INEOS's support for the 1851 Trust provides (as the charity puts it) 'inspirational sporting contexts, expertise and funding'.

The INEOS-sponsored UK challenge for the America's Cup is documented at much greater length in the Sports chapter. Meanwhile two of the 1851 Trust's charitable programmes – known as STEM Crew and Rebels Crew – I will describe here.

STEM Crew

Established in 2014, STEM Crew uses its link with the America's Cup to inspire young people and to open their eyes to their own potential. It emphasizes that any success of the sailing team would extend far beyond the eleven strong crew. On the contrary, it would involve more than one hundred and twenty people in many different roles, and with many different skillsets.

The programme provides a range of teaching resources, targeted at eleven to sixteen year olds. It is designed to leave children feeling confident in their personal abilities, knowing that they could pursue a career as an athlete, as a designer, as a scientist or as an engineer. As Ben Cartledge, CEO of the charity, commented:

'We want to give them opportunity and ambition. It's all about making the experience as real as possible and relevant to their day-to-day lives. The America's Cup is a real combination of technology and teamwork . . . It's a coming together of different people from a lot of different backgrounds and skillsets, with the single aim of making the boat go as fast as possible.'

What support means in practice is that each week, around eight school groups attend workshops hosted at STEM Crew's base in Portsmouth, UK – the base which it shares with INEOS Britannia.

There they learn about the science behind sailing as well as behind conservation and sustainability. They also have access to interactive, hands-on exhibits which highlight the innovative technologies and materials used on the INEOS Britannia's America's Cup boat. From the techniques used in its construction to learning about hydraulics and hydrofoils, students come away with a much better understanding of how science and sport are linked.

In 2020 alone, more than three thousand teachers and two hundred thousand young people benefited from the STEM Crew programme. This is cutting-edge stuff, 'cool' in the way that much equally 'educational' material thrown at school-age children might not be. As Ben Cartledge says, teachers choose to use the resources because 'the content really delivers and it excites and inspires their students'.

Rebels Crew
This programme is targeted specifically at eleven- to fourteen-year-old students from disadvantaged backgrounds. As such, it aims particularly both to remove any barriers and to dispel the widespread myth that sailing is exclusive or unaffordable for those not coming from a privileged setting.

Through their schools, participants join a six to eight week sailing programme that not only gives them a taste of the sport but also helps them develop vital life skills. They are taught by a network of highly qualified instructors as well as being inspired by short films from INEOS Britannia sailors.

INEOS's support has allowed the programme to expand far beyond the sailing team's Portsmouth base to reach disadvantaged children right across the UK, in areas which include London, Liverpool, Manchester and Edinburgh. Before the COVID-19 pandemic forced the programme to pause its operations, three thousand pupils from sixty schools in some of the poorest communities in the UK had benefited from the opportunity to learn to sail. Nor is the benefit confined to those who take part directly. As Ben Cartledge commented: 'We find that the behaviour and motivation at school improves not only for those who are directly taking part but the rest of the school feels the benefits as well.'

London Business School

This is one charitable initiative in which I need to declare an interest. As dean of the London Business School (LBS) at the time, I was deeply concerned that we could lose our flagship building in Regent's Park when our lease ran out. We are constantly ranked among the best business schools in the world, but unlike the big US business schools, we do not have the endowment to make big payments of the kind which were needed to renew the lease.

So in 2016 I talked to Jim Ratcliffe, an alumnus of the school who graduated in 1980, about the possibility of financial help to get our lease extended as part of the first major fundraising campaign. According to *The Alchemists* – the book produced to mark the first twenty years of INEOS – at LBS Jim 'met ambitious, engaging and intelligent young high-fliers from all over the globe: an eclectic group of future business leaders for whom LBS was a nursery – a training ground for eventual entry into the highest levels of corporations round the world. He seemed to thrive in this environment . . .'

This seems to have been true, because, thrillingly for us, he provided the whole amount needed in order to give the school another one hundred and twenty-five years in the building. So our future in our current home (an iconic building designed by John Nash in 1823) was assured and the school has gone from strength to strength. As I said at the time:

'This will mean that future generations of students will have the benefit of studying in one of London's most beautiful and historically important buildings.'

As important as the gift itself was the signal that it gave to any future donors that one of the LBS's most successful alumni was prepared to back it. This undoubtedly helped the school to exceed its appeal target the year after the donation. It is also a pleasure for me that the relationship between the London Business School and INEOS has flourished since then, with the school helping to train many INEOS managers.

COMMUNITY

The Community Fund

Seeing as INEOS's plans are often a big presence in their communities, there has long been a recognition that the company has local responsibilities outside the factory gates. For Jim Ratcliffe it is clear: 'Being present in a community, it's the right thing to do.' It was the challenge of the COVID pandemic, however, which was the direct stimulus for setting up the INEOS Community Fund. It was then in particular that the company recognized that local charities and community organizations have a very special role to play in reaching some of the most vulnerable people in communities, in developing trusted relationships and in implementing support programmes. INEOS was also aware that the pandemic would threaten the very existence of some of these organizations.

The basis of the fund is that INEOS employees are asked to help identify and to support important local organizations that are most in need near their site or office. Grants of up to £10,000 are available to those addressing urgent social need created by the pandemic. This has included providing protection and care for the elderly, homeless, disabled and otherwise vulnerable, supporting food banks facing increased demand and providing support for those who have been the victims of domestic abuse and poor mental health. There has also been support to fund existing services such as hospices and care homes which were struggling with their finances because of the pandemic.

By the end of 2022, sixty-seven sites in fifteen countries have engaged with the fund – with nearly one hundred and sixty grants made. An example of what this means in practice for one single site – in this case, the Grangemouth plant in Scotland – is featured below.

The Community Fund in Grangemouth

The Grangemouth complex plays a huge role in the economy of Scotland, and the plant management takes relations with their local community – a large number of whom work there, of course – very seriously indeed.

The policy document that guides philanthropic giving by the plant identifies three elements that constitute what they call their Social Investment Strategy: supporting the local community; education (with the emphasis on encouraging science and engineering); and enterprise (described as 'leveraging our expertise to promote growth in the local economy and Scotland'). These three elements define the criteria for support, both financial as well as 'in kind' support through employee volunteering.

Andrew Gardner, chairman of INEOS Grangemouth, emphasized to me that he is not only keen to help locally. He believes also that the process of helping is important in terms of how those working in the plant see themselves in relation to the community around it. He is proud of the widespread involvement through volunteering by the Grangemouth staff, especially in relation to education. The web of local connections is strengthened in all sorts of ways. As well as personal involvement, he commented to me: 'Our charitable giving goes a long way to joining us with our own employees, and through them to the local community.'

He believes that this is particularly important bearing in mind the pockets of deprivation which exist very close to the plant, and it is with this in mind that the employees help out locally. For example, Kersiebank Community Project, based in Grangemouth town centre, provides a food bank as well as activities, support and learning opportunities for the local community.

The main impetus for local giving comes from employees who nominate local charities that they feel deserve support, as well as an initiative with the local union. Some charities have been supported over several years – the Kersiebank Community Project is one example. Another is Zetland Park, close to the Grangemouth plant, which has been renovated and was reopened after a big works programme in August 2022. The renovation received the help both of national charities and of the local authority. In this case, the aim of INEOS in providing funding was not only to help the park, but also to provide its volunteers with the means to raise other funding. A third source of regular funding is of Dux awards to Grangemouth High School.

As well as these examples, a wide variety of causes and projects have received specific donations. Some are local branches of national charities, such as Macmillan Cancer Support, the Scottish Association for Mental Health or Cerebral Palsy Scotland. Some are purely local causes, such as contributions to the Strathcarron Hospice, or to the Forth Valley Hospital children's ward's cystic fibrosis and diabetes team.

As is often the case with INEOS activities, there are links to the themes both of physical exercise and of young people. Some are specific grants, such as providing rugby kit for the local girls' team. Another example is support for any child wanting to attend Falkirk Football Club if accompanied by an adult, together with free coaching for children of employees.

Other initiatives are more long term. Grangemouth is active as part of the wider INEOS Tour de France initiative, in which teams undertake to match the kilometres cycled by the Tour de France competitors. Teams that complete every stage win €2,000 to donate to a children's charity of their choice. The Tour de Forth – a fundraising cycle ride around the river Forth on behalf of the Cash for Kids appeal, is another recipient of charitable funding, meeting multiple desirable criteria: being local, involving exercise and having a focus on children. The company commented:

'As a landmark along the route, the Grangemouth petrochemical site has been a feature of the Tour de Forth for many years and we recognise the importance of a healthy lifestyle . . .The Tour de Forth Challenge promotes the benefits of healthy exercise and having fun.'

Putting all these efforts in context, it is worth quoting from the company's Social Investment Strategy policy document, which states that the Community Fund initiative has a number of distinct priorities:

- Being regarded as a world class business and a force for good in the local community
- Being a good neighbour, being regarded as a trustworthy and positive influence
- Being recognized as a significant contributor to the local economy: an employer of skilled people who are excellent ambassadors for the site
- Ensuring we retain an excellent reputation in all we do – a reputation that has to be earned. Running a safe, efficient and reliable operation is our number one priority and underpins everything we do
- Ensuring that our activity is in line with business affordability

Grangemouth is only one of INEOS's sites but it is unquestionably one of the most important, and as such it needs to be a model for the company's philanthropic and community-based behaviour. Its significance is very clearly recognized and there is no question that

INEOS's management, both centrally and on the site, accords Grange-mouth the importance which it deserves.

Trash-4-Treats

In 2022, INEOS started to pilot a new primary school education pro-gramme based in challenged townships in South Africa, to teach children about responsible waste management.

Working with Caroline Hughes of INEOS South Africa and charity marketing consultancy [dot]GOOD, INEOS ran a pilot challenge for ten primary schools in the Western Cape area around Cape Town: the one which collected the most plastic, glass, cans and paper would get the chance to win about €3,000. 'The idea was to turn what is perceived as a chore into a fun habit', said Caroline, 'and also to show the children that waste has value.'

The schools chosen to take part in this Trash-4-Treats pilot were first briefed by a local recycling company, Waste Want, which was set to weigh and to dispose of the rubbish collected. Rubbish mascot Trashy issued starter kits to each child, to show what could and what could not be recycled.

After the competition ended, the thirteen thousand children were found to have collected more than five thousand kilogrammes of waste in just seven weeks. This total included more than a thousand kilo-grammes of plastic: the same weight (as someone who knows such things put it) as 3.75 black rhinos.

The winning school was Mitchell Heights Primary, which amassed fifteen hundred kilogrammes of recyclable waste. 'I have noticed a big difference in our learners since we started Trash-4-Treats,' said a teacher at the school:

'They now take pride in their school grounds and berate others who litter. It has been wonderful to witness children take an active interest in caring for their environment. We have started a clean revolution at Mitchells.'

All of the schools plan to continue their involvement with the local recycling centre, which pays for the rubbish. Caroline said that the recycled plastic was especially in demand locally. 'Many of the teachers and children were amazed to discover what happens to plastic bottles that are recycled,' she said.

For Caroline and the team at INEOS, the biggest benefit has been a change in mindset. 'Many of the children simply didn't know why rubbish was a problem,' said Caroline. 'But the hope is that now – having seen the financial and environmental benefits of managing their waste – these children will continue to keep their neighbourhoods tidy.'

In future, INEOS plans to develop Trash-4-Treats and take its popular mascot Trashy to more schools in South Africa. Having been a success, the scheme has obvious potential to be rolled out more widely.

Mavis's LEJOG

Although not really in the category of a separate initiative, the INEOS website proudly proclaims the story of its support for pensioner Mavis Paterson. It is a remarkable and very affecting story which well merits retelling.

81-year-old Mavis got in touch with the company regarding her plan to become the oldest woman to cycle the length of the UK (from south to north, from Land's End to John o'Groats, so 'LEJOG'). The ride was in support of Macmillan Cancer Support, which she had been supporting after losing both her mother and her sister to cancer.

She had by then lost all three of her adult children within four years, due to a heart attack, viral pneumonia and an accident. It is a truly appalling sequence that is hard to imagine – like something from a previous age. In response, Mavis had set out – very admirably – to raise £20,000 for Macmillan's work providing specialist health care, information and financial support to people affected by cancer, thinking too (rightly perhaps) that the challenge would distract her from her own grief.

Significant INEOS support came in the form of cash of £10,000 for her cause, as well as motivational videos, equipment and publicity through social media channels from the INEOS professional cycling team.

Battling health conditions of her own, Mavis finished a cycle ride of almost a thousand miles and duly took the title of oldest woman to cycle the route. Not surprisingly, as she commented afterwards, it was anything but easy:

> 'It was the most difficult thing I have ever done. The hardest part was on the third day when I wasn't feeling well and there were so many hills. I struggled to cycle, and I was in tears.'

The weather was almost unrelentingly miserable: she cycled through what seemed almost constant downpours of rain. She fell off her bike four times (fortunately not hurting herself seriously). And she kept going when she felt ill, relying upon little more than her resources of what Jim Ratcliffe would certainly refer to as grit. 'I made myself do it,' she said.

When she finally reached the end, in John o'Groats, she could hardly believe that the ordeal was finally over: 'I thought – gosh, we've done it. The whole journey I was so tired ... It was really tough.' With hindsight, though, it was worth it: the result was a sum raised for Macmillan of £80,000 – four times her original goal. She was well-entitled to feel very proud of what she had achieved.

CONSERVATION

Endangered Wildlife in Tanzania

Southern Tanzania has one of the highest concentrations of lions and other wildlife in the world, but these animals are under threat from humans in general and from poaching. This part of the country does not attract as many tourists as its more famous national parks and has tended to be out of the public eye. Despite being the size of the US state of New Jersey, Southern Tanzania is visited by only a handful of travellers every year. The INEOS initiative in the region is to support sustainable development by teaming up with an eco-tourism company, Asilia Africa, which is also funded by the Norwegian sovereign wealth fund.

Asilia is currently operating three luxury safari lodges in the region within two ecosystems which cover more than one hundred thousand square kilometres of conservation land. The Roho ya Selous camp is in the heart of the Selous Game Reserve, a wild and unspoiled area that is larger than Switzerland. The Jabali Ridge and the Jabali Private House are situated in the Ruaha National Park, reckoned to be home to 10 per cent of Africa's (which these days means the world's) lion population, estimated to be between thirty thousand and a hundred thousand animals.

The logic of the initiative is that increased tourism will increase awareness of the region's beauty and importance as well as bringing additional local jobs. This emphasis on local benefit has been part of the initiative from the start. The two camps and the lodge were built using local labour, and food and goods made locally are also used where possible. About a third of the company's six hundred plus staff live in the remote rural villages close to the safari camps. More than simply providing income, the initiative is intended to empower local people. 'We see people and nature as inseparable partners,' said Clarissa Hughes, positive impact co-ordinator at Asilia Africa. 'The development of one must mean the development of the other.'

So the way of working is for Asilia to partner with communities, authorities, non-governmental organizations and other tourism companies. As one example, INEOS provides schools with the basic things that they need such as desks, books and pens. Another example is that it helps local students who cannot afford higher education with scholarships for training at the Veta Hotel and Tourism Training Institute in Njiro. 'We believe that education is key to lifting people out of poverty and providing them with alternative livelihoods to poaching and unsustainable farming,' according to Clarissa Hughes. In addition to what the company does in its own time, guests contribute a levy (currently US$5 per night) to help take forward the work with communities.

Another aim of the project is to raise public awareness of the richness of the region and of its need for protection. 'There would be an international outcry if someone said we might lose all the elephants in the Serengeti, but if someone said the same of the Selous Game Reserve, most people wouldn't even know where it was,' comments Katie Fewkes, commercial manager of Asilia Africa. 'We aim to change that.'

As well as the three lodges, a research facility in the area is being supported to monitor both the local wildlife and the environment. 'I have visited southern Tanzania many times', Jim Ratcliffe commented:

'. . . and I know what an extraordinary place it is. As has been seen so clearly in the Okavango Delta, when a local community benefits from high quality employment from tourism, poaching flips to protection to preserve those jobs. This is a huge opportunity to create a long term, sustainable and ecologically friendly safari tourism business.'

He added:

'Gregg Hughes and his colleague Brandon Kemp are working on expanding some very exciting conservation work in Southern Tanzania at the Usangu camp and beyond.'

The Icelandic Six Rivers project

This initiative is based on the knowledge that the future of the Atlantic salmon is critically endangered. It is already extinct in Germany, Holland and Belgium and it is virtually extinct in North America. Iceland is one of only a handful of countries where the fish still enjoys healthy rivers. The project seeks to reverse the decline of the North Atlantic salmon by increasing the number of salmon that successfully breed in rivers in North East Iceland – the Selá, the Hofsá, the Vesturdalsa, the Midfjardara and the Sunnudalsá. All of these rivers feature in the top league worldwide for salmon caught per rod per day.

Support for the project from INEOS comes in a number of forms. One is to reduce the pressure on the salmon stocks by allowing only a limited number of rods on the river at any one time and limiting the number of hours for fishing each day. As an illustration of the very precise and specific nature of the rules, here are those for the Selá river:

- 100% catch and release
- maximum fishing time is four hours per session or eight hours per rod per day
- maximum catch is four fish per rod per session or eight fish per rod per day
- all rods are to be guided at all times
- no weighted flies or sinking lines
- floating lines only
- maximum two fish per pool per session
- no hooks larger than size ten
- no fishing above the second ladder

Another form of support is investment in the river systems to improve breeding results. Fish ladders are one example of what this means. These 'ladders' are actually steps cut in the rock at a height that allows fish to jump from one river pool to another. They provide access for the salmon to the upper reaches of a river and increase the breeding area and therefore the number of salmon that a river can service. They are important when there is a natural obstacle (such as a waterfall that is too high for them to jump) that limits the salmon's journey upriver. Financial support is required because fish ladders are expensive and need considerable technical skills not just to construct, but to overcome any environmental threat that they pose.

The tagging of smolts (maturing salmon) – in order to discover where they go after leaving Icelandic waters – is another aspect of this initiative. The data is used to help the scientific and academic teams build statistical models on survival rates and travel patterns to guide conservation work.

Another form of support is to improve the food available to the 'parr' – the young salmon. This can involve reforestation and revegetation to improve the delicate ecosystem surrounding the rivers and thus improve what is available to eat. It also involves egg planting in the more inaccessible parts of the river.

To these charitable donations are added revenues from payment by visitors for stays at the fishing lodge, which are reinvested in the conservation programme.

A scientific programme has been underpinning the conservation efforts. Conducted together with research partners at Iceland's Marine and Freshwater Research Institute and scientists from Imperial College London, the programme is intended to connect international researchers and to share best practice. For example, the researchers tagged parr and smolts in the Vesturdalsa using very small tags which give the fish a unique identity. As the researchers describe it:

'The Vesturdalsa was equipped with antenna up and down the river to enable us to chart their movements and so gather new data on how many parr survive to become smolts, and how many smolts leave the river then survive to return to the next year as adult fish ready to spawn. Alongside this, by starting to measure food sources and the demands of the fish for food, we have set about the task of estimating the carrying capacity of the river, something that's never been done before.'

As part of the scientific research programme, in January 2020 the first international symposium on North Atlantic salmon was convened, in order that work might be shared and a discussion joined upon future plans. This was then followed by a second conference held in September 2021.

Reforestation in Zambia

INEOS has been working since 2018 to develop community enterprise schemes protecting a forest reserve area in the centre of Zambia by collaborating with local chiefs to halt and reverse deforestation while improving the livelihoods of local farmers.

This one hundred and twenty square hectare region, which has seen some areas completely deforested and degraded with further areas under significant pressure from illegal charcoal production, logging, mining, poaching and encroachment, is beginning to see its fortunes turned around by the efforts of the project, including by ensuring that there are vital 'forest corridors'. In doing so, the programme is helping the local community to create sustainable businesses on surrounding land. The long-term aim is to rebuild the local ecosystem in order to support several endangered species, eventually protecting the region through the gaining of National Park status.

To illustrate what this means in practice, among the projects in this initiative are:

- monitoring and policing illegal activities in the forest, through supporting local law enforcement

- designing an efficient wood burning stove, which is simple to build for free and easy to operate. Working in tandem with local leaders and often the women who use the stoves daily, each results in a family saving at least two tonnes of firewood per year, and reduces the time involved in meal preparation from several hours a day to less than an hour

- providing alternative sustainable sources of income to families whose current livelihood depends on illegal logging and charcoal sales

- supporting the teaching of more efficient farming techniques in partnership with local farmers. This covers planting methods and timings, crop rotation, composting and water management. These enable families to grow nutritious food for their own needs with any leftover cash crops sold through cooperatives. The farmers are as a result replanting trees to support their fields' ecosystems (providing shade, wind protection, water retention) and to provide new crops (e.g. fruits)

- educating local leaders and influencers through workshops, supporting farmers to attend initial in-person teaching and creating a strong local network to share this better practice in the wider community

- teaching farming families how to produce effective natural fertilizer (compost) from their land, and enabling former 'convicted' charcoal burners to set up compost businesses instead. One effect of this is to reduce the area's reliance on fertilizer supplies

- providing families with beehives, to begin generating income from local honey. The small amount of profit derived from these sales is being reinvested in the programme to expand it further by providing more hives. The project also creates a link between financial rewards and the health of the forest, since in order to produce honey, the bees need to have access to trees

- experimenting with simple tree nurseries to repopulate damaged forest with new trees. This means exploring the most cost-, time- and ecologically efficient species and methods of growing indigenous trees to find the solutions that work best locally

- deepening the scientific understanding of forest monitoring through open source tools such as Google Maps and using readily available data from flights and drones so that this area can be cheaply surveyed whenever needed.

On the basis of the initiative, INEOS has commented:

'By empowering locals and stimulating the local economy alongside enhancing the health of the forest, a positive feedback loop is created locally enabling Mkushi farmers to become stewards of their surroundings. INEOS has provided its business expertise in efficient farming methods, while reducing middlemen with a social enterprise model ensuring that economic success is fully reinvested in the community and can continue in the long term'.

Concluding reflections

INEOS's philanthropy naturally reflects the personalities of the founders. It carries their personal mark in terms of their interests and priorities, which are rooted in concerns for social deprivation, the value of the quality of life (particularly in education), scientific endeavour in medicine and in the importance of conserving the natural world. Sometimes it is combined with the philanthropic aspect of personal sporting interests – as in the run for fun initiative, for instance. Conspicuously absent from this list are the arts. 'We are not opera types,' one of the founders told me.

These priorities also reflect the founders' belief that giving should make a difference, that action should be decisive and that once a decision is made it should be effective, with delivery swiftly following a decision to get involved. It is no accident that such decisiveness and speed mirror the business style of the founders. And as with their business decisions, philanthropic choices can be made quickly, because bureaucracy is kept at a minimum. This remains true even though, in response to the greatly increased philanthropic activity, a charitable committee was set up in order to provide essential vetting for grants. This charitable committee also distributes a sum which is set aside each year precisely in order for it to give at its discretion.

There is also a clear desire throughout the company to get involved in philanthropic work when this would be useful. As the text accompanying the Oxford INEOS Institute puts it: 'INEOS believes that it is important for the company to "put back" into society and to do so in a meaningful way, where it can add more value than simply funding.'

In the case of the INEOS Oxford Institute, this includes putting their project management expertise to work on behalf of the institute. This is not something that will be easy to pull off. Research institutes might well be cautious about being told what to do by donors, no matter how successful they might be at project management! There is evidently goodwill on both sides, but the hands-on aspects of the relationship will clearly have to be handled with care.

The characteristics of INEOS's philanthropic activities are based on, and made possible by, the fact that this is a highly successful private company dominated by a group of three founders. This is in stark contrast to many of its industry peers – public companies with accountability to outside shareholders, having to use carefully drafted and legally screened policy documents and being much less agile in decision-making. It is a world away from charitable foundations, with boards of trustees and assessment teams, or from public bodies subject to scrutiny by the press and the legislature.

I asked Ursula Heath, INEOS group communications manager, whether this approach and style gave rise to any problems. Does she find, for instance, that the press is always looking over her shoulder? Or are outsiders in general always keeping an eye open for – and half willing – any mistakes? Her response was that:

'. . .there must remain, nevertheless, some element of risk attached to the relatively informal nature of the approval process. Not having a bureaucratic process of vetting has huge advantages to donor and recipient alike, but it does possibly leave the donor organization vulnerable to irresponsible or unscrupulous recipients.'

Then there is the question of whether INEOS's philanthropy is 'greenwashing': that is to say, using philanthropy as a way of making acceptable to society activities which are otherwise unacceptable in some way. INEOS, in common with the other firms in the petrochemical industry, has regularly been accused of trying to buy respectability, and Operation Clean Sweep®, the international initiative from the plastics industry to reduce plastic pellet loss, flake or powder into the environment, has been named as one example. Sir Jim Ratcliffe was quoted in *The Financial Times* in March 2022 on his plastic production in relation to his support of the Icelandic salmon fishing initiative:

'We couldn't survive without plastics. Look at COVID. Everyone wanted masks, rubber gloves, hypodermic syringes, ventilators. All that stuff's made of plastic. You want an alternative? There's always paper.'

As a recipient of INEOS philanthropy on behalf of my institution, I am unlikely to have a wholly unbiased view of this, but I would note that it is virtually impossible for any person or organization involved with philanthropy to rebut this argument, whether in the petrochemical industry or indeed just as a citizen with good intentions. The more the moral high ground is assumed, the more it sounds like special pleading.

While the defence has to be about motive – 'We have done this to do good, not to advance our own interests' – motive can in reality never be proved. Understanding this, Jim Ratcliffe commented simply that the majority of us are innately moral. 'It's in most human beings to do some good.'

A reasonable question that might be asked about the philanthropic programme as a whole is: why is it not better known? Indeed, many of the initiatives are barely known about even inside the company. The answer again mirrors the company's commercial past – INEOS has been as diffident about publicizing its philanthropic activity as it was about publicizing its arrival as a force on the commercial scene.

For many years it was a badge of honour to be 'the biggest company you've never heard of'. Indeed, when I asked about the publicity that the company gave to its philanthropy, Jim Ratcliffe commented that 'trumpeting is not our thing'. Perhaps that is the 'northern grit' coming through: you just don't 'big yourself up', so to speak.

So this chapter may just be the first time that details about the whole range of philanthropic activities in which INEOS is involved have appeared in print, although none is a secret of any kind. For someone who is willing to search the company and other websites, virtually all the information in this chapter is already in the public domain. But you do have to work to get hold of it. The approach continues to be low-key.

Another question about the programme concerns how effective it is in addressing the problems that are the subject of the philanthropy. Here at least, INEOS has a record in setting clear objectives and following up the consequences. Much more so than in many charitable institutions, results are carefully tracked and reflected upon.

The quotes throughout this chapter – and indeed throughout this book – are evidence of INEOS's intense interest in successful outcomes, not simply in good intentions. Indeed, the term 'businesslike' might not seem unreasonable as a description of the way that initiatives are followed through, even if sometimes the objectives might not have been pinned down as effectively as might be desirable.

Could it be argued that the company should have a different set of philanthropic priorities? Certainly it is not unusual for charitable bodies and for public bodies supporting causes of various kinds to be faced with precisely this question. In the case of publicly quoted companies and those companies with outside shareholders, the argument is often that their role is not to make charitable donations, but rather to pay dividends to the shareholders, who can then decide for themselves whether they want to make charitable donations.

INEOS does not have any such conflict. The managers *are* the owners and if the company makes charitable donations, it is at their own expense. In terms of whether the priorities are 'right' or 'appropriate', that is a very individual verdict: certainly the owners of INEOS are clear that – just as with most of us – the charitable causes that they choose reflect their own particular interests. It would be strange indeed were this not true – and would reflect, I think, a lack of engagement.

Some, of course, might make different choices. But few would complain that these causes are not very worthwhile ones. Unlike in the public sector, meanwhile, almost none would grumble about the execution.

9

From the Horse's Mouth, CEO Insights

INEOS Leadership

THE TRUE STORY OF COURSE always comes from within! Never listen to the chairman! In keeping with the first book, *The Alchemists*, I invited the execs to reflect on the last few years in their own words. There was no set agenda, just a few suggestions such as culture, why so few people leave, growth.

In no particular order, the responses are set out below.

Please show forbearance where English is not the mother tongue!

Ashley Reed, Chairman

Wrong side of sixty-five and still working.

After twenty-seven years in BP, heading for fifty, retirement was already discussed.

My then colleagues are now all having long lunches.

INEOS came as a breath of fresh air.

Exciting, fun, challenging, rewarding, sometimes a bit scary, I still can't quite believe it.

My family can't really believe it.

Forty years in the chemicals business, finding yourself in a super-cool fashion brand, and managing the market entry of a new car company.

Of course that's a dream.

But no, I'm awake, this is life in INEOS.

A very special company and why?

It's the people, it's the ambition, it's the culture, it's the Boss!

Bob Learman, Chairman

When I worked for Dow Chemical, I was asked to lead the divestment of the GAS/SPEC and ethanolamine businesses in 2001 so that Dow could get FTC clearance to merge with Union Carbide. I vividly remember being asked to make a presentation to INEOS, and not a single member of my team had any idea who they were. At that time, no one could have possibly imagined how wildly successful and intriguing INEOS would become in just twenty-five years. The long list of accomplishments by Jim, John and Andy is stunning – what a great ride for them and their employees. My friends used to ask me what INEOS did; now they ask what's INEOS going to do next!

People seldom leave INEOS to work for our competitors. Working for INEOS is like being part of a perennial World Champion sports team. Nobody wants to leave a winning team with great team-mates and Hall of Fame coaches. Everyone is highly motivated to keep winning and a tremendous sense of pride and loyalty develops.

There are many reasons for the company's success, but ultimately Incap's vision, courage and decision-making speed must be paramount, followed closely by the absolute clarity of expectations provided to every business.

The INEOS culture is one of the company's greatest assets. The sporting and fitness emphasis is particularly powerful and is quickly embraced by employees. How many company owners genuinely care about their employees' health and fitness and provide all the tools, motivation and most importantly time for a successful outcome? The

INEOS chairman's passion for fitness is legendary. It is blatantly clear that many INEOS employees will live a longer, healthier and happier life as a direct result of Jim's encouragement.

Simon Laker, Group Operations Director (GOD!)

To many external bodies INEOS can appear an enigma.

We continue to be relentlessly acquisitive yet constantly achieve world-class Safety and Reliability, whilst at the same time achieving highly competitive cost performance. We take on businesses with very challenged EBITDA performance yet within a year or so this is totally turned round.

We announced in 2020 a 13 billion euro Major Projects Programme and from a standing start with almost zero project managers, construction managers and not even a major projects procedure, within a year we have all of this. Within three years we are commissioning the first of the projects safely, on time, on budget and they work!

A common refrain from the external finance and insurance markets we work with is that they see integration of new businesses as a significant risk to the acquiring company that often derails both parent and acquired.

We see the opposite. How do we do it?

Basically, don't get too cute. Apply a few things, but do them extremely well and thoroughly. Don't try to slam a new business into a whole new set of engineering standards or force them into a complex shared service functional structure of Safety, HR, IT, Engineering or Projects departments.

We buy good businesses from blue-chip companies and all they often need is a good dose of rigour.

We have a tried and tested toolkit.

In the first six months a 20 Principles Safety audit is carried out, gaps found and closed. The seven Life Saving Rules are implemented and consequences for not following them made very clear and enacted.

Each site carries out a gap analysis of the INEOS Group Guidance notes – these essentially describe how we expect our facilities to operate, maintain and grow. Work on any gaps starts immediately.

Every site receives an Asset Care audit to ensure it is in the condition we expect a highly complex processing plant to be. Resources are allocated and work begins. The Asset Care audit becomes a bonus gate for all employees within the first year. Don't look after your plant, no bonus.

We typically find that this approach is manna from heaven for the acquired businesses. Often their last few years have been as an unloved entity. Entering INEOS as a highly desired new business, they immediately see we are serious about people, safety, operations, investing and growing.

Wrapped around all this is our culture.

If culture is the outcome of actions then ours is of smart, friendly, well-mannered, high-performing people who look for a solution not a defence. Motivated to keep looking until the problem is understood, the answer found and issue fixed. In a nutshell, relentless.

As people become excited about this highly proactive way of working, performance improves, sites start to look good again and this creates a re-confirming cycle. For those who enjoy such an environment it becomes highly attractive to stay. Those who don't like the responsibility or exposure and would rather take a step back typically self-select and leave. And that's fine. We wish them well, it's not for everyone. But for those who do, an exciting, fulfilling, value-adding career amongst a friendly, often sporty and certainly healthy bunch of great people lies ahead.

Rob Nevin, Chairman

Curious sustainable longevity of people
Flexible atmosphere
Simple lines up to the top
No politics

A senior team that gets on
Strong alignment on objectives
Understandable direction, not complex
Direction is easy to find
No superstructure of large multinationals
People have to create their network, not given
No age discrimination!
Experience is valued
Constant flow of new ideas
Refreshing changes that stimulate new ideas
Fair bonus targets
Well paid
Flexible working locations for seniors

Gerd Franken, Chairman

Having spent quite a few years in different companies, I often wondered what company culture really is. In the case of INEOS, why the company has always rapidly integrated new businesses and sites without any cultural debates, without adversarial arguments? With apparently a unifying force at work, like gravity. So what in INEOS's case constitutes gravity?

- Common sense, good business sense. Rationale over style.
- Given chemicals are at the heart of the company, a singular focus on safety. This is reassuring for staff, but also for neighbours, the environment. And safety has been shown to go hand in hand with reliable operation.
- Staff with a sense of ownership – for the asset and for the business. Inspired by a leadership from the top that avoids stereotypes and boring formalism, so often dominating the communication in other organizations.

319

This resulted in a uniquely successful twenty-five years for staff from very different heritages. It is hard not to embrace the INEOS culture . . .

Graeme Leask, Head of Treasury

This is actually quite hard to do, as all of the observations I made for the twentieth anniversary still hold true!

Nevertheless, I have a couple more I could throw into the mix:

I often paraphrase the Greek philosopher Heraclitus when I describe the company to newcomers: 'The only constant in INEOS is everything changes.' This is one of the key reasons why we all enjoy working here so much – there is always so much going on, there is never a moment to get bored!

Working at INEOS often reminds me of the phrase my old mentor at PWC, Bill Teasdale, used to quote to me: 'Any fool can do one job at a time.' I certainly can't think of any other company where the Group CFO would also end up designing and implementing the company website at the same time!

Leen Heemskerk, CFO and Football Manager

I don't know what books you were reading when you were young, what movies you watched or what outdoor games you played, but I think all young children love a good adventure.

My best childhood memories are about going out with a group of friends and creating some havoc in our neighbourhood. Our world was as big as a few streets and this havoc was limited to ringing a few door-bells or hiding a few bikes but still it was a proper adventure and a good laugh. Similar in my teens or student days, the best memories have this element of a group adventure. Nothing beats a group of friends creating some chaos at school, sailing together dangerously across a big lake (in the dark) or just being stupid on a night out. I am sure this is also why we like sport so much as the great substitute drug for any retired hunter-gatherer.

When thinking about these books, movies and personal experiences, I think a good adventure needs to have a sense of purpose, it needs to have a simple storyline; good versus bad, us versus them. A good adventure is full of action and you want to be in the thick of it. The chances of success are higher with a group and it is definitely more fun chasing goals together.

I guess by now you get the bridge to INEOS. INEOS is a bit like a young children's adventure book. When you tell the history of INEOS to other people you are quickly becoming a true storyteller. We like clear storylines; we buy, make and sell things. We are not active in services, consulting, crypto or any other business too difficult to explain. Our business model is simple; we hunt in groups, small teams with full responsibility and accountability. Our objectives are always clear; deliver and grow, reasons no excuses. And we want action; do stuff, movers and shakers, don't sit on your hands, keep going at it with a smile on your face. Grit, rigour and humour.

Even after twenty-five years this series of INEOS adventures is not stopping. We continue to find new chemical adventures in Europe and the USA and we have now also started our big China adventure. We are building a massive chemicals site in Antwerp, we own lots of big boats, we are building our own car and we are now even having our own sport ventures. How much closer can you get to a true adventures classic!

This in my view makes the INEOS success very explainable; we are not one but a series of ventures. We select our ventures well. For each business the objectives and challenges are crystal clear. We put dedicated teams in place of professional people fully committed to delivering these challenges. This is how we are maximizing our chances of success, and this is why people stay with INEOS and will put their hands up again for the next adventure.

This book is not finished yet!

Jonny Ginns, Head of M&A

I have often pondered on what makes INEOS so unique. And more so on why so few at the top retire. And my conclusions are:

- The job is challenging, varied, enjoyable, and simply could not be replicated elsewhere
- We make it personal
- It's like a good book: you just want to keep reading to see what happens next

For the M&A world I live in, what makes us successful is the personal aspect – for the INEOS team, it is personal. We care about the result, and we want to find the solution so as to get the job done. We take responsibility for it, even if it's not specifically our role. For our oppos, it's just a job. They're happy for it to just grind on, with a void as to who, ultimately, is taking responsibility.

The key to longevity is replicating the current INEOS leadership. Jim is training a team of entrepreneurs who think the same way, who won't take no for an answer, and who are constantly striving for improvement and success. It is this team who will lead INEOS into the next generation.

John McNally, CEO

It never ceases to amaze me how nimble INEOS can be compared to other companies we do business with. Decisions are made quickly and efficiently, with delegation of authority crystal clear. No matrix decision trees! In fact, the word 'matrix' is one that we avoid carefully when speaking with the owners. Accountability is sharply defined; there is nowhere to hide if things go wrong, but plenty of space to shine when things go right – just the way it should be!

It really does dawn on you how surprisingly unique this method of working is when you look at some of the acquisitions we have made. I remember one of our operations directors lining up the operational managers in the Control Room on a key site of one of our acquisitions. 'OK, which one of you is responsible for this unit on the map over here?' All the operational managers looked uneasily at each other around the room. 'Well, it's not that simple,' hazarded one of the managers . . . 'It depends on what you want to do with the unit as to which of us together would take a decision.' So this company had devised a matrix of matrices to run a chemical unit. Amazing. That didn't last too long, I can tell you!

ExCo sessions are a microcosm of the INEOS ethos. Each Business Board presents to the owners for a couple of hours the state of their business. The good, the bad, the wins and the challenges. And of course the opportunities! The attention by the owners is undivided and absolute. No phones ringing (and may God help you if one of your Board has forgotten to put their phones on silent!). No secretaries rushing in to whisper in Jim's ear. No ten-minute breaks for one of the owners to take an urgent call . . . All conducted politely with mutual respect, and a good dose of injected humour when the opportunities present!

Jill Dolan, Head of HR

The last five years have been somewhat eventful. Putting COVID-19 to one side (where it belongs), INEOS has continued to grow not just in Chemicals but also Energy, Sport and Philanthropy, not forgetting a car named after a pub! What binds such audacious growth is clarity of purpose from the top, and unrelenting teams whose grit and rigour translate vision into reality. If you add in team camaraderie, a good dose of humour, mutual trust and friendship, then you get a picture of how INEOS operates and why so few leave the company.

How did INEOS grow to what it is today?
It's quite a mystery, many would say

But those on the inside know a lot more
It's based on INEOS culture, that's for sure

Teams pulling together with clarity and drive
Enjoying the challenges, learning to thrive

In INEOS Jim sees no limits, we find a way
Hard working teams delivering each day

During COVID lockdown, we learnt to adapt
Acquisitions continued, that's a fact

Hard work and wellness moved on-line
Gym and yoga classes helped us feel fine

But it's being together that makes us our best
Part of our DNA, the INEOS Crest

Grit, rigour, humour, good manners are key
It's important to us, and we want all to see

It's what makes INEOS stand out from the crowd
Our people and team spirit, makes us feel proud

Adding Sport and Philanthropy, it's a good place to be
Respect and friendship . . . and always a plan B

Tom Crotty, Communications Director

Why am I sitting here at my desk almost five years after my 'official' retirement age? I don't need to work, but why would I stop when instead of looking back on a forty-plus-year career in the industry I just keep looking forward to the next adventure over the horizon, and I think the same is true of so many people in INEOS. There is always something new around the next corner and we operate in a culture that is unique in industry and is summed up perfectly in the three words Grit, Rigour and Humour. People don't leave, because they are given responsibility and support to do exciting jobs and Incap reward loyalty with loyalty.

David Bucknall, CEO

I joined INEOS just over a year ago. I have been amazed at how much you can get done when you cut out the wasted effort found in large corporates. The people who work here love it. It's a simple but very effective formula and a joy to be part of.

Brian Gilvary, Chairman

A unique combination of like-minded teams that are agile, focused on the outcome and how we get there – driven, focused, gritty, humble, and led by the sheer bloody-mindedness of the leader who created it.

Always tell it as it is, backed up by hard evidence and rigorous analysis, and you will be the last one standing in any negotiation.

Lynn Calder, CEO

Why did I join INEOS? Audacious, bold, ploughing its own furrow, happy to be a bit different. But always with business rationale and the strongest foundation in the fundamentals of running a business.

Why do I stay? A culture that is performance driven; no-nonsense, direct, northern communication style, nowhere-to-hide accountability, but all with a sense of humour and a bunch of decent people. Works for me.

Oh, and who knows where the next career turn may take you . . .

Kevin McQuade, Chairman

I have been with INEOS almost eighteen years and what has struck me about what is different from the other companies I've worked for (Mobil Chemical, BASF) is the level of responsibility and accountability I have been given in my roles compared with my former employers. Many companies say they want entrepreneurial spirit, but INEOS truly embodies that with freedom to operate and truly gives you the opportunity to run your own business. It is why I think that fundamentally INEOS has been so successful in growth and profitability over the years. The federated structure with truly empowered boards has led to energized individuals focused on the successful development of their separate companies. It also has generated some good-spirited competition between the CEOs/Companies in terms of profitability or beating budget. We are all aware of the Company leader charts – in keeping with the competitive sports nature in INEOS. With all this comes a level of *trust* from Incap that is important – it is earned through results – but once gained it allows you to press even further to develop the business. There is a true openness within INEOS to push the envelope in terms of new, unorthodox ideas to grow the company.

The above description is why I believe people don't leave – INEOS is unique for the level of responsibility and accountability it gives to people at all levels in the organization. The federated structure allows for a small company environment within one of the largest chemical companies in the world. When I see the people who left Styrolution to go back to BASF it was because they felt uncomfortable with the level of accountability and exposure relative to the safety of the BASF bureaucracy – but for the people up for the challenge they thrived and loved it. Those type of people stay with INEOS as that kind of work environment is rarely found elsewhere.

A lot above speaks to the culture, but key words for me are entrepreneurship, challenging, rewarding, competitive, and with a good amount of good-natured fun also.

Maybe one last thought – it is exciting to be part of something that is dynamic, and growing and the company continues to be committed to growing and expanding globally. I think that's something people experience and want to be part of. What's next? – cars, ships, China, sports teams . . .

When so many other players in our industry are all about portfolio management and re-alignment, it is a great sign to all INEOS employees how firmly we are committed to profitable growth and expansion of the company. Even after twenty-five years, exciting times still lie ahead.

David Brooks, CEO

In addressing Jim's mail, my mind went back to my very first meeting with INEOS, back in late 1999, when my business ICI Acrylics had been acquired. Calum Maclean turned up armed with one slide (an acetate!) which had ten bullet points – nothing else. I can't remember all the ten, but three or four stick in my mind, which have remained to this day: Work Safely, No Politics, Quick Decision Making, Lean Structure. If we look at our business today, some twenty-four years on and immeasurably bigger, these four still hold true – also the principle of turning up to make a presentation without a catalogue of slides. It's clear we've held true to some of the founding beliefs throughout, no doubt a reason for our continued success.

I'm immensely proud to say I work for INEOS. I'm not alone in this and believe most employees feel the same. When I talk to people inside and outside our industry it's clear that INEOS is held in the highest regard, recognizing the achievements made in a relatively short period of time – BASF was formed 157 years ago! We've done this while keeping a strong moral and commercial compass that is respected across the world.

The early years of course were characterized by believing we could run bulk commodity chemical companies better than the traditional blue chips. Time after time this has proved to be correct and there can be little doubt that without INEOS's management approach the UK and European Petchem industry would have a much smaller footprint than it has today. INEOS's approach was probably nowhere better demonstrated back in the 2008–9 crash, when all of our industry peers went through huge restructuring exercises whilst INEOS didn't need to as it had got its house in order on costs years earlier.

This rapid growth has allowed people to have rewarding careers with strong individual performance being recognized and therefore little need for managers to seek careers elsewhere. New grads coming in have a real sense of a company going places and an understanding of what they need to do to reach their full potential.

A final point is that the federal structure of the company has driven focus, understanding and problem solving down to a level that most companies never achieve. This allows rocks to be turned over and costs driven out. It allows Boards the time to address the critical issues of the business with the rigour needed for the long-term success of the business. The Org structure has driven the right decision making on investments and holds Boards accountable for their actions.

Fran Millar, CEO

I've only been in INEOS since March 2019 – so I am but a newbie to this business. And in contemplating this question I wanted to produce something funny and clever – as that's how I have found most of the people I've worked with since arriving here. I failed. So instead, I thought maybe just giving an insight to my experience in my four short years might speak to how special it is here, better than any attempt at humour.

I came into INEOS via their acquisition of Team Sky – the six-time Tour de France-winning cycling team. I was CEO of the team and thought my life had seen some pretty unbeatable highs. Little did I know. Within the first two weeks I was asked to shortcut the transition between the team branding by two months, changing the entire hundred-person, twenty-five-vehicle, 250-bike team from Team Sky to Team INEOS, not after the Tour de France in July as had originally been planned, but before the Giro in May. We managed it, and we won the Tour in July as Team INEOS – oh, and we came second too – INEOS, unheard of in our sport four months before, blazoned across the two top steps of the Tour podium.

Midway through the team transition we were asked to support INEOS's attempt to break the two-hour marathon barrier with Eliud Kipchoge – an idea first formulated in December 2018 and a project I started working on in April 2019 that we successfully delivered, in its entirety in October 2019. INEOS, unheard of in running five months earlier, the catalyst and architects of breaking one of the last great barriers in athletics.

Hot on the heels of Eliud and 1:59 came the pandemic. In February 2020, as the world ran out of hand sanitizer, we were asked 'because you guys are good at logistics' to distribute the thousands of litres of hand sanitizer being manufactured by INEOS in Newton Aycliffe, Herne and Lavéra. INEOS provided a rapid response to a global crisis within weeks of discovering the issue and did it for free to any hospitals in Europe that needed it.

In September that year, as the pandemic raged and the team attempted to race through the chaos, I had an informal chat with our chairman, Rob Nevin, about what my future may hold in INEOS. Having done so much in such a short space of time, cycling had begun to feel humdrum. Careful what questions you ask! Ten days later I was made CEO of Belstaff, the struggling fashion brand owned by INEOS since 2017. Two years to turn it round – that was the challenge. From a double-digit deficit to profitability – a feat no other owner had achieved. We did it. INEOS, a 'petrochemical' business has saved a hundred-year-old British clothing brand from extinction – and put it on course for a bright and profitable future.

So what makes INEOS special? The belief that if you apply grit and rigour to any problem, you can solve it. The belief that if you challenge the norms and push yourself beyond what people tell you is possible you can achieve anything. The fact that we don't take no for an answer – go back, ask again, how do we make that a yes? The fact that INEOS empowers people to be the best they can be – the opportunity is given to you, the freedom is provided and the support and backing to deliver is around you every step of the way. It isn't easy, but no truly high-performance environments are. You never quite know what you will be doing next, or what will be asked of you – but you can guarantee that if you let yourself go all in, you will have the time of your life.

Rob Ingram, CEO

Not sure whether this is helpful, but as one of the longest-serving members of the INEOS family, and basically the first external hire that INEOS made directly after the MBO, I thought some reflections on my first day at INEOS might be interesting.

In 1998, I left a large global petrochemical company to join INEOS and was excited to become part of the adventure that had been described in my interview. I arrived bright and early on my first official day in my new job. INEOS was just starting the process of setting up home at 30 Bell Street, Romsey – an old townhouse in a small Hampshire market town.

I knew the atmosphere at INEOS was not going to be formal, so I knew not to wear a tie, but I was wearing a suit, just in case this helped to make a good first impression. I was met at the door of the building. The entrance lobby was stacked with desks, chairs, filing cabinets, telephones, computers, and printers. 'Good that you're here early. Get rid of that jacket. We've got to move all this up to the first and second floors.' I literally had to roll my sleeves up and get stuck in.

Looking back, this was a perfect introduction to INEOS: no airs and graces; no nonsense; do what is needed; get things done – roll up your sleeves and get stuck in. I think this culture has always been one of the main strengths of INEOS and has been a key contributor to the amazing success of the company over the last twenty-five years.

What a ride it's been!

Steve Harrington, CEO

People talk about the myth of meritocracy. From my experience, I can attest that the true spirit of meritocracy is at the heart of INEOS culture.

Having graduated from a good (but not best) university with a good (but not great) degree, my first job was as a laboratory technician. In how many other world-leading chemical companies is it possible to progress through the ranks from a laboratory technician (whilst receiving the necessary experience and hands-on training), to be entrusted with the reins of running one of its largest businesses?

Throughout my career in INEOS, I can say hand on heart that the core values of the company include appointing the best person for the role – regardless of sex, creed, colour, religion, etc. A real-life testament to this is a recent leadership team of mine; eight people – eight different nationalities across five continents (hint: includes an Aussie), each bringing a unique cultural perspective and value to the team.

We can argue the merits of positive discrimination and quotas – but for me, the proof is in the pudding.

Andy Bell, CEO

I recently found myself in an airport lounge in Buenos Aires after having visited the Vaca Muerta Shale basin, one of the largest shale plays in the world. With my colleagues Oli Hayward-Young and Ricky Simonson, we were evaluating the prospects of new ethane exports to support our growing global ethane demand.

About an hour before my flight boarded, a tall, slender gentleman plopped his white North Face backpack down next to me. As he sat down he looked over at me with a smile and a cheerful 'Hello'. His face was weathered and wrinkled, his hair bushy and unkempt under a well patinaed cap. On his backpack was strapped a climbing helmet and a water bottle. I asked if he had been out hiking and he said he was from Australia and had been in the Patagonia for a month. I took him to be an older gentleman doing some basic hiking around the Andes. He looked at my urban backpack and an extra gear bag I had clipped on with a carabiner. He pointed to the bag and said 'I started that company.' It was a Sea to Summit branded bag. He explained he was no longer part of the company and had split ways with his partner years before. He then asked if I knew the origin of the company name, Sea to Summit. I did not, and he explained that he had previously summitted Mount Everest in 1984 and was challenged by a friend to complete the full 8,848 metres (29,032 feet) by starting at sea level. Which he did in 1990 with a swim in the ocean and then a 700+ mile hike to Everest Base Camp and a final climb to the top of the world.

Suddenly, I realized I wasn't talking to your average backpacker, this seemed a much more serious mountaineer. We talked briefly about the 1996 Everest tragedy (since he'd been hanging around Everest during that time), climbing 14ers in Colorado (fifty-four peaks in the State of Colorado are above 14,000 feet) and my own aspiration one day to hike up to the top of Mont Blanc. He offered a simple point of advice – that for any great adventure you have to spend time getting your mind in the right place. You must find the inspiration that will push you to carry on and not quit when the going gets tough. Then a tap on my shoulder from my INEOS colleague reminded me we had to go to our gate. I asked the gentleman his name and he said Tim Macartney, and with that I bid him a safe journey back to Australia.

Once on the plane I scrambled on my phone to google this Tim Macartney and verify his story. Much to my surprise, Tim Macartney-Snape is a bit of a mountaineering legend. First Australian to summit Everest in 1984 with a climbing partner via a difficult new route without supplemental oxygen. He put up new routes on Annapurna II, made a second-ever ascent on a new route up Gasherbrum IV and then his Sea to Summit expedition where he soloed, unsupported, Mount Everest without supplemental oxygen and depleted from being sick. Clearly, I had no clue who I'd been talking to. He is now sixty-seven, and his Instagram page is full of pictures of himself climbing with three young mountaineers for the last month on some major rock faces like Fitz Roy and other legendary Andes mountains.

I kept coming back to his Sea to Summit expedition and reflected on its similarity to INEOS over the past twenty-five years – even more personally in relation to the Ethane Export project I had worked on for the last ten years, which brought me to Buenos Aires in the first place. The same hallmarks in both pursuits I believe are why INEOS is able to attract and retain an excellent motivated team of people. They include:

Big and Bold. Just as Macartney's Sea to Summit was Big and Bold, so has INEOS been in its brief history. BP Acquisition 1, BP Acquisition 2, Sinopec Joint Venture, Project 1, Grenadier to name just a few. Ethane Exports started the same way, pundits challenging whether ethane could even be put on a ship, let alone build a virtual pipeline with Dragon Boats to shuttle low-cost feedstocks to European Chemical Plants. It was Big and Bold, but with sufficient research and engineering INEOS became convinced that it was not only possible but commercially viable. Doing things Big and Bold makes for exciting projects, infectious enthusiasm and is motivating.

Grit and Determination. To hike nearly 750 miles from the Bay of Bengal, across the Indo-Gangetic Plain, through the Himalayan foothills to the top of Mount Everest was an amazing feat with countless obstacles to overcome. He had limited support and no team of Sherpas, making for a greater challenge and grind. As with INEOS over the years, it has not always been a smooth path: the 2008 financial crisis, Grangemouth Union, politicians unsupportive of the chemical industry, and countless other obstacles. And with the Ethane Export project the very outset saw a major partner walk away at signing, requiring INEOS to step up and take on additional infrastructure commitments without the underlying feedstock secured. But INEOS believed in the shale economics and with hard work developed new relationships with the largest independent producers in the US, securing for the long term the necessary ethane. Working through difficult situations forms bonds amongst team members that last a lifetime. In its simplest form it can be seen in a group of employees suffering through a difficult CrossFit or spinning session on an idle Tuesday afternoon. The growth and real value are in the grind, not the finish.

Entrepreneurial and Decisive. In his expedition Tim had to ad lib, find solutions, and take action. When refused entry at a border crossing into Nepal, he ran one and a half times a marathon for five straight days to make it to an alternative border crossing 200 miles away. When faced with a major river crossing and no bridge, he swam its chilly waters. Quick, decisive action. INEOS has been built on quick, decisive, entrepreneurial action, closing major deals in a fraction of the time normally spent between companies. With the Ethane Export project, major contracts were done in two to three months that normally took one to two years. Unique pricing structures, multiple export locations, product-flexible ships made for a diversified robust supply chain. INEOS remains the only company exporting ethane to have built such a system and it has suited us well. Doing things differently and quickly creates a can-do mindset and keeps people moving from challenge to challenge.

Humble and Understated. If you watch any documentaries on Tim, he is a humble, understated person. Clearly a man of strong will and views, but not boastful or overbearing. He was that way in my conversation with him. And with INEOS, it has always quietly gone about its business building one of the largest

Petrochemicals in the world. Humble in knowing things can turn against you, yet determined to work through it all. With the Ethane Export project, I took pride with my boss David Thompson signing major multi-billion-dollar deals in small discreet coffee shops. Changes to our supply chain, whether new sources of supply or customers, were simply announced by where our ships turned up. We celebrate our successes, but then move quickly on to the next opportunity. That is how we roll, and it creates pride amongst our teams in how we handle ourselves.

All of the above makes for highly motivated people invested in each other. It creates stickiness to the company. It is how we also retain suppliers and customers. It fosters the inspiration in us all to do uncommon things and do them well. That for me is INEOS.

Geir Tuft, CEO

- Hugely successful, of course, but also devoid of any of the crap that creeps into large organizations. I think the relentless focus on real, actual value (cash) avoids us running down holes looking for 'intangible' values that some big blue chips do and distract them from making real changes or progress.

- Growth pace is massive. I think key has been that we have stuck to what we know and repeated it so many times that we ultimately have become very proficient at it.

- The lack of a 'strategy' is liberating – i.e. not chasing some goal like 'by this time we will be this type of company'. Value and opportunity focus.

- Culture. The willingness to challenge the status quo. The question 'why' is an excellent representation of how we approach change and improvement without it necessarily implying that current practice is not good. Opens people's eyes to change.

- Our willingness to measure ourselves and raising the bar for improvements when it is clear we need to in order to continue improving (e.g. LOC to LOC10)

- In my mind, people leave companies because they get bored. The rate of growth and change that we have with the opportunities it gives our people makes it very hard to replicate in a different company (e.g. ethane pipeline from US, the Grenadier as well as the 'classical' acquisitions of which there of course have been a very large number). Add to that our no-nonsense, direct culture with short decision routes. And not the least a very enjoyable work environment with great colleagues.

- I think a lot of us who have been around for significant parts of this journey can say the same as me: it has provided some of the hardest moments of my career (e.g. Grangemouth), but also so many enjoyable moments and highlights and the feeling of real achievement when I look back at fifteen years now in February.

Joe Walton, CEO

Stayed a private company
- Eliminates cumbersome governance associated with a public company's filings.

- Insulates company from the latest themes of financial analysts and NGOs that often drive inconsistent strategies and actions at a public company. INEOS can make a play on out-of-favour businesses.

- Examples include Shell facing legal threat in the Dutch courts; BP's CEO jumping through hoops to reconcile profitable fossil fuel investments and its changing perspective on sustainability milestones.

Senior Leadership continuity
- Incap has been a 'firm hand on the tiller'. Provided a consistent message on company direction and values. INEOS has avoided the abrupt changes companies can undergo when a new CEO is installed.
- Leadership values have to an extent been codified and promulgated in the INEOS Compass.
- Keeps unproductive intra-company politics to a minimum. No rival factions jostling for the top job.

Senior Leadership experience
- Experience is valued at INEOS. CEOs / LTs predominantly have a wealth of experience in the businesses they lead. Substance is valued over style. A track record of delivery is demanded.
- INEOS retains this experience far longer than rival companies that internally set mandatory retirement ages.

'Risk On' culture
- INEOS is at its best when pursuing new opportunities, be it acquisitions or new projects. Growth is the unifying driver.
- INEOS has an enviable track record in successfully executing and integrating acquisitions. I have seen other companies botch M&A deals multiple ways.
- INEOS has a lean management structure for such a large company – an element many companies claim to desire but fail to replicate. A lean management structure means fast decision making, no 'analysis paralysis'.
- INEOS puts great store on accountability, no hierarchy to hide in.
- INEOS avoided large group-level functional organizations. BUs focus on front-line issues not overly burdensome initiatives from Group.

High level of employee retention
- INEOS is an exciting place to work. People like to be associated with a winner. INEOS has the most compelling growth story in the global petrochemical industry.
- The move into sports has only added glamour to the INEOS brand and heightened public awareness. Some of that 'halo effect' rubs off on employees.
- INEOS has avoided periodic large layoffs through downturns, in contrast to, say, Dow or BASF. A consequence of staffing for the BOC. Employees take note of this history.

Tobias Hannemann, CEO

I was very lucky to join INEOS in the early days. When INEOS acquired the Phenol business in 2001 the change in company culture could not have been more extreme. What previously was a boring, slow and very politically organized German chemical company was suddenly enlivened with fresh energy, grit, rigour, and a lot of humour.

Personal ownership and responsibility irrespective of your age or your level in the organization are encouraged and honoured. Treating company money as if it is your own is part of our culture. Taking bold decisions and never standing still is a daily exercise, keeping everyone excited.

All of this continues to encourage and motivate a lot of bright people to work for INEOS and more importantly many young talents joining to become a part of INEOS.

Mike Nagle, CEO

Reflections
- **Genuine safety focus**. I have worked in both the refining and chemical industries, and I have worked for public and private

companies. Without a doubt, INEOS has the most thorough safety program that I have seen, and I am proud about the systems we have in place. Many companies have rigorous programs for personnel safety, and INEOS certainly does as well. But beyond that, INEOS has a genuine focus on process safety – High Potential incidents, Losses of Containment, overdue inspections, and Asset Care. All of these safety topics are covered in detail during each Executive Committee meeting, and there is deep discussion and engagement on any issues and findings. Safe operations is our licence to operate, and it is a commitment we make to our employees, contractors and communities.

Growth

- **Willingness to take risks**. The US shale revolution created energy self-sufficiency and enabled manufacturing reshoring. INEOS saw the transformation and competitive advantage of our US business and initiated a project to explore the possibility of exporting ethane to Europe. At the time, this had not been done anywhere in the world, and moreover, it had not even been contemplated. The challenges were many, but the opportunity was large. And there was an underlying willingness to take a calculated risk on a transformational proposition. Working with partners around the globe, INEOS built a virtual pipeline system of pipelines, storage tanks and ships to move hydrocarbons from the US to Europe. Now, shale gas has transformed our European business as well. Since then, other companies have seized on the idea, but it was INEOS that conceptualized, demonstrated, and pioneered the concept.
- **Perseverance**. We identified a high-growth market with limited suppliers, and after reviewing our technology, we believed that we could make an analogous product in an innovative way. We challenged our product development, manufacturing and sales teams to figure out a way to design, make and sell this material

for us. It took roughly five years of work across the organization, with many failed attempts along the way, but grit and perseverance ultimately paid off. The market has grown far beyond our expectations, and the product is highly successful to the point where we are evaluating debottleneck opportunities on our asset. The collective focus across the organization – along with a determination to not give up and find a way forward – was instrumental in delivering a very successful and profitable product for the business.

Culture
- **Entrepreneurial**. INEOS has grown primarily through acquisitions in the petrochemical industry. But that entrepreneurial thinking goes beyond traditional markets and products. Several years ago, our business was contacted by a customer who was interested in selling their business. They admired INEOS as a supplier, and they wondered if we would be interested in buying them. We had never considered a downstream integration, but after studying their market and business, it seemed like a good idea. After a brief discussion with INEOS Capital, we decided to buy the business. The acquisition turned out to be a very strategic addition, and we have since opened new facilities and made further acquisitions to build the business into a market leader. This entrepreneurial mindset and creative thinking has fuelled the growth of INEOS.
- **Quick decision-making**. INEOS is designed with a federal structure with an extremely small headquarter office. Each business is empowered to make decisions which are in their best interests. This enables quick decision-making and eliminates uncertainty and churn which is typical in large organizations. Moreover, as a private company with stable ownership, major decisions are likewise very fast and are usually made within the construct of a single discussion.

- **Rigour**. I worked in a public company where a senior vice president told me that the secret to getting a project approved was to walk into a management meeting with a large stack of papers in order to give the impression that a lot of work has gone into the analysis. In INEOS, that would never work. We value substance over style, and we value rigour and depth of knowledge. Moreover, our challenge is to make the complex simple, and that can only be done with a deep understanding of the topic.

Why people stay
- **Real challenges**. We recruit some of the best and brightest individuals, but what sets INEOS apart is that we give them real assignments and real challenges very early in their careers. People don't spend several years bouncing around functional and project groups – they hit the ground running. From there, we give them new opportunities to challenge themselves, such as the Namibia challenge where they run, bike and hike through the desert for six days. When combined with our lean corporate structure, this gives people meaningful work and tangible successes which builds a lasting bond between the company and its employees.
- **Sustainability**. When the topic of sustainability arises, I remind people that INEOS employees are environmentalists as well. We live and raise families in the communities where we work, and we want to create a better world for everyone associated with our business. We have already made significant commitments to reduce our greenhouse gas footprint and to incorporate recycled plastics and bio-feedstocks into our products. Our employees see this commitment and the future that we have outlined, and they are excited to be a part of creating a new future for the business and INEOS.

Steve Dossett, CEO

When I joined INEOS in 2005 the company was not particularly well known, even in the town of Lyndhurst, where it was headquartered then, as I discovered when asking for directions for the office on my first visit. It's all different now. Game-changing acquisitions, bold investments and step-outs into the world of sports, fashion and automotive have raised the company's profile immeasurably, and for the better. Graduates and apprentices are keen to join the organization and few people want to leave, or have to. The number of asset disposals or business sales are few and far between. People in the organization know the company stands for growth, opportunity and adventure, be that in the world of manufacturing and business or outside the work place in sports and community support, and most want to hang around. One doesn't know what the next year will bring, but one can be pretty sure there will be surprises. It's never dull.

There have been some bumps along the way. The financial crisis of 2008–9 was difficult for a lot of companies and INEOS was impacted, but unlike many organizations that spent years licking their wounds, INEOS was out there very quickly, looking to add to its portfolio cheaply as others restructured, moved away from commodities and chemicals in search of a quieter (and arguably less rewarding) life. For me personally the experience has been great. They say you shouldn't take your work home with you, but I do wittingly, and some of the INEOS culture has rubbed off. Family members are all fit, healthy, hardworking and have an appetite for adventure. They love to get involved in the skiing, cycling, running, etc., and are keen to up sticks and live and work abroad, some of which I attribute to stories I bring home from the world of adventure that is working for INEOS.

Hans Casier, CEO

Being with INEOS since the beginning (and its predecessor) I have thought a lot about this over the years.

- Not easy to define but there is always this 'thrill/vibe in the air' of new ideas, growth, challenges, unexpected things. Every year I'm curious what will come around.

- The striving to be number one, to be the best, to be the largest, to grow and not to be complacent.

- This requires the ability to drive, to adapt and jump on the wagon but also to be able to change and look at things differently, and be creative.

- The people who love this stay on; the ones who want to be safely hidden in a large corporate organization don't last very long and leave.

- To me one of the main reasons why we have been successful is ownership, and this comes with our company structure where people work for a very clear defined entity/division/site/responsibility and also run it and are recognized and rewarded for it.

- Without these people (and the drive, the challenge, set-up and support of Incap/Sir Jim obviously) it would not have been possible to realize what we have done over the course of twenty-five years.

- In general there is a good atmosphere amongst colleagues and some fun/humour is never far away (at least where I have been working, Oxide, Phenol, Nitriles).

David Thompson, CEO

As for the growing of the INEOS business, I'm sure you have had many comments regarding the formula used by Incap:

- Clear ambition to grow demonstrated by the shareholders (sets the tone)

- Target on blue-chip assets
- Good market positions
- Focused in petchems
- Looking for distressed sales (in that someone was looking for an exit)
- Which means opportunities to buy good assets, good people, good market – at a low cost

And then add Jim's ingenuity in financial engineering to fund the acquisitions, plus empowering the management to develop and deliver a strategy – to give successful growth.

The culture doesn't appeal to all. But the brilliance is the short management chains used through the company. This avoid tiers of middle management and their associated reporting requirements (to enable those middle managers to know some of what is happening). Cutting it out, avoiding any unnecessary paperwork, keeping the focus on the deliverables, has been the core of the culture. This gives nowhere to hide if that's your view of life (hence why it doesn't appeal to all). Having that 'can-do' culture, being positive and encouraging an approach of trying to find ways to enable everyone to make a difference in their roles.

We say that so few leave – but many left in the early days of the acquisitions, including those who didn't buy in or those who didn't want to find themselves taking responsibility. That meant that there was opportunity for the remaining staff to grow and develop in their jobs, without having tiers of managers causing a fog of uncertainty above them. As a result, there is in INEOS a general level of satisfaction in being able to really influence the performance of the business. That isn't the case in many other companies, where the bureaucracy can easily stifle the efforts being made.

And general reflections:

- The stability of the management team, that so many know each other, has really helped.

- Killing the equity scheme was genius – it was creating unnecessary tension in the federal structure that was contrary to achieving maximum overall performance.

- Adding the encouragement to take time to participate in sport and in considering your own health has been so positive in so many ways, not only as a policy, but in providing facilities to get involved.

- It's been fun but hard work.

Andrew Gardner, Chairman

Reflections on how we grew so successfully
Very few rules, but the ones we have are very simple – e.g. CEOs have to sign off on all new core roles, which stops empires being built and followed by big redundancy programmes, which is what happens in the oil majors every two years, seven lifesaving rules, twenty principles, etc.

Almost all the CEOs are the same in that at their core they just get on and get stuff done.

Humour is a big part of our lives.

Most people love sport and now it's a big part of our INEOS daily business also.

Accountability – it's amazing what gets achieved by individuals at all levels when it's crystal clear that they are accountable, and how so many other companies fudge accountability, resulting in people being unclear of their roles, or able to hide, which just means less is achieved.

Whatever takes your fancy
Most of us are still from the North.

Why so few people leave
Only a few simple rules.

Feels like you own the business you run/work in – it's yours.

Given our current stock levels – free hand sanitizer for everyone!

Pete Williams, Head of Technology

If I had now to choose what really distinguishes INEOS from just about every other organization I know, it is span of control coupled with insistence upon excellence. By span of control, I mean splitting the organization into entities in such a way that the span of control of each CEO and team perfectly suits the needs of each different business area. This brings focus, simplicity and speed. By excellence I mean the quality of being outstanding or extremely good.

I think INEOS is:

Creative: the use of imagination or original ideas to create something; inventiveness.

Entrepreneurial: entrepreneurial spirit thrives on meeting the next challenge.

Intolerant of bullshit: stupid or untrue talk or writing; nonsense (vulg).

Intolerant of bureaucracy: over-concern with procedure at the expense of efficiency or common sense.

Willing to delegate the day-to-day business: entrust (a task or responsibility) to another person, typically one who is less senior.

Insistent upon excellence: the quality of being outstanding or extremely good.

Impatient: restlessly eager.

So add that up. INEOS is successful because:

. . . it is restlessly eager to take on the next challenge, creative in overcoming it, intolerant of untrue talk, nonsense and fussy procedures whilst doing it, willing to trust its business teams to get on with things in the meantime and demanding of excellence in whatever it does.

Stuart Collings, CEO

Run businesses the right way

Each board being accountable for running their business is key. They own the success and take responsibility for making things happen. Our focus is on things we can control rather than worrying about the things we can't. We understand our businesses much better than our competitors and make quick, informed, smart decisions.

Work hard, play hard with a smile

Our culture is 'full on'. We maximize our impact in work by working hard, cutting out BS and focusing. We do what it takes to get the job done. Outside of work we do lots of sport and enjoy a beer or two. Throughout this we enjoy a healthy dose of humour and good manners. This all goes hand in hand, and we attract and retain people who love this culture and thrive in it.

Do deals that no one else thinks possible

Throughout our history we have been very clear about what we are trying to achieve in deals and are relentless in achieving it. My best example is the formation of Inovyn, where we assembled the best collection of plants in Europe by combining our business with Solvay's. This took canny negotiating, relentless drive to gain clearance, and determination to make the deal work. I could point to many other examples (e.g. Styrolution, FPS, Innovene) that no one else would have been able to achieve.

Xavi Cros, CEO

What makes INEOS different?

- INEOS has a unique company culture, clearly coming from the top, but also impressively spread around all of us.

- Grit, rigour and humour summarizes it well and make us 100 per cent different from others.

- It is simple but amazingly shows how we work (and live!) in our daily activities. Impressive, looking at our daily work, how this culture makes us different (and better!).

- Again, interesting to see how this culture goes well beyond our work hours to everything (sports, health, family, friends . . .).

- Talking with other industry players (where I have continuing relationships) or even friends working in other businesses (Swiss banks to big Swiss food company . . .), they do not share this attitude. More bureaucratic, less focus, less delivery . . . in essence, less grit, rigour and humour. And in essence, all of them are jealous of our having it . . .

- And maybe that answers why so few people leave. INEOS is a great place to work, that makes us proud and goes well beyond the workplace. It just makes all of us better.

- And just let me finish with an example: which other company will take graduates to Namibia and make them something that is a life-changer on the way they will approach life/work challenges? And which other company will give this opportunity to senior people (like me) to be part of it? . . . None, outside of INEOS!

Andrew Miller, CEO

As a pretty new CEO (December last year) and someone who was acquired by INEOS at the end of 2019, I don't quite have the depth of twenty-five years' INEOS experience but I can at least give my views on culture and growth so I'd like to do that here.

I don't think I will be writing something you haven't heard already, let's see.

I previously worked at Dow and Ashland and expected similar (bureaucratic, corporate) fare when acquired by INEOS. How wrong I was. I find the INEOS approach of 'just get on with it' really refreshing.

We truly hold people accountable for results and progress them when they deliver. It is why the company is so successful and few people leave. With a few years in tenure I am proud to be a CEO of the Composites business. We work hard and rigour is taken to a new level, and I have enjoyed pretty much every minute of it!

Paul Rands, CEO

- As a relative newcomer to the CEO group, what strikes me at CEO days/gatherings is how much of a 'Village Community' feel there is in that group when it gathers. So many of the group have worked, interacted and socialized together for such a long time, that everybody seems to know each very well, it is very comfortable and informal – as a newcomer it feels like walking into the village pub for the first time when you've just moved into the area (but I've been warmly welcomed so far, without having to stand a round of drinks!).

- As to why people stay with INEOS so long, I think that is largely down to the key elements of the culture, especially clear accountabilities, simple reporting lines and speed of decision-making/approvals, coupled with the level of autonomy you get as leader (although obviously this has to be earned). For people with the confidence to accept accountabilities, this makes INEOS a relatively simple and hence a great place to work, much less complicated than other 'blue chip' companies I've worked for earlier in my career.

Appendix 1: Dealmaking in Our DNA, Deal List

Throughout its history, INEOS has actively pursued strategic acquisitions, restructuring, joint ventures (JV), JV buyouts and disposals to grow the business. Here is a list of the 162 such deals since its founding in 1998.

YEAR	EVENT	TARGET BUSINESS	COUNTERPARTY	INEOS DIVISION
1998	Acquisition	Ethylene Oxide (Antwerp, Belgium), to create 'INEOS'	Inspec	INEOS Group
1999	Acquisition	Antifreeze	BP	INEOS Group
1999	Acquisition	Acrylics	ICI	Individuals
2001	Acquisition	Acetate Esters	BP	INEOS Group
2001	Acquisition	'INEOS Fluor', 'INEOS Silicas', and 'INEOS Oxide' (INEOS renamed 'INEOS Oxide')	ICI	INEOS Group
2001	Acquisition	Buyout of Murray Johnstone investment in Oxide	Murray Johnstone	INEOS Group
2001	Acquisition	Ethanolamine and Gaspec	Dow	INEOS Group
2001	Acquisition	Phenolchemie (phenol and acetone business)	Degussa	INEOS Group
2001	Acquisition	Enterprises (B&W, Baleycourt, ETB, Atlantik, IACC jv) and Chlor businesses	ICI	Chlor group
2002	Acquisition	Majority shareholding in EVC plc	Publicly listed	Vinyls group
2003	Acquisition	Paraform	Degussa	Paraform
2004	Acquisition	Sulphur Chems	Rhodia	Chlor group
2002	Acquisition	Remaining shares in EVC plc, to become 'INEOS Films', 'INEOS Vinyls', 'INEOS Compounds'	Publicly listed	Vinyls group
2005	Acquisition	Styrenics	Nova Chemicals	INEOS Group
2005	Acquisition	'Innovene' business	BP	INEOS Group
2005	Acquisition	Cumene plant (Port Arthur, US)	Chevron Phillips	INEOS Group
2005	Acquisition	Melamines	Cytec	INEOS Group
2005	Restructuring	Spin-out of Atlantik business	-	-
2005	Restructuring	Healthcare (spin-out from Silicas)	-	-
2006	Acquisition	Vacuum salt business	Salt Union	Enterprises group
2006	Acquisition	Ethylene Oxide/Ethylene Glycol	BP	INEOS Group
2006	Restructuring	Moving Chlor group into main INEOS Group	-	-
2006	Restructuring	Moving Films and Compounds groups into main INEOS Group	-	-
2006	Restructuring	Merger of Chlor and Vinyls business divisions, to 'INEOS ChlorVinyls'	-	-

Year	Type	Description		
2006	Restructuring	Spin-out of Vinyls Italian business	-	-
2006	Acquisition	Acquisition of Wingles site (deferred acquisition of part of Innovene)	BP	INEOS Group
2007	JV	Acquiring 50% ABS plastics business 'Lustran Polymers'	Lanxess	INEOS Group
2007	Disposal	ChlorVinyls EPVC business	Vinnolit	INEOS Group
2007	JV	Merger of respective styrenics businesses in the US, to create 'INEOS-NOVA US'	Nova Chemicals	INEOS Group
2007	Restructuring	Moving Enterprises group into main INEOS Group	-	-
2007	Restructuring	Spin-out of ETB business division	-	-
2007	Acquisition	50% of Noretyl cracker and polyolefins business (Norway)	Borealis	INEOS Group
2007	Acquisition	Ferrous chloride plant at Runcorn, UK	HIGH Chemicals	INEOS Group
2007	Acquisition	Silica gels business in Baltimore, US	Lyondell (Millennium Chemicals)	INEOS Group
2007	JV	Establishing Champlor (biodiesel)	SICLAE / Thywissen	Enterprises
2007	JV	Establishing 'Jiangxi InTech' JV to produce Anhydrous Hydrogen Fluoride	Zhejiang Xing Teng	INEOS Group
2007	Acquisition	Glebe Mines, UK	Individual	INEOS Group
2007	Disposal	Gas storage caverns (UK)	GDF	Enterprises
2008	Acquisition	Kerling (Norwegian chlorvinyls plus remaining 50% of Noretyl cracker)	Norsk Hydro	INEOS Group
2008	Disposal	INEOS Acrylics minority holdings	Individuals	Mitsubishi
2008	JV	Merging INEOS Silicas business with PQ Corporation	Carlyle private equity	INEOS Group
2008	Acquisition	Ethyl acetate ('Etac') and vinyl acetate monomer ('VAM') plants (Hull, UK)	BP	INEOS Group
2008	Acquisition	Acrylonitrile plant (Seal Sands, UK)	BASF	Nitriles
2008	JV buyout	Acquiring remaining 40% of INEOS Asiatic Chemical Company Limited ('IACC')	EAC	Enterprises
2008	JV	Acquiring 75% of the publicly listed ABS Indian business	Lanxess	INEOS Group
2008	JV	Acquiring 50% of 'Great Plains', for the development of biodiesel	Individuals	Enterprises
2008	JV	Establishing a Refining trading division, as a quasi JV	Morgan Stanley	INEOS Group
2008	Acquisition	INEOS Bio technology	Individual seller	INEOS Group
2009	JV buyout	Acquiring remaining 50% of ABS business	Lanxess	INEOS Group
2009	Disposal	Minority JV interest in Cires (part of Kerling acquisition)	Shin-Etsu	INEOS Group
2009	Restructuring	Spin-out of various business divisions into new 'Industries' group	-	-
2009	Disposal	Vinyls PVC plant (Italy)	Safi (Fiorenzo Sartor)	Vinyls group
2009	Restructuring	Ownership of gas storage caverns transferred to Geosud SAS (France)	-	-
2009	JV	Energy-from-waste project in Runcorn, UK	Viridor	ChlorVinyls
2010	Acquisition	Oil terminal at Dalston, Scotland	BP	INEOS Group

Year	Type	Description	Party	Division
2010	Acquisition	Additional land (Seal Sands, UK)	BASF	Nitriles
2010	Disposal	Fluorochemicals business	Mexichem	INEOS Group
2010	Disposal	50% interest in Jiangxi In-Tech JV	Zhejiang Xing Teng	INEOS Group
2010	Disposal	Film manufacturing site (Assemini site, Sardinia)	Mr Scanu	Industries
2010	Disposal	Land and buildings at Whiting site	Tilde	INEOS Group
2010	Disposal	Sale of interest in the 'Great Plains' biodiesel JV	Individuals	Enterprises
2010	Restructuring	Spin-out of ChlorVinyls from main banking group into Kerling sub-group	-	-
2010	Restructuring	Swiss restructuring and establishment of INEOS AG	-	-
2010	JV	French 'Exeltium' project relating to nuclear electricity supply	EDF and various industry players	INEOS Group
2010	JV	Establishing a Naptha trading division, as a quasi JV	BP	INEOS Group
2010	JV	Establishing a joint venture to build a commercial plant in Vero Beach, Florida	New Planet Energy	Industries
2010	Disposal	Global films business	Bilcare	Films group
2011	JV buyout	Acquiring remaining 50% share of INEOS-NOVA	Nova Chemicals	Industries
2011	JV	Merger of respective Styrenics and ABS business, to form 'Styrolution'	BASF	Industries
2011	Restructuring	Spin-out of ABS Addyston site	-	-
2011	Restructuring	Spin-out of Styrenics EPS business	-	-
2011	Restructuring	Spin-out of Enterprises into a separate 'group'	-	-
2011	JV	Refining business carved out, to create 'Petroineos'	PetroChina	Petroineos
2011	JV	Infrastructure assets at Grangemouth placed into a JV with Petroineos	PetroChina	Petroineos
2011	Disposal	IP in the Healthcare business	Cytochroma	INEOS Group
2011	Disposal	Glebe Mines, UK	Cavendish Minerals	INEOS Group
2011	Acquisition	Chlorvinyls business (Belgium and France)	Tessenderlo	ChlorVinyls
2011	Acquisition	55 mile Seminole Pipeline (Texas, US)	Enterprise	INEOS Group
2012	Restructuring	Spin-out of ICT business	-	-
2012	Restructuring	Separation of O&P Europe into O&P UK, O&P South and O&P North		
2012	Disposal	A22 plant at Runcorn, UK	Fenix Fluor	INEOS Group
2012	JV	Wood acetylation project, 'Tricoya'	Accsys Technologies	Industries
2012	Disposal	ABS business 'Elix Polymers SL' (Tarragona, Spain)	Sun Capital	Styrolution
2012	Disposal	IACC business (Thailand)	Siam PVS Chemicals	Enterprises group
2012	Acquisition	US shale gas import project	Range Resources / Sunoco	INEOS Group
2013	Acquisition	Solvents business	Sasol	Solvents

			Banners	ChlorVinyls
2013	Disposal	UK packed chlorine business		
2013	Acquisition	Barex business	Mitsui	INEOS Group
2013	Restructuring	Closure of VAM site	-	-
2013	Restructuring	Spin-out of Compounds business from Kerling group	-	-
2013	Restructuring	Moving O&P UK outside of main banking group	-	-
2013	JV buyout	Acquiring remaining shareholding in Champlor JV	Colsit	Enterprises group
2013	Restructuring	Spin-out of combined Barex business into a standalone group	-	-
2013	JV	HDPE new-build in the US, referred to as 'Gemini'	Sasol	INEOS Group
2014	JV buyout	Acquiring remaining 50% of the Styrolution JV	BASF	Industries
2014	JV buyout	Buyout of Bio royalty interests	Individual seller	Industries
2014	JV	Merger of Compounds business with Doeflex Compounding	Individual shareholders	Industries
2014	Restructuring	Spin-out of US technologies business	-	-
2014	Restructuring	Spin-out of O&P South business division into its own group	-	-
2014	Restructuring	Transfer of various assets out of ChlorVinyls and Kerling businesses	-	-
2014	Acquisition	UK shale gas licence	BG Group	Upstream
2014	Acquisition	UK shale gas licence	Reach	Upstream
2015	JV	Merger of ChlorVinyls with Solvay chlorvinyls business to create 'Inovyn'	Solvay	Inovyn
2015	Acquisition	Shale licences (onshore UK)	iGas	Upstream
2015	Acquisition	Grangemouth CHP unit	Fortum	Industries
2015	Disposal	Chlorvinyls remedy assets (various)	ICIG	Inovyn
2015	Acquisition	Phenol and cumene assets	Axiall Corporation	INEOS Group
2015	Acquisition	UK oil and gas licences	Fairfield	Industries
2015	Acquisition	UK oil and gas business 'DEA UK'	Letter One	Industries
2015	Acquisition	Spanish Sulphur Chems business	Befesa	Enterprises
2016	JV buyout	Acquiring remaining 50% interest in Inovyn	Solvay	Inovyn
2016	Restructuring	Closure of Barex business	-	-
2016	JV buyout	Buyout of Compounds minority holders	-	-
2016	Acquisition	Calabrian Corporation	SK Capital	Enterprises
2016	Disposal	EPS (Styrenics) business	Synthos	Enterprises
2016	Acquisition	Oxide business	Celanese	Oxide
2016	Acquisition	Shale licences and entities	Moorland	Upstream
2016	Acquisition	WL Plastics - HDPE pipe manufacturer	Individual sellers	O&P US

Year	Type	Description	Party	Division
2016	Acquisition	K-Resin® styrene-butadiene copolymers (SBC) business	Chevron Phillips	Styrolution
2017	Acquisition	Oxo alcohol business (including stake in Oxochimie JV)	Arkema	INEOS Group
2017	Acquisition	INEOS aviation business (jets)	CTC Aviation	Aviation
2017	Acquisition	Shale gas licence portfolio	Engie	Upstream
2017	Disposal	Oil and gas licences in Rosebank (UK)	Suncor	Upstream
2017	Acquisition	Danish oil and gas business 'DONG'	Dong Energy	Upstream
2017	Acquisition	North Sea Forties Pipeline System and Kinneil Terminal, to become 'INEOS FPS'	BP	FPS
2017	Acquisition	Shale interest (onshore UK)	Total	Shale
2017	Acquisition	Belstaff Group	JAB Luxury	Industries
2017	Acquisition	Oil and gas licences	Siccar Point Energy	Upstream
2017	Acquisition	Swiss Football Club, 'Lausanne FC'	Alain Joseph	INEOS Group
2018	JV	America's Cup racing 'sponsorship' deal, as a quasi JV	Sir Ben Ainslie	Industries (Sports)
2018	Disposal	Baleycourt and ChloroToluenes businesses	Valtris Specialty Chemicals	Enterprises
2018	Acquisition	Polystyrene production sites in China	Total	Styrolution
2018	Disposal	VinyLoop business at Ferrara, Italy	Benvic	Inovyn
2018	Acquisition	Intermediates business (Joliet, US), to become 'INEOS Joliet'	Flint Hills Resources	Enterprises
2018	Acquisition	Ethoxylation plant (Lavéra, France)	Wilmar	Oxide
2019	Acquisition	INESCO combined heat and power plant (Belgium)	RWE	Oxide
2019	Acquisition	INEOS Grenadiers' cycling team (prev. Team Sky)	Sky	Industries (Sports)
2019	Acquisition	TiO2 business (Ashtabula, Ohio), to become 'INEOS Pigments'	Tronox (Cristal)	Enterprises
2019	Disposal	Melamines and Paraform business units	Prefere Resins	Enterprises
2019	Acquisition	US onshore oil & gas (Giddings Field, TX)	Crawford Hughes	O&P US
2019	Acquisition	'OGC Nice' Football Club	Individual sellers	Industries (Sports)
2019	Acquisition	Global composites business, to become 'INEOS Composites'	Ashland	Enterprises
2019	JV	China Technology JV with Sinopec	Sinopec	INEOS Group
2020	Acquisition	Spirit Energy's Danish interests	Spirit Energy	Upstream
2020	Restructuring	Moving Styrolution and Inovyn groups into a new 'Quattro' group	-	-
2020	Acquisition	Acetyls and aromatics business, to become 'INEOS Acetyls' and 'INEOS Aromatics'	BP	Quattro
2020	Acquisition	Naperville site (US)	BP	Quattro
2020	Acquisition	Additional land (Lavéra and Sarralbe, France)	BP	INEOS Group
2020	Acquisition	Acquiring remaining 50% interest in Gemini HDPE plant	Sasol	O&P US

Year	Type	Description	Company	Division
2021	Acquisition	Hambach automotive production site	Mercedes-Benz	Automotive
2021	Disposal	Sulphur Chemicals business (Spain)	ICIG	Enterprises
2021	Disposal	Norwegian oil and gas business	PGNiG	INEOS Energy
2021	Acquisition	Oil and gas licences in Denmark	HESS Corporation	INEOS Energy
2021	Acquisition	Minority investment in HydrogenOne	Publicly listed	INEOS Energy
2022	Disposal	Entire 75% equity interest in INEOS Styrolution India	Shiva Performance Materials	Styrolution
2022	Acquisition	1/3 interest in Mercedes Formula 1 team ('MBGP')	Daimler	Industries
2022	Acquisition	Pipe manufacturing plant (Titusville, US)	Charter Plastics	O&P US (WL Plastics)
2022	Acquisition	'The Grenadier' pub in London	Green King Group	Industries
2022	Acquisition	KOH/chlorine plant 'ASHTA Chemicals'	Bigshire Mexico	Enterprises
2022	JV	50% interest in SECCO petrochemical complex	Sinopec	INEOS Group
2022	JV	50% China ABS business (Ningbo)	Sinopec	Quattro
2023	Acquisition	Mitsui Phenols Singapore	Mitsui Phenols	INEOS Group
2023	Acquisition	Chesapeake's South Texas O&G assets	Chesapeake Energy	Industries - Energy

Appendix 2: INEOS Financing Transactions

YEAR	GROUP	DESCRIPTION	AMOUNT	ACQUISITION FINANCING?
1998	Group	Secured bond	€0.1bn	Acquisition of Oxide business
2000	Acrylics	Secured bond	€0.1bn	Acquisition of ICI Acrylics business
2001	Group	Term loans	€0.8bn	Acquisition of Fluor & Silicas business from ICI
2002	Group	Term loans and secured bonds	€1.0bn	Acquisition of Phenol business from Degussa
2004	EVC	Secured bonds	€0.2bn	
2005	Group	Term loans, secured and unsecured bonds	€9.0bn	Acquisition of Innovene from BP
2010	Kerling	Secured bonds	€0.8bn	
2010	Group	Secured bonds	€0.7bn	
2011	Styrolution	Secured bonds	€0.5bn	Formation of JV with BASF
2012	Group	Secured bonds	€1.3bn	
2012	Group	Term loan B and secured bonds	€3.0bn	
2013	Group	Term loan B and secured bonds	€1.8bn	
2014	Grangemouth	Secured bonds	€0.3bn	
2014	Styrolution	Term loan B	€1.1bn	Buyout of BASF 50% share in JV
2014	Group	Secured bonds	€1.0bn	
2014	Group	Term loan B	€0.4bn	
2014	Group	Project finance facility	€0.5bn	Formation of JV with Sasol
2015	Energy	Reserved based lending	€0.2bn	Acquisition of Breagh business
2015	Group	Term loan B	€0.8bn	
2015	Group	Term loan B	€3.2bn	
2015	Group	Secured bonds	€0.8bn	
2016	Inovyn	Term loan B and secured bonds	€0.8bn	Buyout of Solvay 50% share in JV
2016	Group	Secured bonds	€1.1bn	
2017	Energy	Reserved based lending	€0.6bn	Acquisition of DONG business
2017	Group	Term loan B	€4.4bn	
2017	Group	Term loan B and secured bonds	€4.4bn	
2019	Enterprises	Term loans A & B	€1.4bn	Acquisition of Composites business
2019	Grangemouth	Term loan	€0.3bn	
2019	Group	Schuldschein loans	€0.2bn	
2019	Group	Secured bonds	€0.8bn	
2020	Inovyn	Term loan B	€1.1bn	
2020	FPS	Term loan	€0.1bn	
2020	Enterprises	Term loans A & B	€1.4bn	
2020	Group	Term loan B	€0.6bn	
2020	Group	Term loan B and secured bonds	€0.7bn	
2020	Styrolution	Term loan B and secured bonds	€1.2bn	
2020	Quattro	Term loan A and bridge facility	€4.0bn	Acquisition of Aromatics & Acetyls business from BP
2021	Quattro	Term loan A & B, secured and unsecured bonds	€5.0bn	Acquisition of Aromatics & Acetyls business from BP
2021	Styrolution	Project finance facility	€0.4bn	New Chinese ABS facility
2021	Group	Term loan B	€1.2bn	
2022	Enterprises	Term loan A	€0.4bn	Acquisition of Ashtabula business
2022	Group	Term loan B	€2.0bn	
2022	Group	Term loan	€0.3bn	
2022	Group	Term loan	€0.6bn	Acquisition of 50% of SECCO from Sinopec
2023	Group	Project finance facility	€3.5bn	New cracker project in Antwerp
2023	Group	Term loan B and secured bonds	€2.7bn	
2023	Quattro	Term loan B	€0.9bn	

About the Authors

Sir Jim Ratcliffe – Chapter 1

Sir Jim Ratcliffe began his career at Exxon Chemicals, where he completed his MBA at the London Business School. He moved to Courtaulds and in 1992 led the successful buyout of Inspec Group plc.

He left in 1998 to acquire INEOS plc from Inspec and has been chairman of INEOS ever since.

Under Sir Jim's leadership, INEOS has grown to become one of the world's biggest chemicals companies, while also expanding into oil and gas, automotive, sport and consumer goods.

Dominic O'Connell – Chapter 2

Dominic O'Connell is the business presenter on Times Radio, having previously done the same job on BBC Radio 4's *Today* programme. Before that he was business editor of the *Sunday Times* for six years. He has won several national journalism awards including the Wincott Award, the premier award for business writers and broadcasters, in 2017. Born in New Zealand, O'Connell also writes a weekly column for *The Times* business section.

Quentin Willson – Chapter 3

Motoring journalist and transport campaigner Quentin Willson is one of Britain's best known motoring media faces. He presented BBC Two's *Top Gear* for fifteen years along with Channel 5's *Britain's Worst Driver*, *The*

Classic Car Show and BBC Two's *The Car's the Star* and has written eleven global motoring books. He's won the British Press Awards Motoring Writer of the Year, co-founded the FairFuel campaign, saving over £120 billion in planned fuel duty rises, and also founded FairCharge, an electric vehicle lobby group to help make EV transition accessible, affordable and to push the government to deliver more charging infrastructure.

Well known in Westminster and auto industry boardrooms, he's been campaigning on UK automotive and transport issues for over thirty years, writes for car magazines and newspapers and is a regular transport commentator on TV and radio.

Patrick Barclay – Chapter 4

Former Sports Writer of the Year Patrick Barclay covered football for a succession of national newspapers. He began at the *Guardian* in 1976 and moved first to the *Independent*, then to the *Observer*, the *Sunday Telegraph* and finally *The Times*. Barclay travelled extensively in following the sport's evolution, attending nine World Cups, ten European Championships and four Africa Cup of Nations. Afterwards he concentrated on writing biographies of football managers: José Mourinho, Sir Alex Ferguson, Herbert Chapman and Sir Matt Busby.

Most recently, finally fulfilling a desire for a change of subject, he started work on the life story of Harry Rée, a British hero of the French resistance during the Second World War.

Barclay lives just a couple of miles upriver of Fulham Football Club, where he has a season ticket, although the true love of his football life is, always has been and always will be represented by the dark blue of Dundee.

Sean Keach – Chapter 5

Sean Keach is one of the world's leading technology and science journalists with over a decade of experience in the media industry. He has worked in London and New York for some of the world's best-known media brands including News Corp, Future Publishing and Time Inc.

Sean has produced thousands of articles on tech and science read by tens of millions of readers around the world. He currently leads an international team of world-class journalists at the *Sun* and the U.S. *Sun* as head of science and technology, delivering fast-paced specialist reporting to a global audience. Sean has featured as an expert on TV and radio to talk about technologies of the future, including appearances on Sky News and TalkRadio.

He has covered a wide range of beats including consumer technology, artificial intelligence, space, energy and climate, gaming, cryptocurrency and the metaverse. Sean has interviewed industry leaders, delivered world-first exclusives, and is one of the industry's most prolific writers.

He was born and raised in Birmingham, and graduated with a BA Hons Journalism degree from Southampton Solent University.

Steph McGovern – Chapter 6

Award-winning broadcaster Steph McGovern is the presenter of the eponymous *Steph's Packed Lunch*, broadcast daily on Channel 4.

Prior to this, Steph worked in financial journalism for over fifteen years and spent seven years as part of the *BBC Breakfast* family.

Steph travelled all over the UK to cover economic and business news for the BBC and broadcast live from over 500 businesses. Whether talking to workers in factories or interviewing FTSE 100 chief executives in the studio, Steph made it her mission to find out what was going on in the real economy.

Steph also co-presented BBC One's *Watchdog*, Channel 4's 2021 Paralympics coverage, her own primetime BBC One programme *Shop Well for Less* and children's TV show *Pocket Money Pitch* for CBBC.

Lord Sebastian Coe – Chapter 7

Lord Coe is the president of World Athletics, where he is serving his second term and non-executive chairman of CSM Sport & Entertainment.

As an athlete he won Olympic gold medals in the 1500 metres in 1980 and 1984 and set twelve middle-distance world records. He retired from athletics in 1990 and two years later was elected as member of parliament for Falmouth and Camborne, a seat he held until 1997, when he became private secretary to William Hague, the leader of the opposition. In 2000 he was appointed a life peer and took the title of Lord Coe of Ranmore. He chaired the London Organising Committee of the Olympic and Paralympic Games (LOCOG), delivering the Games in 2012.

Coe has four children and has received numerous honours throughout his career. He was the BBC's sports personality of the year in 1979 and in 1982 he was appointed a Member of the Order of the British Empire (MBE). Eight years later he was promoted to Officer of the same order (OBE). Following his appointment as a life peer, Coe was promoted to Knight Commander of the Order of the British Empire (KBE) for his services to sport, and in the 2013 New Year's Honours List he was appointed to the Order of the Companions of Honour (CH).

In the summer of 2020 Lord Coe was approved as an International Olympic Committee (IOC) member at its 136th IOC Session.

Professor Sir Andrew Likierman – Chapter 8

Andrew Likierman is professor of Management Practice at the London Business School and was its dean from 2008 to 2017. His current research is in judgement in management.

Andrew has had many non-executive roles, including the Bank of England, Barclays plc, insurance company Beazley plc and the market research firm MORI. He has twice worked in central government, had non-executive roles in local government, the health service and public enterprises and is a former president of the Chartered Institute of Management Accountants. He is currently a director of a listed Australian pharmaceutical company and a start-up bank.

Index

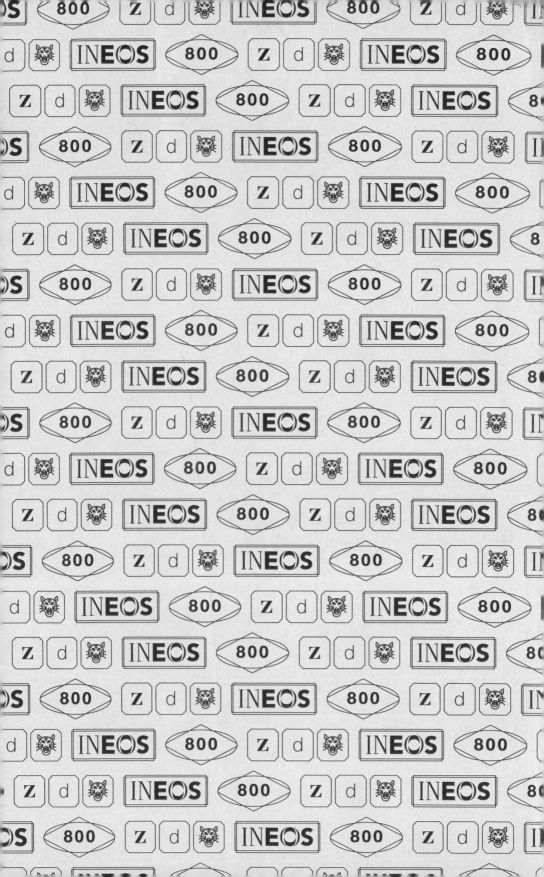